THE ONE SHOW

THE ONE SHOW

Judged To Be Advertising's Best Print, Radio, TV. Volume 7
A Presentation of The One Club for Art and Copy

RotoVision

Published by Rotovision S.A. Geneva

The One Club
For Art and Copy

Ron Berger
PRESIDENT

Mike Tesch
CHAIRMAN, PUBLICATIONS COMMITTEE

Angela Dominguez
DIRECTOR

Michelle Fisher
MEMBERSHIP COORDINATOR

Mike Tesch
DESIGNER

Cathi Mooney
DESIGN ASSISTANT

Ryuichi Minakawa
ART DIRECTOR

Robert Ammirati
COVER PHOTOGRAPHY

Frank DeLuca
LAYOUT AND PRODUCTION

Elise Sachs
EDITORIAL COORDINATOR AND INDEX

Fisher Composition, Inc.
TYPESETTING

Dai Nippon Printing Co., Ltd., Tokyo, Japan
COLOR SEPARATIONS, PRINTING AND BINDING

PUBLISHED BY
Rotovision S.A.
10, Rue de l'Arquebuse
Case Postale 434
CH - 1211 Geneve 11
Switzerland
Telephone 22 - 21 21 21
IN ASSOCIATION WITH
The One Club for Art and Copy, Inc.
3 West 18th Street
New York, New York 10011
(212) 255-7070
U.S. DISTRIBUTION
R.M. & R.E. Silver
95 Madison Avenue
New York, New York 10016
(212) 686-5630
WORLDWIDE DISTRIBUTION
Rotovision S.A.
10, Rue de l'Arquebuse
Case Postale 434
CH - 1211 Geneve 11
Switzerland
Telephone 22 - 21 21 21

First Printing.
ISBN 0-960-2628-7-3
ISSN 0273-2033

Contents

The Board of Directors

President's Message

If there is one point to be made about award shows in general, and the 1985 One Show in particular, it is that award shows have arrived.

After years of being criticized by some agencies (usually the ones that never won anything) as nothing more than the advertising industry patting itself on the back, award shows have now, without question, taken on great significance in our industry.

They obviously are important to agencies. Why else would some agencies invest as much as 35 or 40 thousand dollars on entry fees alone?

Today, awards also mean something to clients. If you don't think so, just win an award and see who the second person is who wants one for his(or her)office. (Clients somehow are always second because account people always beat them to it.)

But, fortunately, the one thing that hasn't changed is that awards are most important to the copywriters and art directors who win them.

Which is as it should be.

Because, above all else, awards give creative people the emotional impetus to continue to produce work that both they and the advertising industry can be proud of.

On that note, I would like to thank all of you who helped make the 1985 One Show, with nearly 10,000 entries from over 500 agencies throughout the world, the most successful in history.

And, congratulate those creative people who emerged victorious.

Ron Berger

Judges Panel

Jim Aaby
Wells, Rich, Greene

Hy Abadi
Ally & Gargano

David Altschiller
Altschiller, Reitzfeld, Solin

Ralph Ammirati
Ammirati & Puris

Larry Anderson
Cunningham & Walsh

Tony Angotti
Angotti, Thomas, Hedge

Ron Arnold
Ally & Gargano

Charlie Ashby
McKinney Silver & Rockett

Ellen Azorin
McCann-Erickson

Alan Barcus
Benton & Bowles

Greta Basile
Young & Rubicam

Paul Basile
Della Femina, Travisano & Partners

Mike Becker
Ted Bates

Ron Becker
Altschiller, Reitzfeld, Solin

Howard Benson
Biederman & Company

Norman Berry
Ogilvy & Mather

Rea Potterfield-Brown
Geer DuBois

Walter Burek
McCaffrey & McCall

John Caggiano
Doyle Dane Bernbach

Neil Calet
Calet Hirsch Spector

Gene Case
Jordan, Case, McGrath

Jay Chiat
Chiat/Day

John Clapps
Isidore & Paulson

Peter Cornish
Ketchum Advertising

Neil Costa
Campbell-Ewald

Jack Cowell
Albert-Frank Guenther Law

Vincent Daddiego
Young & Rubicam

Boris Damast
Saatchi & Saatchi Compton

Libby Daniell
Saatchi & Saatchi Compton

Ed Davitian
Bozell & Jacobs

Tony DeGregorio
Levine, Huntley, Schmidt & Beaver

Jerry Della Femina
Della Femina, Travisano & Partners

Lou DiJoseph
Young & Rubicam

Brian Dillon
Young & Rubicam

John Doern
Saatchi & Saatchi Compton

Neil Drossman
Drossman Lehmann Marino

Dick Earle
Saatchi & Saatchi Compton

Bernie Eckstein
Saatchi & Saatchi Compton

Arthur Einstein
Lord, Geller, Federico, Einstein

Malcolm End
Ogilvy & Mather

George Euringer
Ally & Gargano

Gene Federico
Lord, Geller, Federico, Einstein

Steve Feinberg
Cunningham & Walsh

John Ferrell
Young & Rubicam

Carole Anne Fine
Scali, McCabe, Sloves

Bob Fiore
Warwick Advertising

Steve Frankfurt
Kenyon & Eckhardt

Alan Fraser
Needham Harper Worldwide

Lee Garfinkel
Levine, Huntley, Schmidt & Beaver

Bill Giles
Grey Advertising

Amy Gold
Sacks & Rosen

Irwin Goldberg
Nadler & Larimer

Hal Goluboff
The Bloom Agency

Roy Grace
Doyle Dane Bernbach

Stephen Graff
Doyle Dane Bernbach

Paula Green
Paula Green Advertising

Barry Greenspon
Doyle Dane Bernbach

Ray Groff
Needham Harper Worldwide

Charles Guarino
Warwick Advertising

Bill Hamilton
Rumrill-Hoyt

Jim Handloser
Ally & Gargano

Mary Ellen Harris
SSC&B

Joel Harrison
Benton & Bowles

Sirje Helder
NW Ayer

Bill Hentz
Foote, Cone, Belding

David Herzbrun
Doyle Dane Bernbach

Bob Hildt
Martin Sturtevant Silverman & Marshall

Peter Hirsch
Calet, Hirsch, Spector

Martha Holmes
Needham Harper Worldwide

Mike Hughes
The Martin Agency

Tony Isidore
Isidore & Paulson

George Jaccoma
George Jaccoma & Associates

Dick Jackson
Dick Jackson Inc.

Murray Jacobs
Doyle Dane Bernbach

Caroline Jones
Mingo-Jones Advertising

Dick Joslin
Joslin, Walker

Walter Kaprielian
Fearon, O'Leary, Kaprielian

Jack Keane
Nadler & Larimer

Richard Kiernan
Grey Advertising

Murray Klein
Smith/Greenland

Diana Kramer
Warwick Advertising

Andy Langer
The Marschalk Company

Chet Lane
D'Arcy MacManus Masius

Karen Larson
HBM Creamer

Bob Levenson
Doyle Dane Bernbach

Paul Levett
HCM

Ann Marie Light
Epstein, Raboy Advertising

Dick Lopez
Scali, McCabe, Sloves

Peter Lubalin
TBWA

Joseph MacKenna
HCM

Joel Maliniak
Young & Rubicam

Mike Mangano
Doyle Dane Bernbach

Dan Marshall
Martin Sturtevant Silverman & Marshall

Stan Mazzius
Muller Jordan Weiss

Ed McCabe
Scali, McCabe, Sloves

John McCullough
Firestone & Associates

Arthur Meranus
Cunningham & Walsh

Tom Messner
Ally & Gargano

George Miller
BBDO

Marvin Mitchnick
Nadler & Larimer

Richard Moore
Muir, Cornelius, Moore

Roger Mosconi
BBDO

Charlie Mullen
Isidore & Paulson

Frank Murakami
AC&R Advertising

Peter Noto
Shaller, Rubin & Winer

Gerry O'Hara
Epstein, Raboy Advertising

Bob Oksner
NW Ayer

Stephen Olderman
Geer DuBois

Bernie Owett
J. Walter Thompson

Bruce Palmer
J. Walter Thompson

Steve Penchina
Penchina Selkowitz

Phil Peppis
NW Ayer

Ellen Perless
J. Walter Thompson

Jim Perretti
Ally & Gargano

Ted Pettus
Lockhart & Pettus

Charles Piccirillo
Leber Katz Partners

Stuart Pittman
McCann-Erickson

Jerry Prestomburgo
Warwick Advertising

John Prizeman
Laurence, Charles & Free

Tony Pugliese
Grey Advertising

Frazier Purdy
Young & Rubicam

Jim Rainere
Bozell & Jacobs

Velva Rickey Rankin
Ogilvy & Mather

Donn Resnick
Grey Advertising

Les Richter
Ted Bates

Mike Robertson
Grey Advertising

Ron Rosenfeld
Rosenfeld, Sirowitz & Lawson

Warren Rossell
Colarossi & Griswold

Tom Rost
Ogilvy & Mather

Nat Russo
Bozell & Jacobs

Mike Scardino
J. Walter Thompson

Rheinhold Schwenk
Jordan, Case, McGrath

Tod Seisser
Levine, Huntley, Schmidt & Beaver

Ted Shaw
McCaffrey & McCall

John Siddall
Siddall, Matus & Coughter

Murray Skurnick
Venet Advertising

Don Slater
Slater, Hanft, Martin

Ernie Smith
Sudler & Hennessey

Marty Solow
Durfee & Solow

Helayne Spivak
Ally & Gargano

Lynn Stiles
Lord, Geller, Federico, Einstein

Bob Sturtevant
Martin, Sturtevant, Silverman & Marshall

Bob Sullivan
D'Arcy MacManus Masius

Pat Sutula
The Marschalk Company

Bob Tabor
Foote, Cone & Belding

Peter Tanen
Benton & Bowles

Gene Tashoff
Campbell-Ewald

Jay Taub
Levine, Huntley, Schmidt & Beaver

Judy Teller
Wells, Rich, Greene

Richard Thomas
Lord, Geller, Federico, Einstein

Tom Thomas
Angotti, Thomas, Hedge

Michelle Tiberio
Geer DuBois

Joe Toto
D'Arcy MacManus Masius

Ron Travisano
Della Femina, Travisano & Partners

Bob Tucker
Doyle Dane Bernbach

Rodney Underwood
Scali, McCabe, Sloves

Steve Versandi
Needham Harper Worldwide

John Walsh
NW Ayer

Gerald Weinstein
Benton & Bowles

Peter Whitelam
Ohlmeyer Advertising

Bob Wilvers
Plapler Russo Wilvers & Associates

Mike Winslow
McKinney Silver & Rockett

Mike Withers
Ally & Gargano

Bill Wurtzel
Hicks & Greist

Mark Yustein
Della Femina, Travisano & Partners

One Club Members

Jim Aaby
Michael Abadi
Jeffrey Abbott
Francine Abdow
Erik Abel
Charles Abrams
Robin Albin
Carl Ally
J. Gregory Alderisio
Hal Altman
David Altschiller
Jeffrey Antman
Sharon Appleman
Brian Arcarese
Mark S. Archer
Victoria Atoraguan
Thomas Augusta
Pamela Averick
Ellen Azorin
Catherine W. Bahlke
Carol Ann Baker
Deborah Gaines Bannister
Stanley Banos
Lucia Barrientos
Sidney M. Barrier, Jr.
Heather Bartling
Brenda Basken
Allan Beaver
Brian Belefant
Lois Bender
Noel Berke
Ron Berger
Sandy Berger
Herbert Berkowitz
Debbie K. Bernstein
David Berstein
Neil Billings
Paul Blade
Charles Blakemore
Ilene Block
Marylou Blomer
Jack Bloom
Richard Bloom
Chris Bodden
Frank Boehm
George R. Bonner, Jr.
Kathy Botas
Michele K. Boyko
Harry M. Braver
Harvey L. Briggs
Isaac B. Brooks
Pamela Brooks
Lonnie Brown
Scott Lewis Brown
Wolfgang Brucker

Casey Burke
Ron Burkhardt
Penny Burrow
Dirk Burrows
Ed Butler
Noel R. Caban
Larry Cadman
Darlene Cah
Michael Campbell
John Caples
Bob Carducci
Robert Cargill
David Carlin
Michele Carlo
John Carrigan
Susan Carroll
Cherly Casronuove
Earl Carter
Maria Carzis
Christen Caudle
Earl Cavanah
Ronald Cesark
Sara Chereskin
Karen Cherniack
Audrey Chernoff
Joe Chiffriller
Marcia Christ
Lisa L. Chu
Joanna Cilento
W. Hunt Clark
Andrew Cohen
Dale Cohen
Deanna Cohen
Adrienne Collier
Kay Colmar
John Colquhoun
Angela Competello
Catherine Jo Cook
Lynn L. Corley
David Corr
Stephen B. Cowles
Robert B. Cox
Allison Lipe Cross
Jane L. Cross
Bruce S. Cumsky
Tom Cunniff
Dale Cunningham
Lisa Cushman
Bill D'Ambrosio
James M. Dale
Boris Damast
Debra Daum
Marilyn Davis
Michael Descul
Lewis deSeife
Brian Dillon
Bob Dion
Mary Ann Donovan
Shelley Doppelt

Stephen Doyle
Lynne Doynow
Carol Dronsfield
Neil Drossman
Miriam Dunn
Paula Dunn
Laurence Dunst
Jim Durfee
Tina S. Dyes
Charles Eaton
Arthur Einstein
Bernadette Elias
Nancy Fairstone
Suzanne V. Falter
Gene Federico
Oksana Fedorenko
Bob Feig
Corinne Felder
Steve Feldman
Jerry Della Femina
Sarah Fendrick
Jerry Fields
Peggy Fields
Sal Finazzo
Carole Anne Fine
Chuck Finkel
Carol Fiorino
Kathleen M. Fitzgerald
Marieve Fitzmaurice-Page
Daniel Flamberg
John Follis
Mel Freedman
Susan Friedman
Harvey Gabor
Bob Gage
Gretta Gallivan
Bertrand Garbassi
Amil Gargano
Rich Garramone
Paul Gary
Judith Gee
Stephen G. Gelber
John Georges
Robert Gerardi
Gary Geyer
Frank Ginsberg
Lynne Ginsberg
Sharon Glazer
Irwin Goldberg
Jennifer B. Goldin
Charles Goldman
David Goldring
Jo Ann Goldsmith
Gayle J. Goodman
Milt Gossett
Herbert Graf
Alison Grant
John Grant
Paula Green

Irma Greenfeld
Jayne Greenstein
Dick Grider
Josclynne Grier
Mary Vanderwoude Gross
Siegfried Gross
Brenda Seidler Guber
Delores Gudzin
Olivia Gushin
Robert Haigh
Jim Hallowes
Barbara Hamilton
Fred Hannaham
Keith A. Harmeyer
Joel P. Harrison
Donna Tedesco Hartmann
Paul Hartzell
Nancy Hauptman
Richard A. Headly
Mary-Lynn Hedison
Juliet Heeg
Bill Heinrich
Joan Helfman
Roy Herbert
Rony Herz
Joan Orlian Hillman
Peter Hirsch
Barbara Hood
Patrick E. T. Horne
Mike Hughes
Kate Humphrey
Linda Huss
Tony Isidore
Nik Ives
George Jaccoma
Ellen Jacobs
Harry M. Jacobs, Jr.
Corrin Jacobsen
Craig R. Jackson
Richard Jackson
Gary C. Johnson
James J. Johnson
Caroline Jones
Jessica Jossell
Alysa Anne Kadin
Charles Kane
Marshall Karp
Daniel S. Karsch
Stephen Kashtan
Nancy Beth Katsin
Linda Katz
Paul Kaufman
Richard Kaufman
John Keil
Gail Kennedy
Dana Warren King
Rhea Kirstein
Mary Kleve
Karen M. Kliewe

Esther Kong
Lois Korey
Haruo Koriyama
Judy Kostuk
Max Kovins
Helmut Krone
Richard Kuklis
Richard Kullander
Shep Kurnit
Henry Kwok
Anthony E. LaPetri
Larry Laiken
Lucille Landini
Steven Landrum
Ava Lang
Andrew Langer
Patricia Sutula Langer
Doris Latino
Mary Wells Lawrence
Lisa T. Lebduska
Bruce Lee
David L. Leedy
Jean Lehman
Dany Lee Lennon
Robert Lenz
Dorothy Leonard
Robert Levenson
Robert B. Levers
Victor Levin
Barbara A. Levine
Diana G. Levy
Stacy Lewis
Steven M. Libowitz
Lana Licht
Susan Lieber
Marsi S. Liebowitz
Lou Linder
Steve LoPresti
George Lois
Forrest Long
Allison Longo
Jeanne-Marie Lonza
Regina Lorenzo
Cecile T. Lozano
Peter Lubalin
Alden R. Ludlow, III
David Luhn
Karen Lundstrem
Lisa Lurie
Tony Macchia
Ellie MacDougall
Malcolm MacDougall
Georgia Macris
Ira Madris
Joel Maliniak
Renee Mandis
Carol Mann
Michele Mar
Martha J. Marchesi

Howard Margulies
Rodney Marquardt
Gina Mastrogiacomo
Simi J. Matera
Ed McCabe
Ruth L. McCarthy
Bill McCullam
Tom McElligott
Lynne McNamara
Robert McPherson
Peggy McVeigh
Mary Means
Leslie Stokes Mechanic
Jerome Meddick
Sid Meltzer
Debra Mendel
Barton Mercer
Mario G. Messina
Tom Messner
David C.N. Metcalf
Lyle Metzdorf
Lou Miano
Mark W. Millar
Pat Miller
Steven J. Miller
Jayne Millman
Jonathan L. Mindell
Erik Mintz
Michael Miranda
Robert Mizrahi
Thomas J. Monahan
Rafael Morales
Linda Morgenstern
Syl M. Morrone
Roger P. Mosconi
Vivian R. Moy
Norman Muchnick
Brian Mullaney
Linda Mummiani
Thomas Murray
Ed Nagler
Thomas Nathan
Jim Nealey
Chris Nehlen
Bruce S. Nelson
Eileen Norton
William Oakley
Larry Oakner
Brian Bory O'Brien
Dick O'Brien
James Offenhartz
David Ogilvy
Bunmi Ojugbele
Robert Oksner
Joe O'Neill
Philip Orenstein
Curvin O'Rielly
Jill Ottenberg
Sally Bond Ours

Maxine Paetro
Stephen V. Parker
Joanne Pateman
Richard J. A. Pels
Steve Penchina
Ellen Perless
Lynn Piasecki
David Piatkowski
Charles Pierson
Linda Pinero
Larry Plapler
Beth Player
Angelo Pocchia
Chris Pollock
Shirley Polykoff
Joseph Pompeo
Stan Quash
Elissa Querze
Brian Quinn
Jane Rabin
Richard Raboy
Jim Raniere
Ted Regan
Jan Rehder
Michael Reid
Anne Reilly
Ann Reinertsen
Bob Reitzfeld
Perry Rengepis
Donn H. Resnick
Robert Resnick
Nancy Rice
Cheryl Richman
Ruthann M. Richert
Bruce Richter
Dorrie Rifkin
Bill Ringler
Sylvia Rivera
Nancy Robbins
Phyllis Robinson
Ashley Rogers
Susan Rogers
Julie Rosenbaum
Ron Rosenfeld
Robert Rosenthal
Tom Rost
Mark Rothenberg
Leonard Ruben
Bobbie Rubin
Jane Rubini
Ken Rubman
Marchelle Rush
Dale Rushing
John Russo
Trish Russoniello
Steve Rutter
Mike Rylander
Susan Sacks
Bonnie Salkow

Joseph Sanchez
Kenneth Sandbank
Laird Sanders
Jon Sandhaus
Harry Sandler
Bob Sarlin
Carol Schaeffer
Nancy Schaffir
Louis E. Schiavone III
Joyce Schnaufer
Sy Schreckinger
Jay Schulberg
Hutcheson Schutze
Amy Schwabacher
Tom Schwartz
Ron Seichrist
Ray Seide
Mark Shap
Melisse Shapiro
Renee Sheivachman
Brett Shevack
Jamie Shevell
Virgil Cox Shutze
John Siddall
Katherine Siegmeth
Alan Silver
Sheralyn Silverstein
Ann Silvi
Susan Simmons
Karen L. Simon
Claudia Simpson
Leonard Sirowitz
Bill Sklazie
Sara J. Slater
Mike Slosberg
Jo Smith
Laurie Smith
Stephen Smith
Alan Solomon
Richard Solomon
Martin Solow
Mark Spector
Susan Spelman
Andrea Sperling
Helayne Spivak
Dean Stefanides
Robin M. Steinberg
Lesley Stern
Diane Stiles
Stan Stoj
Ray Stollerman
Debora Stone
Andrea Stout
Ira Sturtevant
Len Sugarman
Randall Swatek
Joseph M. Sweet
Ilene Cohn Tanen
Norman Tanen

Jack George Tauss
Judy Teller
Marty Tempkin
Mike Tesch
Barbara Thompson
Beckwith Thompson
Deepak Thosar
Daniel Tilles
Janice Tisch
Juanita Torrence-Thompson
Ron Travisano
Barri Lynn Tretiak
Amy Tufel
Don Turner
Jerry Turner
Carol Turturro
Micheline D. Turturro
Nancy Tynan
Diane Unger
Sharon Vanderslice
Joan Van Der Veen
William F. Vartorella
Annette C. Vendryes
Pieter Verbeck
Gloria Viseltear
Ned Viseltear
Evelyn Vogel
Peter Vogt
Nina Wachsman
Judy Wald
Marvin Waldman
Matt Warhaftig
Thomas Weber
Bruce Weinberg
Carol L. Weinfeld
Gary Weinraub
Riva B. Weinstein
Lisa Weintraub
Frank Weiss
Mark Evan Weitzman
Lynn Welsh
Garth A. White
Thomas E. White
Anne V. Whitney
Richard Wilde
Cynthia Williamson
Kurt Willinger
Kevin Willis
Renee Wilson
Robert W. Wilvers
Cindy Wojdyla
David Wojdyla
Connie Kail Wolf
Mark Wolf
Tracy V. Wong
Sandra Wright
Elizabeth Wynn
Terri Yenko
Mark Zucker

GOLD, SILVER & BRONZE AWARDS

Consumer Newspaper
Over 600 Lines: Single

1 GOLD
ART DIRECTOR
Amy Schottenfels
WRITER
Bruce Richter
PHOTOGRAPHER
Alan Dolgins
CLIENT
Perdue
AGENCY
Scali McCabe Sloves

2 SILVER
ART DIRECTORS
Jeff Vogt
Tony Angotti
WRITER
Tom Thomas
DESIGNER
Jeff Vogt
PHOTOGRAPHER
Cailor/Resnick
CLIENT
BMW of North America
AGENCY
Ammirati & Puris

3 BRONZE
ART DIRECTOR
Gary Johnston
WRITER
Laurie Brandalise
PHOTOGRAPHER
Ron Avery
CLIENT
Apple Computer
AGENCY
Chiat/Day-Los Angeles

WHO CARES
WHERE THE BEEF IS?
Frank Perdue

1 GOLD

THE HIGH-PERFORMANCE VEHICLE ON THE LEFT NOW USES THE SAME KIND OF BRAKING SYSTEM AS THE ONE ON THE RIGHT.

2 SILVER

Apple announces a technological breakthrough of incredible proportions.

3 BRONZE

Cars aren't built to last forever.
But there's one 1984 automobile that's destined to remain on this planet decidedly longer than most of today's other cars.

It's a Volvo.

Because while the average life expectancy of today's cars is 11 years, statistics show the average life expectancy of today's Volvos is over 16 years.*

Which could mean years of traversing the globe in a car that will fare well against the elements. Because

Volvos are dipped in a rust resisting bath that coats them with a layer of zinc three times thicker than cars coated by conventional electrogalvanizing.

Years of superb maneuverability from an automobile that literally hugs the earth thanks to a specially tuned suspension system.

Years of being surrounded by a car ergonomically designed to be so thoroughly comfortable and efficient to use, there's even a footrest for the drivers left foot, so both feet will be on the same

plane, thereby reducing muscle tension.

Of course, these are just but a few of the amenities you'll find on a Volvo.

To experience the pleasures afforded by the others, visit your nearest Volvo dealer.

After all, statistics show we could make it to the next century.

And that's more than we can say for such possible endangered species as today's Mustangs, Cougars, Firebirds, Thunderbirds... **VOLVO**
A car you can believe in.

IN 2000 A.D., WHILE TODAY'S VOLVOS ARE STILL ROAMING THE EARTH, OUR COMPETITION WILL BE AN ENDANGERED SPECIES.

4 GOLD

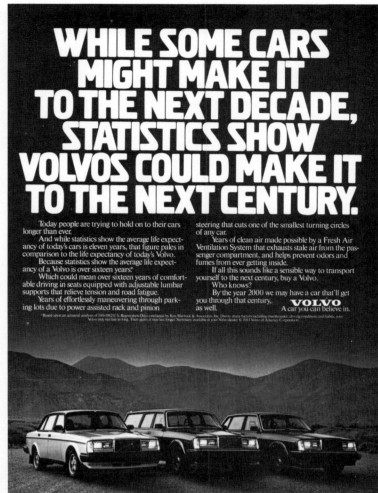

**Consumer Newspaper
Over 600 Lines:
Campaign**

5 SILVER
ART DIRECTOR
Richard Osborn
WRITER
David Morris
PHOTOGRAPHER
Terry Ellis
CLIENT
The Australian Government
AGENCY ,
Weekes Morris & Osborn/
Australia

ELEPHANT KILLED BY BRACELET.

An ivory bracelet means one less elephant. And there aren't too many elephants left. The Australian National Parks and Wildlife Service has always been concerned with the protection of wildlife.

The Australian Government has now proclaimed the Wildlife Protection Act 1982, which consolidates Australian controls over international trade in wildlife into the one Act.

The Act lists species in Australia and overseas, endangered by exploitation.

This list includes crocodiles and turtles, pythons and lizards, elephants and plants. From now on the import and export of protected wildlife will be more strictly controlled.

If you return from overseas with endangered species or products made from endangered species, you risk their confiscation and a fine of up to $100,000.

If you import or export commercial quantities of these endangered species without a permit you risk greater penalties.

Before you consider buying or trading in wildlife, make sure you're not endangering a species or endangering yourself.

Send to: Director, Australian National Parks and Wildlife Service. Attention: Wildlife Protection Section, G.P.O. Box 636. Canberra. A.C.T. 2601.

APW 11 1811 103

Name_____ Address_____ Postcode_____

I don't want to endanger a species. Please send me literature on wildlife protection. I am interested in ☐ Commercial Trade ☐ General

5 SILVER

PYTHON KILLED BY BELT.

A python belt means one less python. And there aren't too many pythons left.

The Australian National Parks and Wildlife Service has always been concerned with the protection of wildlife.

The Australian Government has now proclaimed the Wildlife Protection Act 1982, which consolidates Australian controls over international trade in wildlife into the one Act. The Act lists species in Australia and overseas, endangered by exploitation. This list includes crocodiles and turtles, elephants and plants, pythons and lizards.

From now on the import and export of protected wildlife will be more strictly controlled.

If you return from overseas with endangered species or products made from endangered species, you risk their confiscation and a fine of up to $100,000.

If you import or export commercial quantities of these endangered species without a permit you risk greater penalties.

Before you consider buying or trading in wildlife, make sure you're not endangering a species or endangering yourself.

LEOPARD KILLED BY RUG.

A leopard-skin rug means one less leopard. And there aren't too many leopards left.

The Australian National Parks and Wildlife Service has always been concerned with the protection of wildlife.

The Australian Government has now proclaimed the Wildlife Protection Act 1982, which consolidates Australian controls over international trade in wildlife into the one Act. The Act lists species in Australia and overseas, endangered by exploitation. This list includes crocodiles and turtles, elephants and plants, pythons and leopards. From now on the import and export of protected wildlife will be more strictly controlled.

If you return from overseas with endangered species or products made from endangered species, you risk their confiscation and a fine of up to $100,000.

If you import or export commercial quantities of these endangered species without a permit you risk greater penalties.

Before you consider buying or trading in wildlife, make sure you're not endangering a species or endangering yourself.

Finally, a produce section with some meat to it.

Two years ago Ukrops made a decision to grow. Carrots, beans, nectarines, melons, artichokes, broccoli, oranges, avocados, even bamboo.

We wanted to have the largest selection of fresh produce in the area.

And we wanted more than choice, we wanted quality.

Pineapples had to be field-ripened to the peak of sweetness and flown in twice a week from Hawaii.

Overgrown cucumbers wouldn't do. (Too many seeds.)

So instead of just getting on the phone, we got on a plane.

We visited grape growers in California. We tasted grapefruits in Florida. We looked for the most flavorful fruits and vegetables in the country.

Today, over 175 different produce items are delivered fresh to Ukrops stores. And unlike many supermarkets, we make sure they stay fresh.

Our produce clerks are constantly watering, trimming and restocking items. We dig through the potatoes looking for bruises. And any bad apples are weeded out.

Ukrops also has a customer alert program to keep you informed on such things as the availability, flavor and nutritional value of particular items.

So if you want your pick of the finest fruits and vegetables available, come to us. If it's in season, chances are it's in Ukrops.

Ukrops

6 BRONZE

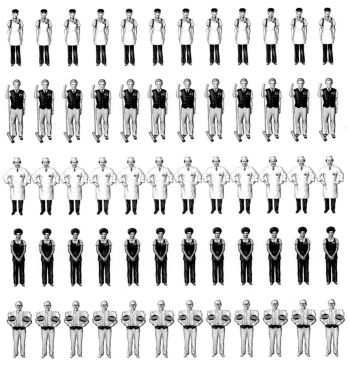

Ukrops has more of these hard to find items than any other supermarket.

At some supermarkets the hardest thing to find is help. Not at Ukrops.

What other stores spend on stamps, games and promotions, we spend on employees.

In fact, according to an independent survey, Ukrops has nearly twice as many employees per store than the average Richmond area supermarket.

That means if you have trouble finding something there's always someone close by to help you.

And we won't just point you in the general direction. We'll take you to it.

Having more people means a number of other things, too. For instance, there's always someone looking after the produce. Watering, trimming and restocking fresh fruits and vegetables.

Unlike many supermarkets, we don't trim the hours of our butchers. If we're open, there's always a butcher on duty to help you.

Even when we're not open people are working. Restocking shelves at night so you don't have to walk around boxes and cartons during the day.

And every Ukrops employee attends regular educational meetings. We believe the more you know about your business, the more you'll enjoy doing your job.

Perhaps all of this is why Richmond shoppers recently rated Ukrops as having the friendliest personnel, fastest checkout service, most attractive interiors, best meat and produce departments, cleanest stores and most orderly arrangement of items of any other supermarket in the area.

Visit Ukrops. It's hard to find a reason not to.

Ukrops

Not every supermarket's deli can cut the mustard.

You'd have to go a long way to beat the delicatessens in Ukrops.

Maybe all the way to New York.

Ukrops' delis have over 60 different meats to choose from.

Italian salamis. Spicy pastramis. Roast beef from rare to well-done.

And we're really full of bologna. Ten different kinds, including special low-salt and no-sugar.

You can buy ham that's baked, smoked, or boiled. Fresh baked turkey breast. Corned beef. Even, if you have a taste for it, smoked tongue.

Ukrops delis have a huge selection of cheeses, too. Over 35 varieties, from nine different countries. And, like our meats, we'll slice each one to the exact thickness you ask for.

And what's a thick deli sandwich without deli bread? Ukrops delis bake more than 25 assorted breads and rolls fresh each day. From Vienna to pumpernickel.

Now, many other delis would stop right here. (Most supermarket delis wouldn't

get this far.) At Ukrops, it's just the beginning.

Our deli salads are meals in themselves. Your choice includes seafood, macaroni, chunky chicken, shrimp, pasta and three varieties of potato salad.

Our two cole slaws are second to none.

And have we got kosher food for you. Hebrew National and Best meats, great bagels, Challah bread and, of course, kosher dill pickles.

Many of our delis sell fresh dried pasta. Several even offer delicious Southern fried chicken. And all of them will make up party trays full of assorted meats and cheeses, relishes, dips, open-faced sandwiches or whatever else you may ask for.

So if you want a great selection of deli foods like those we've just mentioned, remember: there are only 14 supermarkets that can cut the mustard.

And they're all Ukrops.

Ukrops

**Consumer Magazine
B/W: 1 Page Or Spread
(Including Magazine
Supplements)**

7 GOLD
ART DIRECTOR
Dennis D'Amico
WRITER
Ron Berger
PHOTOGRAPHER
Robert Ammirati
CLIENT
Timberland
AGENCY
Ally & Gargano

8 SILVER
ART DIRECTOR
Susan Mueller-Roepke
WRITER
Renee Valois
PHOTOGRAPHER
John Posl
CLIENT
WCCO-TV
AGENCY
Carmichael-Lynch/Mpls.

9 BRONZE
ART DIRECTOR
G. Oliver White
WRITER
Linda Satterfield
DESIGNER
G. Oliver White
PHOTOGRAPHER
Jack Richmond
CLIENT
Hersey Custom Shoe
Company

SHOES FOR PEOPLE WHO ARE WEIGHT-CONSCIOUS.

As you can see, Timberland® lightweight casual shoes weigh a scant 11.5 oz. each.

They may be light in weight but, since they're Timberlands, they're long on quality.

They have a special 2-density orthotic innersole (one layer for comfort, the other for support) and a fully padded collar around the ankles that make them ideal shoes for doing lots of walking.

And they're made with full-grained, oil-impregnated leathers (the same tough but supple leathers we use in our handsewns), and a rugged "Morflex"/Vibram®sole. So you can be sure they won't wear out on those long walks before you do.

Finally, they contain another attractive feature you might want to weigh before deciding which lightweight casuals to buy: a price that's as much as $10 less than similar shoes from the competition.

Which, all things considered, should heavily tip the scales in our favor.

Timberland ®

The Timberland Company, P.O. Box 7005, Portsmouth, New Hampshire 03801

*Registered trademarks of The Timberland Company. © 1984 The Timberland Company.

Available at: Jordan Marsh, Macy's New York, Lazarus, Marshall Field's, Dayton's, Macy's California, Burdines, Britches Great Outdoors, Abercrombie & Fitch.

Is this ad worth 28% less because it was written by a woman?

A lot of men must think so, because women in advertising with 5 years of experience earn 28% less than their male counterparts.[1] And that's _better_ than average for working women — who make about 60¢ for every dollar a man earns.[2]

That's not exactly liberty and justice for all.

Find out more about the status of Minnesota's working women and about their pay, power and poverty. Watch WCCO TV's five part "Cover Story." And if you are a woman, get your boss to watch.

Maybe you'll get a raise. [1] ADWEEK Salary Survey, June 1984 [2] U.S. Department of Labor, April 1983

"Working Women" tonight through Thursday night on WCCO TV's 10 PM REPORT.

WCCO-TV

We're thinking news. We're thinking of you.

©1984 WCCO TV

Most Companies Make More Running Shoes In A Day Than I Make In A Year.

And that's the way I want it.

My Hersey Custom running shoes take longer because each pair is custom made. Not made to sort of fit thousands of people who sort of wear your size.

Even before I begin your shoes, I get information about your feet that a mass-producer of running shoes will never have. Like measurements of each foot. And a complete running history.

I want to get to know you and your feet.

—*Bart Hersey*

Because in my workshop you're in control. You participate in deciding how your shoes will fit and perform.

The design of the Hersey Custom is not like any other. Not only do they look different, but wait until you try them out. Every part of my shoe is designed to give the best possible fit and performance. Using the best materials available.

And I challenge you to find a shoe with better rear foot control.

How many pairs of running shoes have you had to throw out because the soles gave out before the uppers? That won't happen to mine. The outsoles are made of Goodyear Indy 500 rubber and I'll replace the entire bottoms the first time they wear out. And you'll pay nothing, except the postage.

And finally, there's workmanship. My name is on every shoe, so they don't leave the shop without my OK. For $150, you should expect beautifully made, handcrafted shoes. I give you just that.

You'll get more information about the shoes by sending for my brochure. An order form comes with it. All you've got to do then, to get me started on your Hersey Customs, is to send back that form with your check.

So, just send your name and address to the Hersey Custom Shoe Co., RFD #3, Box 7390, Framington, Maine 04938. Or call me at 207-645-3015.

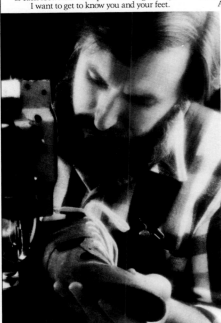

The Hersey Custom
The Shoe For Only A Few.

Consumer Magazine Color: 1 Page Or Spread (Including Magazine Supplements)

10 GOLD
ART DIRECTOR
Gary Johns
WRITER
Jeff Gorman
PHOTOGRAPHER
Mark Coppos
CLIENT
Nike
AGENCY
Chiat/Day-Los Angeles

11 SILVER
ART DIRECTOR
Gary Johns
WRITER
Jeff Gorman
PHOTOGRAPHER
Mark Coppos
CLIENT
Nike
AGENCY
Chiat/Day-Los Angeles

12 BRONZE
ART DIRECTOR
Simon Bowden
WRITER
Frank Fleizach
PHOTOGRAPHER
Harry DeZitter
CLIENT
Volvo
AGENCY
Scali McCabe Sloves

10 GOLD

STATISTICS FOR PEOPLE INTERESTED IN NOT BECOMING STATISTICS.

"A barrier impact at 35 mph can generate between 80,000 and 120,000 lbs of force."

"In a 30 mph front end collision, a 165 lb man hits the windshield with a force of 3 tons."

"A 10 mph increase in impact speed from 30 to 40 mph means that 79% more energy must be absorbed."

Let a bunch of safety engineers slam enough cars into a wall and statistics like these begin to pile up.

The more of them you have to work with, the safer the car you can build.

At Volvo, safety has always been a high priority.

So every year at our Technical Center in Gothenburg,

Sweden, we destroy between 70 and 80 Volvos in crash tests.

And the statistics we've gathered over the years have helped us make the kinds of innovations that have made Volvo the standard of safety for the automobile industry.

Our now famous steel "safety cage," for instance, surrounds the passenger compartment of a Volvo and is designed to keep it from crumpling during a collision. Every weld in it is strong

enough to support the weight of the entire car.

At either end of a Volvo is a built-in safety zone. It's especially designed *to* crumple in order to absorb some of the energy forces of a collision instead of passing them along to the occupants.

To make sure you have protection on all sides in a Volvo, we've placed tubular, steel anti-intrusion bars in all doors.

Even our steering column is designed to collapse upon impact and our laminated windshield is designed

to remain intact.

Of course no car can protect you in a crash unless you're wearing the safety innovation that became standard equipment in Volvos back in 1959: the three point safety belt. (Statistics show that fifty percent of the deaths due to road accidents could be avoided if drivers and passengers were wearing them.)

So if you're interested in not becoming a highway statistic, take a precaution the next time you take to the highway.

Be sure to fasten your safety belt.

And incidentally, it might be a good idea to be sure it's fastened to a Volvo.

VOLVO CRASH TEST RESULTS

VOLVO
A car you can believe in.

**Consumer Magazine
B/W: Campaign
(Including Magazine
Supplements)**

13 GOLD
ART DIRECTOR
Tana Klugherz
WRITER
Stephanie Arnold
CLIENT
McCall's Magazine
AGENCY
Levine Huntley Schmidt &
Beaver

ONE OF THE DRAB HOMEBODIES WHO READS McCALL'S.

McCall's
MORE THAN THE EXPECTED.

13 GOLD

ONE OF THE TYPICAL MOTHERS
WHO READS McCALL'S.

McCall's
MORE THAN THE EXPECTED.

ONE OF THE BORING HOUSEWIVES
WHO READS McCALL'S.

McCall's
MORE THAN THE EXPECTED.

**Consumer Magazine
B/W: Campaign
(Including Magazine
Supplements)**

14 SILVER

ART DIRECTOR
Pat Burnham

WRITER
Bill Miller

PHOTOGRAPHER
Craig Perman

CLIENT
WFLD-TV

AGENCY
Fallon McElligott Rice/Mpls.

14 SILVER

THE PERFECT END TO A PERFECT MARRIAGE.

Bette Davis and James Stewart, together on the screen for the
first time, star in RIGHT OF WAY, a stirring and sensitive drama about
an aging couple's determined struggle to decide their own fate.

WATCH "RIGHT OF WAY" THURSDAY AT 8 PM

32
WFLD TV
METROMEDIA CHICAGO

SEE THE FIRST WOMAN SCHEDULED TO GO TO DA MOON.

One of these days, Alice. Bam. Pow. Zoom. Join other fans in
Chicago's first Raccoon Lodge convention saluting five of the
best loved episodes of The Honeymooners.

WATCH THE BEST OF THE HONEYMOONERS MON-WED 9:30 PM, THURS 9:00 PM.

WFLD TV
METROMEDIA CHICAGO

**Consumer Magazine
Color: Campaign
(Including Magazine
Supplements)**

15 GOLD

ART DIRECTOR
Gary Johns

WRITER
Jeff Gorman

PHOTOGRAPHERS
Mark Coppos
Carl Furuta

CLIENT
Nike

AGENCY
Chiat/Day-Los Angeles

THE CAR THAT COULD SINGLE-HANDEDLY JUSTIFY AN AMERICAN AUTOBAHN.

The world's largest monument to automotive high performance stretches for 7,500 kilometers in Germany. You know it as the autobahn: a network of superhighways where drivers are restrained solely by their cars. BMW engineers know it as one of the major inspirations for the BMW 533i.

To survive autobahn driving—i.e., cruising all day at full throttle, the 533i is equipped with "3.2 liters of six-cylinder, electronically fuel-injected, single-overhead-cam smoothness and ferocity" (Car and Driver). It will do 0 to 60 in what one journalist termed "a stir-

ringly negligible 7.7 seconds" and the standing quarter-mile in 15.8 seconds.

Control of this ferocity is handled by the 533i's patented, fully-independent suspension as well as a power-assisted steering system that "continues a standard by which other systems should be judged" (Road & Track).

What makes this performance even more exhilarating is the fact that it requires no concessions in the area of creature comforts. The 533i offers fully adjustable leather seats, air-conditioning, a two-way sunroof, a digital AM/FM stereo system, and electric windows

and mirrors to name a few.

All of which provides you with a great deal of fun searching out roads that can challenge a 533i, while you await construction of an autobahn in your locale.

THE ULTIMATE DRIVING MACHINE.

16 SILVER

Gold,
Silver
&
Bronze
Awards

**Consumer Magazine
Color: Campaign
(Including Magazine
Supplements)**

17 BRONZE
ART DIRECTOR
Jerry Whitley
WRITER
Joe O'Neill
DESIGNER
Jerry Whitley
PHOTOGRAPHER
Ernst Hermann Ruth
CLIENT
BMW of North America
AGENCY
Ammirati & Puris

THE MOST HONORED MOTORCYCLE IN JAPANESE HISTORY ISN'T JAPANESE.

November 25, 1983, was a face-losing day for Japanese motorcycle manufacturers.

For it was on that day that Japan's fabled buff book, Car Graphic, dedicated an entire buff issue to a German motorcycle. The first time any two-wheeler had been so honored.

© 1984 BMW of North America, Inc. The BMW trademark and logo are registered.

"Occasioned by the announcement of the epoch-making superbikes which BMW calls its K-series," the dedication read, "we at CG have condensed the entire BMW Motorcycle story into this one volume for the enjoyment of our devoted readers."

And devoted they are: To the Japanese enthusiast, Car Graphic is the bible of all motorcycle and automotive writing.

Here then is the gospel according to Shotaro Kobayashi, Car Graphic's premier motorcycle journalist.

"The K turned out to be a bike in which no flaws could be found…built with a precision that far surpasses that of other bikes.

"There is nothing equivocal about the electronically controlled twin-cam engine which begins to push the K 100 smoothly, exuberantly, with a power that is beautiful to experience. The bike holds its course through turn after turn and rights itself smartly…so that the powerful twin-cam, four-cylinder engine can be used to the fullest. Though still unfulfilled, the dream of one

day owning a BMW motorcycle burns continually somewhere in my mind."

Those sharing Kobayashi's dream can make it materialize with a visit to their BMW dealer.

THE LEGENDARY MOTORCYCLES OF GERMANY.

17 BRONZE

Trade B/W: 1 Page Or Spread

18 GOLD
ART DIRECTOR
Rob Tomnay
WRITER
Jack Vaughan
ARTIST
Tony Langmead
CLIENT
The Campaign Palace
AGENCY
The Campaign Palace/
Australia

19 SILVER
ART DIRECTOR
David Garcia
WRITER
Mike Rogers
DESIGNER
David Garcia
PHOTOGRAPHER
Sean Eager
CLIENT
Michelin Tire
AGENCY
Doyle Dane Bernbach

20 BRONZE
ART DIRECTOR
Mark Yustein
WRITER
Rita Senders
CLIENT
USA Cable Network
AGENCY
Della Femina Travisano
Sherman & Olken

The best job ever offered in Australian advertising.

It may sound like advertising overclaim, but it isn't.

Because there's no other way to describe it.
The best job ever offered in Australian advertising.

Which must mean it's the top job at the biggest agency. Or the wealthiest. Or the fastest-growing. Or the most respected.

But it isn't.

Many fine agencies have already reached one or another of these goals. Because they've run their race.

Surely the best job in advertising, when you think about it, is Managing Director of an agency that hasn't yet reached these goals.

Yet is also perfectly poised to reach not one, but *all* of them.

The name of the agency is The Campaign Palace, Sydney.

And if you just hesitated long enough to agree these objectives are possible, perhaps the next thousand or so words will explain why.

A myth shattered.

Of the 340 accredited agencies in Australia, The Campaign Palace, quite simply, aims to be the best of them all.

The myth still persists – to our great advantage – that an agency can either be creative or businesslike, but not both.

To our way of thinking, it is impossible to be one without the other.

This isn't simply a case of offering the best of both worlds.

As far as we're concerned, the two worlds are one and the same.

Hidden Talent.

There's never any confusion at The Palace about what we're trying to do.

While this makes life easier in one respect, it makes it satisfyingly difficult in others.

We strive for the best solutions rather than settle for easy ones.

Whether we're creating a campaign or hiring a Managing Director.

We refuse to accept, for instance, that we will know every possible candidate that exists.

Certainly it's worth talking to big names, and we already are. (You don't need to run an ad to track *them* down.)

But there's also a chance that the very best prospect may not be well known just yet.

Perhaps their path's blocked by a Number One who's as fit as a scrub bull and looks like occupying the chair forever.

Equally, they could be someone waiting patiently for the perfect opportunity to start their own agency.

(And what could be better than starting off with a great client list and top staff?)

High standards.

Whether the name turns out to be well known or not, one thing is certain.

The right person will have a lot going for them already.

For one thing, they will possess the happy ability to get along with others.

People are by far our most important asset, and we definitely include our clients in this group.

Another important prerequisite is that our candidate be in the advertising business.

Even a dazzler who's ideal in every other respect could prove to be a liability while learning the fundamentals.

(We're also convinced it takes years to gain a useful perspective in our profession.)

Considerable emphasis will also be placed upon marketing wisdom.

No specialist will seek the advice of those they don't consider equal.

This could mean someone who might well have been a top Marketing Director, had they not been sidetracked by advertising.

The twin blessings of ambition and dedication will also carry weight.

Nowhere is it carved in stone that an agency can't be large as well as excellent.

(It certainly isn't an attitude we would subscribe to. In the last year, we've managed to more than double our billings.)

It would seem that a growing number of companies are recognising the strong connection between outstanding creative work and outstanding sales results.)

This leads directly into another important requirement; a track record of business building.

A suitable prospect will be able to point to ways in which they've contributed to the growth of their current agency.

We will also, among many other things, be impressed by qualities of leadership, judgement, enthusiasm, business acumen and stability.

All of which may start to sound like a job for Superman or Wonderwoman.

But before you take off your glasses and unbutton your shirt, please be assured you won't have to perform spectacular feats single-handed.

Small, but perfectly-formed.

The Campaign Palace, Sydney, is an agency with the highest calibre of people already in position.

It's not uncommon for us to have Account Directors who've been MD's at other agencies. As well as Writers and Art Directors who've been agency principals in their own right. (Giving them a commercial imperative rare in the breed.)

This touches on a question we're often asked: "Is the Palace creatively dominated?"

Given the current situation we might well reply: "It depends on how creatively you go about dominating it."

Indeed, the Palace does have more than its fair share of creative people. Except that some of them are called Account Directors, Researchers, Production Managers and Media Planners.

Or Managing Directors.

Our policy is to only hire the best possible person for each role.

This tends to mean we don't hire juniors; preferring to appease our industry conscience by teaching students after hours.

Thus our clients deal only with senior people.

And the lines of communication are kept short and clear.

Strategy.

As you can imagine, attitudes like these lead to some excellent work.

Great ads, however, are actually the last thing we do.

None of our work is produced off-the-cuff, out of thin air, or off the top of the head.

Long before Pentels are ever put to paper, we find out all we can about the marketing aspects of a client's business.

Examining every cornerstone and stumbling block of the product, the consumer, the trade and the competition.

Involving ourselves to a degree you might expect of a partner more than an agent.

Armed with all this information, we still don't dash off any ideas.

Instead, we sit down with our client and work out a strategy every bit as unique as the business problem it is designed to solve.

More than being just a guideline for an ad, it's a blueprint for the success of the total brand.

Then, and only then, do we go and do the ads for which our clients' products are famous.

Which may well be the last part.

But by no means the least.

The satisfaction of being accountable.

In the year just past, The Campaign Palace, Sydney won more awards than any other agency in Australia.

(More, some say, than our Melbourne office, though we're too polite to count.)

Nice as this is, it doesn't hold as much fascination for us as the effect we have on sales.

During the last calendar year, clients across the board showed sales increases of between 23% and 125%, in a year of recession.

Clearly, there's potential for enormous job satisfaction.

But ours is very much a business too, and in the end, it all comes down to making some money.

We're offering a package designed to attract even the highest fliers in the business.

To go into details here would perhaps be inappropriate.

Suffice to say at this stage that the right person stands to make their fortune along with ours.

If the job you have now just became second-best, please don't hesitate to call Lionel Hunt, The Campaign Palace, Sydney. (02) 960 3366.

IF YOU CAN MAKE IT HERE,
YOU CAN MAKE IT ANYWHERE.

New York, New York. There's no tougher proving ground in the world, especially for a car. But one, the Volvo, can take just about anything this city can dish out. And it keeps coming back to pick up more.

Fact is, the average Volvo lasts an astounding 16 years; that's one-third longer* than all other cars on the street.

And if a Volvo can make it as a taxi in New York, **VOLVO** just think how well it'll hack it in your hometown.   A car you can believe in.

*Based on an actuarial analysis of 1981-1982 U.S. passenger car registrations including non-taxi vehicles. Registration Data conducted by Ken Warwick & Associates, Inc. Due to many factors including maintenance, driving conditions and habits, your Volvo may not last as long. Then again, it may last longer. Summary available at your Volvo dealer. © 1984 Volvo of America Corporation.

22 SILVER

See how simple financing can be.

Now financing IBM equipment doesn't have to be a whole lot more complicated than signing on our dotted line.

To begin with, our master agreement is a mere four pages long. And you only need to sign it once.

Your signature will get you flexible financing. We offer a wide range of lease or installment purchase options to help you tailor a plan that suits your company's needs.

Your signature also gets you low rates. We're competitive.

And if you want to add or upgrade equipment down the road, a simple supplement to your original contract is all it takes.

So how do you go about getting IBM Credit Corporation financing?

Just call the same person who helps you choose the IBM computer or office equipment you need.

Your IBM marketing representative.

It's that simple.

IBM
Credit Corporation

23 BRONZE

Gold, Silver & Bronze Awards

Trade Any Size B/W Or Color Campaign

24 GOLD
ART DIRECTORS
Dean Hanson
John Morrison
WRITERS
Jarl Olsen
Rod Kilpatrick
PHOTOGRAPHERS
Rick Dublin
Kent Severson
CLIENT
ITT Life
AGENCY
Fallon McElligott Rice/Mpls.

IN 1986, WE'LL HAVE MORE AGENTS IN HONG KONG THAN THE C.I.A. AND THE K.G.B. COMBINED.

For a long time our agents knew there was a very special mission in the offing.

But its exact nature was veiled in secrecy.

Now the story can be told. ITT Life's top-producing salespeople will be rewarded with a trip to our 1986 convention.

In Hong Kong. For six nights.

Along with their spouses Transportation included.

Now, if you can't imagine sitting around an insurance convention for nearly a week, neither can we. So you'll undoubtedly be left with quite a bit of time to kill on your own.

That shouldn't be any trouble. After all, this is Hong Kong we're talking about.

And if you have a really good couple years, we could also be talking about Athens, Bali, Cairo, Honolulu, Melbourne, London and Paris.

Just for starters.

Because after the ITT Life convention, you could qualify for our additional travel bonuses — ranging from two nights in Honolulu to a fifteen-night trip around the world.

By the way, our Hong Kong incentive isn't some unattainable golden carrot.

Any reasonably good agent has an excellent chance.

That is, any agent who's signed up with us.

Which brings us to the point of this ad. For all the details about our current sales opportunities — and about our mission to the Orient —

call ITT Life at (612) 545-2100.

We may not be the only organization that sends its agents to Hong Kong.

But we're the only one that can promise to bring them back.

ITT *ITT Life Insurance Corporation*

ONCE AGAIN, I.T.T. LIFE HITS BELOW THE BELT.

This Fall, ITT Life will embark on a most unusual life insurance promotion. In full page newspaper ads across the country, the *ITT Life $100 Challenge* will offer $100 to any consumer who can produce a whole life policy that we can't beat. All the policy holder will have to do is call us for a free comparison with their present rates. If we can't give them more coverage at a lower premium, we'll give them $100.

Needless to say, this will almost surely elicit calls of "Foul!" from our competitors—most of whom have built their businesses around whole life.

We're no strangers to controversy. In 1981, we declared "whole life is dead" and stopped selling it altogether.

We introduced a new line of plans that provided customers with more coverage at lower premiums than whole life.

When exercise became a national pastime, we offered a Good Health Bonus that rewarded those who keep fit. In the same way, our non-smokers policies gave liberal premium concessions to those who shunned cigarettes.

All of these measures have earned us the brand of "maverick" and "renegade" in the industry.

Not that that has hurt us. In two years, our total premium in force has jumped 74%. Our average premium per case is up 52%. The face value of insurance we issue annually is up 102%. And that doesn't even reflect the jump expected from this year's promotions.

Speaking of which, maybe you'd like to benefit from our $100 Challenge? All you as an agent would have to do is pick up the policies and close the sales.

We'd provide leads and prepare the rate comparisons which are almost guaranteed to sway the prospect.

There's a lot more that we could offer you as an ITT Life agent. National advertising and telemarketing support. Consumer initiated leads. Computer software. Incentives that include a 1986 convention in Hong Kong.

We have the most innovative exchange program in the industry and we're looking for people to put it to use.

Send in the postage-free reply card—or call us collect at 612-545-2100, ext. 32 and we'll give you a complete rundown on the benefits of becoming an ITT Life agent.

Right now you may be uncomfortable with the thought of working for a company that does business as aggressively as ITT Life. You'll get used to it; our own agents seldom complain about our hitting below the belt.

ITT ITT Life Insurance Corporation

HOW 10,000 AGENTS STARTED OUT SELLING THE GOOD LIFE, AND ENDED UP LIVING IT.

It ought to be obvious that the way for a life insurance agent to prosper is by selling the kind of life insurance people want.

But it's apparently not obvious to everyone.

An awful lot of agents are still trying to make it by pushing the same traditional products. The ones life insurance companies want to sell, instead of the ones people want to buy.

At ITT Life, our philosophy is about 180 degrees different. We let the marketplace do the talking, and we listen hard.

For instance, when the rest of the industry was still hanging on to whole life, we let go. Our new line of term-plus-cash accumulation plans was a resounding success.

And when fitness became a way of life in America, we also made it a way of life insurance. Our array of good-health bonuses has been hailed by *Executive Fitness*

Newsletter as the best in the business.

Still, we're not about to rest on our laurels. This summer we'll shake up the marketplace again with the introduction of four innovative new plans.

As you might suspect, we're not alone in our progressive outlook. Since 1981, we've seen a 500% leap in recruitment of new agents.

And they're not sitting around on their hands, either.

In two years, our total premium in force has jumped 74%. Our average premium per case is up 52%. The face amount of insurance we issue annually has increased 102%.

That's good news for us.

But more to the point, our first-year annualized commissions have risen 80%. We pay them weekly. We provide computer software and telemarketing support.

And our conventions and incentives are as exciting as our sales curve. For instance, after our 1986 Hong Kong convention, our top producers can qualify for trips as exotic as a round-the-world junket.

That's good news for our agents.

Finally, our booming sales are opening up tremendous opportunities for talented people who see the wisdom of joining up with a leader.

That's good news for you. Send in the postage-free reply card—or call us collect at **(612)-545-2100, ext. 32**— and we'll give you the whole story of agent opportunities with ITT Life.

Once you've looked into it, you'll understand the simple rule that motivated 10,000 agents to sign on with us:

If you want to live the kind of life everyone wants, you've got to sell the kind of life everyone wants.

ITT ITT Life Insurance Corporation

Ten-year-old Iranian boys are sent onto the battlefield to detonate mines. They are told, "If you return, you'll be executed."

Some of the boys are armed only with plastic keys to heaven because, says Khomeini, if they are killed on the battlefield, they will go directly to heaven. And, they are told, they will be killed regardless.

An original article in the August Reader's Digest reports the grisly facts of the Iran-Iraq war, a war in which 250,000 have already died. How will it end? One Iraqi major answers, "Inshallah" —as God wills it.

The Digest® arms 54 million readers with understanding.

In 1978, a Finnish politician tried to ban Donald Duck. One of the charges against Donald was he hadn't married Daisy Duck.

This attitude, however, is atypical. Today, Donald's films play in 76 countries. And several countries are issuing postage stamps in his honor.

To mark Donald's 50th birthday, an original article in the May Reader's Digest traces the careers of Donald and 79-year-old Clarence Nash, who has *been* Donald from the beginning—ever since he walked into Walt Disney's small studio and rendered "Mary Had a Little Lamb" in Duckspeak.

55 million readers take to The Digest® like ducks to water.

It is known that one way to avoid getting malaria is to sleep with a pig— so mosquitoes bite him instead of you. It is not known what the pig thinks of this arrangement.

A great many mosquitoes (there are some 3000 species and subspecies) would rather dine on some animal other than man. Which, inasmuch as mosquitoes transmit malaria, yellow fever, dengue and encephalitis, you might want to encourage.

The July Reader's Digest sadly reports that swatting a few hundred mosquitoes per day is like "trying to ladle out the ocean with a teaspoon." So "consider giving up and going inside." Perhaps with a pig.

54 million people read The Digest® every month—a very nice arrangement.

A brief case for our portable video system.

Exhibit A. Toshiba's V-X340 VCR.

Even with its rechargable battery, it tips the scales at a mere 7.1 lbs., making it one of the world's smallest, lightest long-play portables.

Yet it plays standard, five-hour cassettes, gives you up to 2 hours, 20 minutes of recording time and a 16-function wireless remote. With its companion tuner, you also get 105 cable channels.

And, as with our home decks, the freeze frame and slow motion are snow free. The variable search capabilities, nearly endless.

Exhibit B. Toshiba's SK-45 CCD camera.

By eliminating conventional pick-up tubes, we've cut the size and weight in half.

With a super-fast, f1.2 lens, 6x power zoom, macro focus, electronic viewfinder and extreme low light capability, to name just a few features, its spec sheet takes up more room than it does.

And better still, it's part of a complete line which includes the IK-2200. A small, light, color video camera with an advanced electronic viewfinder for field review capability. And the IK-2000, its first cousin, with full-color through-the-lens viewing.

And that, in brief, is the evidence proving Toshiba's superiority in portable video. We rest our case. **In Touch with Tomorrow**

TOSHIBA

Toshiba America, Inc., 82 Totowa Road, Wayne, NJ 07470

26 BRONZE

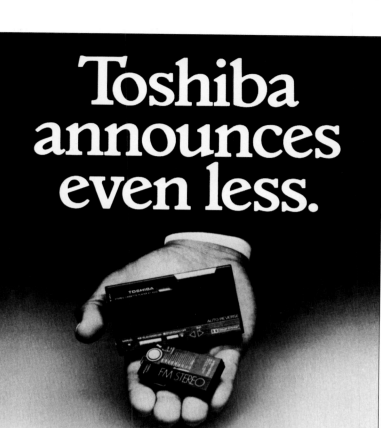

Toshiba announces even less.

This year, the big news goes from tiny to teeny tiny. How tiny is teeny tiny? See for yourself. Pictured here is the Super Mini RP-30, an FM stereo no bigger than a cigarette lighter. A small cigarette lighter. Yet it delivers concert hall-sized sound through ear plug stereo headphones.

And though it's slightly bigger, the Super Mini

KT-AS10 is no less amazing. It's a stereo cassette player even smaller than the standard cassettes it plays. And it offers auto-reverse, Dolby NR,* an AM/FM stereo tuner pack and metal tape capability.

So call your Toshiba Sales Representative. Because the less we offer, the more you make.

*TM Dolby Labs

In Touch with Tomorrow
TOSHIBA
Toshiba America, Inc., 82 Totowa Road, Wayne, NJ 07470

Everything you hear is true.

Toshiba's first CD player opened to rave reviews. One leading buff book called it "an example of how a well-designed CD player should look and work. It offers outstanding performance and a surprising number of features found in more expensive players."

Now Toshiba is proud to introduce second generation CD players that promise to be even more successful than the first.

Take the horizontal front-loading XR-Z50K, for example. With dynamic range

of 90dB, the sound is flawless. No distortion. No wow and flutter. Only pure, concert quality sound.

Or for the audio purist there's the incredible XR-Z70K. It has even more amazing features like a 16-program memory function and wireless remote control.

You'll be hearing a lot more from the XR-Z50K and XR-Z70K. In fact, they're bound to be this year's most valuable players.

In Touch with Tomorrow
TOSHIBA
Toshiba America, Inc., 82 Totowa Road, Wayne, NJ 07470

Gold, Silver & Bronze Awards

Collateral Brochures: Other Than By Mail

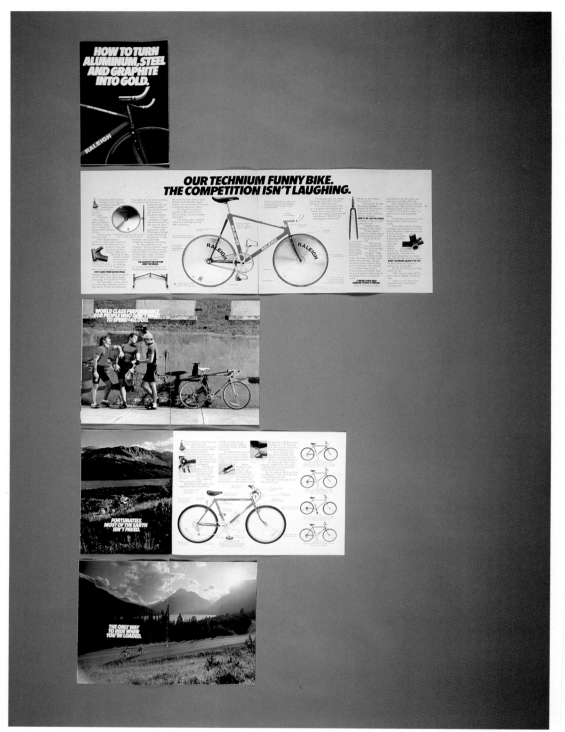

27 GOLD

WARREN LUSTRO GLOSS. A NEW CLASSIC.

Gold,
Silver
& Bronze
Awards

Collateral Direct Mail

30 GOLD
ART DIRECTOR
Carolyn Tye
WRITERS
Bill Westbrook
Robin Stanley
CLIENT
Poplar Springs Hospital
AGENCY
Westbrook/Virginia

31 SILVER
ART DIRECTOR
Tom Kelly
WRITER
Bill Borders
CLIENT
Blitz-Weinhard Brewing
AGENCY
Borders Perrin & Norrander/
Oregon

32 BRONZE
ART DIRECTORS
Bob Meyer
Gordon Hochhalter
WRITER
Gordon Hochhalter
CLIENT
R.R. Donnelley & Sons
AGENCY
R.R. Donnelley & Sons/
Chicago

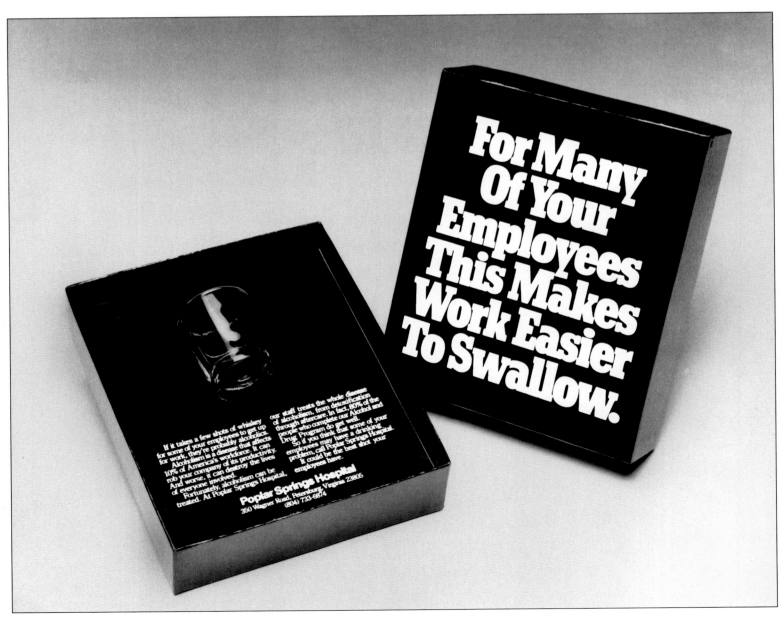

30 GOLD

31 SILVER

32 BRONZE

Gold,
Silver
&
Bronze
Awards

Collateral P.O.P.

33 GOLD
ART DIRECTOR
Mark Moffett
WRITER
Mark Silveira
DESIGNER
Mark Moffett
PHOTOGRAPHER
Bob Gelberg
CLIENT
BMW of North America
AGENCY
Ammirati & Puris

34 SILVER
ART DIRECTOR
Jerry Torchia
WRITER
Jeanette Tyson
DESIGNER
Jerry Torchia
CLIENT
American Marketing
Association
AGENCY
The Martin Agency/Virginia

35 BRONZE
ART DIRECTOR
Corey Stolberg
WRITER
Jill Easton
DESIGNERS
Corey Stolberg
Barbara Thompson
PHOTOGRAPHER
Michael Balderas
CLIENT
San Diego Trust
AGENCY
Phillips-Ramsey/San Diego

DRIVE A BMW WHOSE PERFORMANCE IS UNRESTRICTED BY BAD ROADS, TRAFFIC JAMS AND SPEED LIMITS.

BMW MARINE ENGINES

33 GOLD

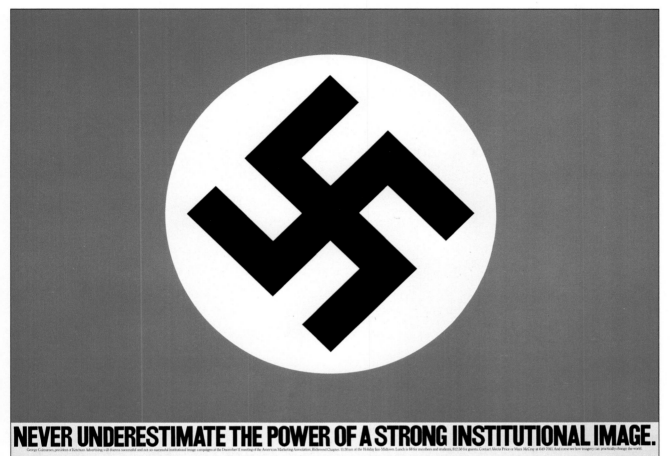

NEVER UNDERESTIMATE THE POWER OF A STRONG INSTITUTIONAL IMAGE.

George Guimaraes, president of Ketchum Advertising, will discuss successful and not-so-successful institutional image campaigns at the December 11 meeting of the American Marketing Association, Richmond Chapter. 11:30a.m. at the Holiday Inn-Midtown. Lunch is $8 for members and students, $12.50 for guests. Contact Alecia Price or Mara McCray at 649-7011. And come see how imagery can practically change the world.

34 SILVER

95 YEARS AND WHAT HAVE WE GOT TO SHOW FOR IT?

VISIT OUR BANK MUSEUM AT THE MAIN OFFICE OF SAN DIEGO TRUST & SAVINGS BANK.
Open on banking days from 10 a.m. to 4 p.m. and by appointment.

35 BRONZE

Outdoor: Single

36 GOLD
ART DIRECTOR
Ron Sandilands
WRITER
Bernie Hafeli
CLIENT
Seattle Aquarium
AGENCY
Livingston & Company/
Seattle

37 SILVER
ART DIRECTOR
Martyn Walsh
ARTIST
Mick Brownfield
CLIENT
Bovril
AGENCY
Ogilvy & Mather/London

38 BRONZE
ART DIRECTOR
Wes Keebler
WRITER
Chuck Silverman
CLIENT
Tahiti Tourism Promotion
Board
AGENCY
Cunningham & Walsh/
California

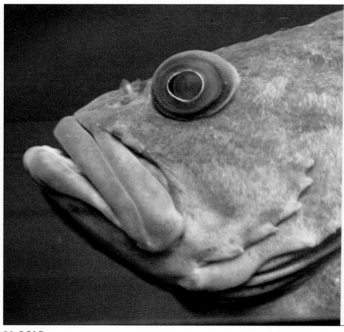

36 GOLD

37 SILVER

38 BRONZE

Outdoor: Campaign

39 GOLD
ART DIRECTOR
Gary Johns
WRITER
Jeff Gorman
PHOTOGRAPHERS
Bill Livingston
Cailor/Resnick
CLIENT
Nike
AGENCY
Chiat/Day-Los Angeles

39 GOLD

Gold, Silver & Bronze Awards

Outdoor: Campaign

40 SILVER
ART DIRECTOR
Dean Hanson
WRITER
Jarl Olsen
CLIENT
7 South 8th For Hair
AGENCY
Fallon McElligott Rice/Mpls.

40 SILVER

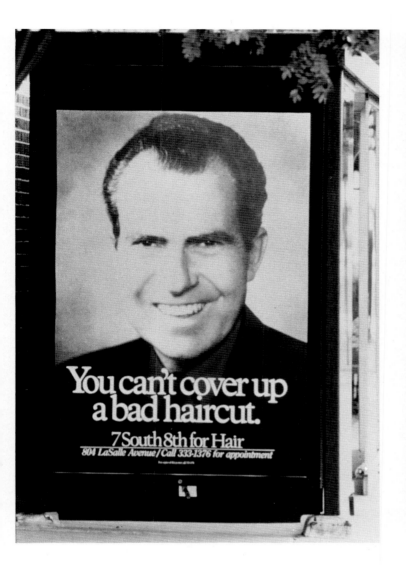

Outdoor: Campaign

41 BRONZE
ART DIRECTORS
Anne Hasegawa
John Bormann
PHOTOGRAPHER
Herb Woodward
CLIENT
Time Magazine
AGENCY
Young & Rubicam

Where Smirnoff makes a splash

Smirnoff® Vodka
SMIRNOFF® VODKA 80 & 100 PROOF DISTILLED FROM GRAIN. © 1984, STE. PIERRE SMIRNOFF FLS (DIVISION OF HEUBLEIN, INC.) HARTFORD, CT — "MADE IN U.S.A." © 1984 Time Inc.

41 BRONZE

Where Hertz drives home its message

It computes for Apple

My name is Evelyn. People call me a Mongol. I wrote this ad.

To help their childrens problems and feelings, I'm sure all Downsyndrome children in this world Like to stop The word Mongal becouse it hurts their feelings.

But They like To be normal and Treated normal. The Whole worlds peoples should help Downsyndrome children and play games with them, To feed Them and To give them Something to Drink.

I shall explain why. They have got 47 chromosomes and the world has got 46 chromosomes.

But we are Different and we can do more work although We are very slow.

But all of us can try to catch up. Downsyndrome children must work harder to keep up.

my name is EvELyn Also I used to go to school for 13 years at least, The Stress is powerful.

So They all call me mongal I dont Like that. But Teachers Dont say that at all and this is good on the Teachers part.

But all of us can try to catch up. I like Nena Weil she has The same problems in the television programme. Downsyndrome children must work harder to keep up.

I love holidays and staying at home But my father did not come when we went on holiday To morocco as he had some work to do and its very hard work, for the meeting in Bristol of Downsyndrome childrens Association.

We have to To Help Those Who have got Downs children or has got anything where They Have got problems.

We must Try To Help Them, The Lot. This is a very important and serious thing.

Its really needs to Be Done also get it Done and Done with.

I Like shopping also going to town. I Like playing my piano so I Love working very much indeed.

We can Breathe in the fresh air; so in the paradise on earth.

I Like Art also reading and writing also games. so I Like Tony Harts paintings.

I can cope on my own also I can run a House so I could Help my children if They got problems. now I do Typing for Scheidegger for A corrispondence Course in Leicester. Its a SwissSchool so I have a Tuter who comes every weekso I Like that.

Outside my front garden Theres A tree in Blossom and its white like there's A person Dressed up in Wedding Dress behind it.

I can get Dressed and Make my breakfast. In the Afternoon I do my typing. But when I get tired I Dont do it as much also I lay the table for all of us to eat then I write Letters to my friends.

This is my every daily Life and the Whole worlds

childrens is the same as us.

We play Tennis all of us are no good but we need practice even our ice-skating so all of us needs more practice.

I Really enjoy Skiing very much indeed. We Like to go to the fair and Art gallery, also museums.

I go swimming its my favourite sport. I have got Three certificates The first one is my gold Award for proficiency in personal Survival at last September 1983.

Thats what we Believe so its Just works. It does work like its Just right, so thats The way To do it. I want To Help Those who have got Downsyndrome children so I Think Thats right to do. so it is a very serious Thing and should be Done.

42 GOLD

43 SILVER

44 BRONZE

**Public Service
Newspaper Or
Magazine: Campaign**

45 GOLD

ART DIRECTORS
Debbie Lucke
Bryan McPeak

WRITER
David Lubars

DESIGNER
Debbie Lucke

ARTISTS
Dom Denardo
Cathleen Toelke

PHOTOGRAPHER
John Holt

CLIENT
Volunteer Services for
Animals

AGENCY
Leonard Monahan Saabye/
Rhode Island

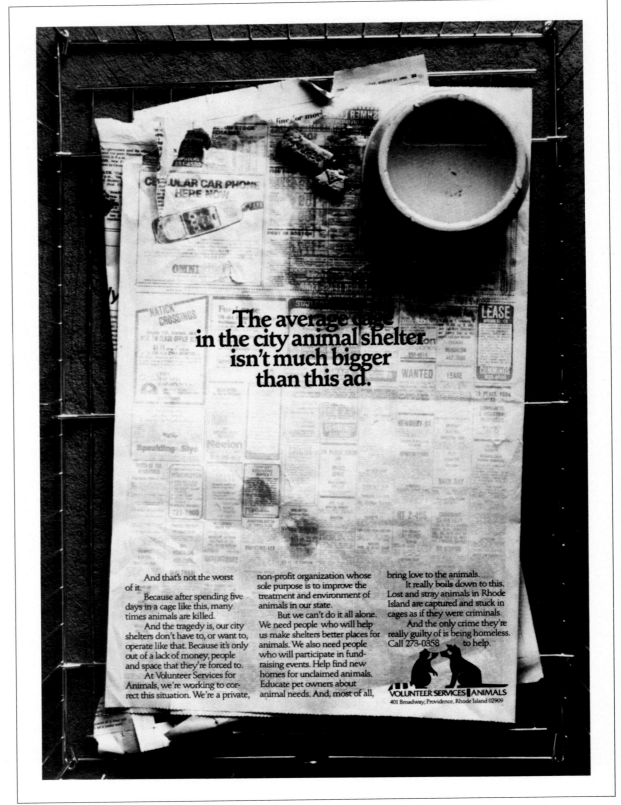

45 GOLD

It's not a dog.
It's a guinea pig.

There is a thriving black market in this country. A dreadful, despicable black market.

A black market where lost and stolen pets are sold to laboratories for experimentation.

And while it's true that Rhode Island has passed legislation that makes selling pound animals for experimentation illegal here, it doesn't mean your pet is safe. Because it's a fact that thieves steal pets and smuggle them into states where selling animals for experimentation is legal.

What can you do?

Well, for your own dog, there are three things. One, don't let him run loose in the neighborhood. Keep him on a leash. Two, when you're not home, don't leave him alone in the backyard. And three, if you don't have ID tags, a license or a tattoo on him, get them immediately.

But there's something else you can do. You can join Volunteer Services for Animals.

We're a private, non-profit organization whose sole purpose is to improve the treatment and environment of animals in our state.

We also help municipalities provide humane services which they couldn't otherwise afford. For example, we have lost and found, adoption, veterinary care, population control, pet therapy and education programs.

So please call us at 273-0358.

And help our animal operation prevent animal operations.

VOLUNTEER SERVICES for ANIMALS
401 Broadway, Providence, Rhode Island 02909

If you lost your dog,
there's a good chance someone
will give him a warm home.

What if you had a dog. And what if he wandered away from home and got lost. And what if he was picked up by the city shelter and stuck into a cage.

And what if, what if after five days you still hadn't found him.

You know what would happen? He might be killed. And then cremated in an oven like this. Or buried in the city dump.

Just think how you'd feel. And think how much worse you'd feel knowing city shelters don't have to, or want to, operate like that. Because it's only out of a lack of money, people, and space that they're forced to.

At Volunteer Services for Animals, we're working with Rhode Island municipal shelters to correct this situation.

We're a private, non-profit organization whose sole purpose is to improve the treatment and environment of animals in our state.

We also help municipalities provide humane services which they couldn't otherwise afford. For example, we have lost and found, adoption, veterinary care, population control, pet therapy and education programs.

But we can't do it all alone. We need your help.

We're looking for volunteers who will help us reunite lost pets with their owners. Find new homes for unclaimed animals. Educate pet owners about animal needs. Participate in fundraising events. Help with shelter chores. And, most of all, bring love to the animals.

Look at it this way.

Last year in one Rhode Island city alone, thousands and thousands of lost and stray animals were destroyed. So call us at 273-0358.

Before the subject of unclaimed pets becomes a dead issue.

VOLUNTEER SERVICES for ANIMALS
401 Broadway, Providence, Rhode Island 02909

THE HOPE DIAMOND.

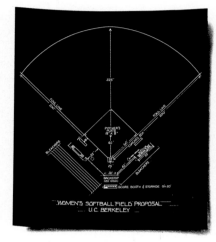

We hope to turn this blueprint into a softball field.

And the sooner the better.

Come next year, our existing women's diamond will be declared unsuitable for conference play.

Guess somebody noticed the broken bleachers.

The funny little scoreboard.

And most embarrassing, the fact that our right field is 35 feet shorter than everyone else's (which makes it nonregulation).

To make matters worse, our funds are in a terrible slump.

Which is also why, every Fall, our women's basketball team has no place on campus to practice.

And why our women's locker room is still shy a few amenities.

Like lockers.

Fortunately, these and other hardships haven't seemed to hurt Cal's trophy collection.

Last year eight of our women's teams were among the top twenty in the country. This year, a few of the same athletes have a shot at winning Olympic gold medals.

But if we're to continue this tradition, we need more than an occasional pep rally.

We need equipment, facilities and scholarships competitive with those schools out to devour our reputation.

In short, we need your help. Your donation to Bear Boosters can help ensure that *all* our athletes have a sporting chance.

We may even be able to give our women what they deserve.

A diamond big as a softball field.

U.C. BERKELEY
It's not the same without you.

U.C. Berkeley Foundation, 2440 Bancroft Way, Rm. 301, Berkeley, California 94720.
Call the Donor Line, collect: (415) 642-4414.

BERKELEY THREATENS RUSSIA.

NOBEL PRIZES

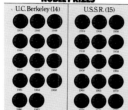

U.C. Berkeley (14)	U.S.S.R. (15)

It's true, Cal's faculty has won almost as many Nobel Prizes as the entire Soviet Union.

Fourteen, to be exact.

That's four more than all of Italy. Five more than Japan and Canada combined.

But hey, who's counting?

Certainly not our professors, they've been too busy.

Discovering plutonium.

Pioneering the first laser beam.

Isolating the virus that would play a key role in conquering polio.

These and other prize-winning achievements reflect an overall academic standard that has for over half a century been consistently phenomenal.

And for that, *you* deserve a medal.

Your contributions have provided our great minds with the resources needed to do great work.

However, now is not the time to rest on our Laureates.

Just ask our latest Nobel winner, economist Gerard Debreu. Upon receiving his award, he had this to say: "The magnificent research environment I have known at this university during the past 20 years ... is threatened by very lean budgets."

So please, contribute all you can. Our professors will gladly repay you. In gold.

U.C. BERKELEY
It's not the same without you.

U.C. Berkeley Foundation, 2440 Bancroft Way, Rm. 301, Berkeley, California 94720. Call the Donor Line, collect, Mon.-Fri., 9am-5pm: (415) 642-4379.

THIS BUILDING IS FILLED WITH MAD SCIENTISTS.

They're some of the most respected scientific minds in the country.

They're also mad.

You would be too if you had to teach and conduct critical research in Cal's Life Sciences building.

There are cracks in the ceilings and cracks in the walls.

And leaks in all the cracks.

Because of the rotten plumbing. Which may be what's causing those terrible odors.

The ones that won't go away, on account of all the ventilation problems.

And it won't be long before we'll have to put laboratories in the lavatories. (We've just about filled up the halls.)

Despite these and other hardships, our Biosciences departments continue to achieve world acclaim for breakthrough research in cancer prevention, brain development, and many other areas.

But the fact remains, Nobel Prize winners and Guggenheim Fellows don't grow on trees. In order to hang on to those we have—and continue to attract top faculty—we need more than a few new beakers and Bunsen burners.

We need your support.

Because largely through private contributions, we hope to begin building a Biological Sciences facility befitting a world class university.

So please call the number below. And help us put a stop to this madness.

U.C. BERKELEY
It's not the same without you.

U.C. Berkeley Foundation, 2440 Bancroft Way, Rm. 301, Berkeley, California 94720. Call the Donor Line, collect, Mon.-Fri., 9-5: (415) 642-4379.

Gold,
Silver
&
Bronze
Awards

**Public Service
Newspaper Or
Magazine: Campaign**

47 BRONZE
ART DIRECTOR
Tracy Wong
WRITER
Michael LaMonica
DESIGNER
Tracy Wong
CLIENT
United Way
AGENCY
Ogilvy & Mather

☐ One 60 minute
massage at
health club.

☐ One week
mental help for
battered wife.

WHICH ONE RUBS YOU
THE RIGHT WAY?
The United Way.

☐ New pair of
running shoes
you only wear
for looks.

☐ New pair of
leg braces that
have nothing to
do with looks.

WHICH ONE BRINGS YOU
TO YOUR FEET?
The United Way.

☐ 1 round of Irish coffees
for you and
your buddies.

☐ 1 day of therapy
for child
burned in fire.

WHICH ONE LEAVES YOU
FEELING WARM ALL OVER?
The United Way.

**Public Service
Outdoor: Single**

48 GOLD
ART DIRECTOR
Jerry Roach
WRITER
Joe Lovering
CLIENT
Young & Rubicam
AGENCY
Young & Rubicam

49 SILVER
ART DIRECTOR
Bill Oakley
WRITER
Michael Smith
DESIGNER
Bill Oakley
PHOTOGRAPHER
David Gold
CLIENT
Victims of Drunk Driving

"Why vote?
Politicians are all the same."

It's a weak excuse for not voting.
Though it's far easier to look back at what has been than to chart the course of what will be, history has proven that all politicians are not quite the same.
And the countries they lead are never quite the same again. YOUNG & RUBICAM INC.

Vote Tuesday, Nov. 6

48 GOLD

Slay Ride.

Don't Drive Drunk.

49 SILVER

College Competition

50 GOLD
ART DIRECTOR & WRITER
Steve Popp
CLIENT
The NFL
SCHOOL
East Texas State University

LEATHER 'N LACE.

Men fight over it. Women once ignored it. But times have changed. And so have you. On weekends and Monday nights during the season, women just like yourself are beginning to watch football.

The excitement. The action. To help you understand the game, the N.F.L. has established a toll-free information line. It's called Timeout. 1-800-TIMEOUT is the number. Just give us a call with any question you might have. We'll connect you with a female analyst who'll give you the answers you need. So when it seems it's you against football, we hope you'll take time out to give us a call.

50 GOLD

CHAUVINIST PIG.

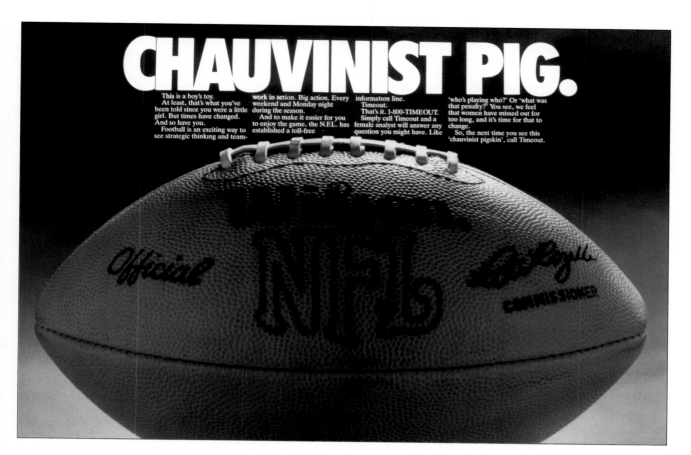

This is a boy's toy.

At least, that's what you've been told since you were a little girl. But times have changed. And so have you.

Football is an exciting way to see strategic thinking and team-work in action. Big action. Every weekend and Monday night during the season.

And to make it easier for you to enjoy the game, the N.F.L. has established a toll-free information line. Timeout.

That's it. 1-800-TIMEOUT. Simply call Timeout and a female analyst will answer any question you might have. Like 'who's playing who?' Or 'what was that penalty?' You see, we feel that women have missed out for too long, and it's time for that to change.

So, the next time you see this 'chauvinist pigskin', call Timeout.

SEX OBJECT.

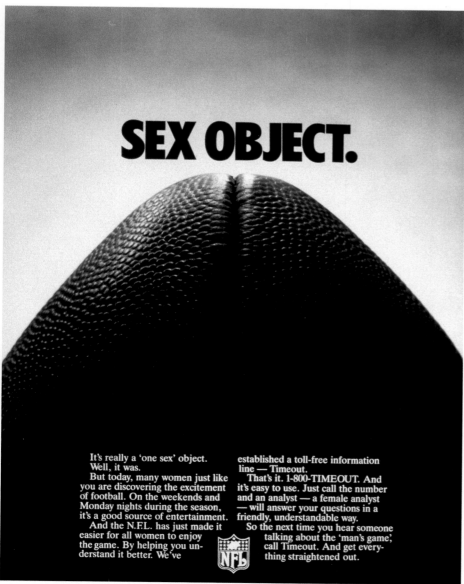

It's really a 'one sex' object. Well, it was.

But today, many women just like you are discovering the excitement of football. On the weekends and Monday nights during the season, it's a good source of entertainment.

And the N.F.L. has just made it easier for all women to enjoy the game. By helping you un-derstand it better. We've established a toll-free information line — Timeout.

That's it. 1-800-TIMEOUT. And it's easy to use. Just call the number and an analyst — a female analyst — will answer your questions in a friendly, understandable way.

So the next time you hear someone talking about the 'man's game', call Timeout. And get every-thing straightened out.

College Competition

51 SILVER
ART DIRECTOR & WRITER
Linda Whitmire
CLIENT
The NFL
SCHOOL
The University of Texas at
Austin

Instantly have something in common with thirty million men.

Find out what makes thirty million men excited.

What do men know that most women don't?

52 BRONZE

MAKE A DATE WITH THE NFL.

WALTER PAYTON. Running back, Chicago Bears.
The greatest running back in the history of the NFL. His style, strength, and grace have earned him the name "Sweetness."
See real sweetness in action this weekend in the NFL.

MAKE A DATE WITH THE NFL.

BRUCE HARDY. Receiver, Miami Dolphins.
His 6 foot 4 inch frame has the moves and agility to have once earned him the distinction of "Athlete of the Year."
Watch the moves this weekend in the NFL.

Consumer Radio: Single

53 GOLD
WRITER
Jarl Olsen
CLIENT
New Orleans Breakers
AGENCY PRODUCER
Jarl Olsen
AGENCY
Fallon McElligott Rice/Mpls.

54 SILVER
WRITER
Joy Golden
CLIENT
Fromageries Bel
AGENCY PRODUCER
Michael Pollock
AGENCY
TBWA

55 BRONZE
WRITER
Jarl Olsen
CLIENT
Pronto Ristorante
AGENCY PRODUCER
Jarl Olsen
AGENCY
Fallon McElligott Rice/Mpls.

Consumer Radio: Campaign

56 GOLD
WRITER
Dick Orkin
CLIENT
Alabama Power
AGENCY PRODUCER
Dottie Martin
AGENCY
Cargill Wilson & Acree/
Atlanta

53 GOLD

ANNCR: The last time the Breakers played the Birmingham Mustangs, Marcus Dupree missed a pitch-out, setting up a turnover that may have cost his team the game. Marcus, what do you have to say for yourself?

MARCUS: I will not drop the ball
I will not drop the ball.
I will not drop the ball . . . (UNDER)

ANNCR: See the continuing education of Marcus Dupree, when the New Orleans Breakers play the Birmingham Stallions this Sunday at the Super Dome. Get your tickets now at any Ticket Master location.

MARCUS: I will not drop the ball . . .

54 SILVER

WOMAN (FAST PACED): Last night my husband woke me and said he had a little craving. I said, "I'll go to the all night super market and get you a little round laughing cow in a red net bag."
He said, "I don't care if she's in lace with high heels, it isn't what I had in mind."
I said, "So what do you want Stuart?"
He said, "Something sort of soft and a little nippy."
I said, "So, you want Mini Baby Bel from the Laughing Cow."
He said, "No."
I said, "So you want Mini Bonbel. It's a little more mild."
He said, "No."
I said, "So what do you want Stuart?"
He said, "Cheese."
I said, "What did you think I was talking about?"
So I went to the dairy case and I bought two red net bags with 5 mini cheeses in each. Mini Bonbel and Mini Babybel. Delicious. Natural. Bite size. Then I went home and I said, "Look Stuart, I brought you a little laughing cow in a red net bag freshly wrapped in wax with an easy-open French zipper."
He said, "Enid don't talk naughty to me."
Then he ate all 10 mini cheeses and said it was the best treat he ever had in bed. So I smacked him.

ANNCR: Mini Bonbel and Mini Babybel. Delectable cheeses by the Laughing Cow. They'll put a smile in your stomach. In your dairy case.

55 BRONZE

ANNCR: Pronto Ristorante's Chef Tomaso.

TOMASO: After exposing Minnesotans to many new Italian words through my big new menu, I would like to take a little time to recognize all of the people who have been helping me with my Minnesotan. Bill and Shelly of Minnetonka— thank.you for telling me about dust bunnies—I look forward to seeing them the next time I am at the zoo. Paul of Blaine contributed Uff-da, Ish and Mopar, very nice words. A special thanks to my friends at the Shriners for all those Sven and Ole jokes—Italians think the Irish are funny, too. I'm sorry if I left anybody out. If you have a Minnesota Phrase, please write it down and bring it to Pronto the next time you have dinner. If I am out, just leave it with the hostess. She is, as you say, my main man.

ANNCR: Pronto Ristorante, an Italian-Italian restaurant. For reservations, call 333-4414.

TOMASO: "Let's have lunch"—that's good-bye, yes?

56 GOLD

DORIS: Oh, Frank, not again.

FRANK: Doris, please, just call Billy.

DORIS: Billy! Your father has an announcement to make.

BILLY: Yeah, Dad?

FRANK: Son, I'm afraid we have to move again.

BILLY: Oh, Dad. I just made friends.

FRANK: I'm sorry, but it's Fall now and if we don't move soon, Winter will be here.

DORIS: North in the Summer, South in the Winter. Sixteen moves in the last four years.

FRANK: It's for our own good. To keep a constant temperature between sixty-eight and seventy-four degrees. I mean, what do you want me to do?

BILLY: Dad, why don't we just get an electric heat pump?

FRANK: Don't be ridic . . . what's that?

BILLY: Just the most efficient all-in-one home heating and cooling system there is.

FRANK: That's impossible . . . isn't it?

BILLY: No, a heat pump is the perfect system for saving energy and money.

FRANK: Cool in the summer?

BILLY: Yep.

FRANK: *And* warm in the winter?

BILLY: Exactly. Everyone's converting to heat pumps.

FRANK: Boy, Billy, you're smart. Isn't he smart, Doris?

DORIS: Yes, he's smart.

FRANK: Where'd you learn about heat pumps, Billy?

BILLY: In science class at school.

FRANK: Can I ask you another science question, Billy?

BILLY: Sure . . .

FRANK: When you erase a blackboard . . .

BILLY: Oh no . . .

FRANK: Where do the darn words go?

BILLY: Dad, I already explained this to you . . .

FRANK: I know, but they're there and they're gone.

ANNCR: The electric heat pump. The all-in-one home heating and cooling system. For more details, call Alabama Power.

MAN: My family lives 2 blocks from here, Mr. Scott.

DICK: Uh huh. So what is it you . .

WIFE: Just tell him, dear.

MAN: Let me get right to the point. We'd like to move in with you.

DICK: You what?

WIFE: Just for the winter.

MAN: See, our furnace went haywire 5 years ago . . .

WIFE: Six, dear.

MAN: Six . . . and because fixing or replacing it is such a big deal, we just pack up and move in with another family each winter.

WIFE: And in the summer, we move in with a family that has air conditioning.

DICK: You're kidding!

WIFE: Oh, no.

MAN: Gosh, we've lived with everyone on this side of the street . . .

WIFE: Except you.

DICK: Is this a gag?

MAN: Oh, no. That's our station wagon all loaded up out there.

(SFX: DOG BARK)

WIFE: Kids, keep that dog in the wagon.

MAN: So whatta ya say?

DICK: Look, why don't you folks just get an electric heat pump like I got.

MAN & WIFE: A what?

DICK: An electric heat pump. It's the most efficient all-in-one heating and air conditioning system around.

MAN: Really?

DICK: Yeah. And it'll save you energy and money.

WIFE: A heat pump?

DICK: Heat in the winter, cool in the summer.

WIFE: Does sound good, dear.

MAN: Sure does. Thanks, Mr. Scott.

WIFE: Yes, thank you.

MAN: But, listen . . . til we get a heat pump, could we move in with . . .

DICK: Well, but . . . okay, but I'll have to tell my wife first.

WIFE: Oh, sure.

MAN: Fine.

(SFX: FOOTSTEPS)

WIFE: (SHOUTS) We have our own bed linen!

MAN: Nice man.

WIFE: Nice house. I hope . . .

(SFX: BLOODCURDLING SCREAM)

MAN: Ooh. I bet he forgot to mention the bed linen.

WIFE: Yeah.

ANNCR: The amazing electric heat pump. Call Alabama Power for more details.

(SFX: DOOR OPENS. IN BACKGROUND "FRED MACHINE")

FRED: Oh, hi George!

GEORGE: I'm returning your hedge clipper, Fred.

FRED: Oh, thanks

GEORGE: Uh . . . Fred?

FRED: Yeah?

GEORGE: What's going on in your house?

FRED: Oh, that's my new heating and air conditioning system. I call it the Fred Machine!

GEORGE: Huh?

FRED: You know my wife, June, over there on the stationary bicycle?

JUNE: Hi, George!

FRED: Okay. Notice the belt running from the bike to the . . .

GEORGE & FRED: The record player?

FRED: Yeah. Well, the record player gives grandpa music he can dance to in his bedroom.

GEORGE: Why is he . . .

FRED: Cuz it drives all the chickens up in the attic really crazy.

GEORGE: Ch—chickens?

FRED: And then they start flapping their wings like mad and that sends heat down into the house.

GEORGE: Heat?

FRED: Yeah. Cuz we got little bar-b-que grills with hot coals sitting all over the attic floor! Neat, Huh?

GEORGE: Fred, have you ever thought about an electric heat pump?

FRED: What's that?

GEORGE: Just the most efficient all-in-one home heating and cooling system around.

FRED: Oh, and for cooling, in the summer we fill the grills in the attic with ice cubes! Isn't that great?

GEORGE: Fred, the electric heat pump would be a lot less trouble.

FRED: Really?

GEORGE: Yeah. Plus it saves energy and money!

FRED: Electric heat pump?

GEORGE: Yeah.

FRED: All in one?

GEORGE: Yeah.

(SFX: THE FRED MACHINE)

FRED: I don't know. I'd miss the excitement.

ANNCR: Efficient, saves money and energy—the heat pump! To learn more, call Alabama Power.

Consumer Radio: Campaign

57 SILVER
WRITER
Joy Golden
CLIENT
Fromageries Bel
AGENCY PRODUCER
Michael Pollock
AGENCY
TBWA

58 BRONZE
WRITERS
Mike Koelker
Mark Vieha
Jake Holmes
Art Twain
CLIENT
Levi Strauss
AGENCY PRODUCER
Steve Neely
AGENCY
Foote Cone & Belding/
San Francisco

Public Service Radio: Single

59 GOLD
WRITERS
Jay Taub
Tod Seisser
CLIENT
Kronenbourg Beer
AGENCY PRODUCER
Bob Nelson
AGENCY
Levine, Huntley, Schmidt &
Beaver

60 SILVER
WRITER
Robert Neuman
CLIENT
American Museum of Natural
History
AGENCY PRODUCER
Tony Wellman
AGENCY
Ogilvy & Mather

---

57 SILVER

WOMAN: My son Arnold said he didn't want peanut
butter and jelly for lunch anymore.
So I said, "I'll give you a little round laughing
cow in a red net bag."
He said his teacher didn't allow animals.
I said, "Tell her it's cheese."
He said, "She'll know it's not cheese when it
starts to moo."
I said, "It doesn't moo, it just sits on a cracker."
He said, "Even if it's quiet, she hates anything
with four legs."
I said, "Hold up the bag and tell her that's what
your mother gave you for lunch."
He said, "If my teacher sees that my mother
gave me a laughing cow in a red net bag for
lunch, she'll send me to a foster home."
I said, "Laughing Cow is cheese, Arnold. Five
delicious bite-size cheeses freshly wrapped in
wax with an easy open zip. Mild Mini Bonbel and
nippy Mini Babybel. Semi soft delicious and
natural. So they're good for you, Arnold."
He said, "You talked me into it, Ma."
So today Arnold went to school with the little
round laughing cow in a red net bag. And
tonight I have to pick him up at the foster home.

ANNCR: Mini Bonbel and Mini Babybel. Delectable
cheeses by the Laughing Cow. They'll put a
smile in your stomach. From Fromageries Bel.
In your dairy case.

---

57 SILVER

WOMAN: My daughter Tiffany said she wanted to do
something totally awesome for her sweet 16.
I said I'll put a little round laughing cow in a
red net bag on a silver platter and surround it
with orchids.
She said that's cute, ma, but it isn't awesome.
Better you should put it in mink and drive it up
in a stretch limo.
I said Tiffany watch my lips. The laughing cow
isn't an animal act, it's cheese.
She said will the girls be impressed with
Laughing Cow cheese on a cracker?
I said Tiffany your girlfriends have so many
birds on their antennae, they wouldn't be
impressed with a dancing bear on a bagel. But
they'll love the Laughing Cow. Mild Mini Bonbel
and Nippy Mini Babybel. Five little round
cheeses in their own red net bags. Delicious.
Natural. Bite-size. Freshly wrapped in wax with
an easy open zip.
She said it sounds good to me ma.
So we served the Laughing Cow at Tiffany's
sweet 16 and all her friends were impressed
except Heather Rubini who expected a real cow
and brought a bale of alfalfa. So everybody had
cheese with a roll in the hay. I want to tell you it
was awesome.

ANNCR: Mini Bonbel. Mini Babybel. Just two in a
selection of delectable cheeses by the Laughing
Cow. Look for all of them in your dairy case.
And put a smile in your stomach.

---

57 SILVER

WOMAN (FAST PACED): Last night my husband woke
me and said he had a little craving. I said, "I'll
go to the all night super market and get you a
little round laughing cow in a red net bag."
He said, "I don't care if she's in lace with high
heels, it isn't what I had in mind."
I said, "So what do you want Stuart?"
He said, "Something sort of soft and a little
nippy."
I said, "So, you want Mini Baby Bel from the
Laughing Cow."
He said, "No."
I said, "So you want Mini Bonbel. It's a little
more mild."
He said, "No."
I said, "So what do you want Stuart?"
He said, "Cheese."
I said, "What did you think I was talking
about?"
So I went to the dairy case and I bought two
red net bags with 5 mini cheeses in each. Mini
Bonbel and Mini Babybel. Delicious. Natural.
Bite size. Then I went home and I said, "Look
Stuart, I brought you a little laughing cow in a
red net bag freshly wrapped in wax with an easy
open French zipper."
He said, "Enid don't talk naughty to me."
Then he ate all 10 mini cheeses and said it was
the best treat he ever had in bed. So I smacked
him.

ANNCR: Mini Bonbel and Mini Babybel. Delectable
cheeses by the Laughing Cow. They'll put a
smile in your stomach. In your dairy case.

58 BRONZE

(MUSIC UP)

SINGER: *She looked too good in her 501's*
She said they shrink to fit her just like a glove
She said they wear forever, boy how about you
I said "yeh, me and Levi's 501 Blues."

501 ain't the time of day-yeh . . .
They're the jeans that shrink to fit men my way
Got empty pockets and button fly, too
But I got you
My 501 Blues-yeh
I ain't got a doubt, no but I got the news
Talkin' Levi's 501 Blues.

58 BRONZE

(MUSIC UP)

MALE SINGER: *Ain't no body like my body*
That's about the size of it (uh-huh)
So I personalize my size with Levi's 501 Blues
They shrink to fit
They're the Blues that make me feel good
Levi's 501 Blues—love them Blues.

Now let me tell ya
Oh, Levi's Blues never die
Got the rivet pocket
Got the button-fly
And a personal kind of a fit every body can use
Oh yeh. . . .
They're the Blues that make me feel good
Levi's 501 Blues—love them Blues.
Oh yeh.

58 BRONZE

(MUSIC UP)

MALE SINGER: *I got the Blues, got 'em real bad*
(hmmm)
The best ol' Blues this body ever had
Kind of Blues you don't want to lose
The Levi's jeans 501 Blues.
I got the Blues, I love how they feel
Yeh . . . if you got the Blues you know that
they're real
The kind of Blues you can use and use
The Levi's jeans 501 Blues.
They shrink down to fit me, yeh
You know what that means
Nobody, no one can fit into my jeans
I ain't no cowboy, I don't got no hat
I'm down to earth, yeh, you know where I'm at
And I love the way they hang 'round my shoes
Those Levi's button-fly 501 Blues
Those Levi's button-fly 501 Blues
. . . . FADES OUT).

59 GOLD

The people at Kronenbourg would like to ask you not to drink and drive. After all, we have a rather small share of the market and quite frankly we'd hate to lose any of you.

60 SILVER

ANNCR: In New York City, there are hundreds of galleries and museums, all displaying original paintings, original sculpture and original designs. But there's only one place in the world today where you can see the finest collection of original . . . people. The new exhibition at the American Museum of Natural History. It's called "Ancestors: Four Million Years of Humanity." Here you'll see some of your long-lost relatives brought together from all parts of the world for this never-to-be-repeated exhibition. Heidelberg Man. Cro-Magnon Man. Neanderthal Man—all told 40 of the nicest folks you'll never want to meet. Not plaster copies. But originals. And if you don't think these people talk much, you're mistaken. They communicate the entire history of the human race. See "Ancestors: Four Million Years of Humanity." At the American Museum of Natural History, 79th Street at Central Park West. You can see original art any time you please. But original people? They're a rarity.

**Public Service Radio:
Campaign**

61 GOLD
WRITER
Bernie Hafeli
CLIENT
Seattle Aquarium
AGENCY PRODUCER
Cindy Henderson
AGENCY
Livingston & Company/
Seattle

ANNCR (SERIOUS SOUNDING): Come to the Seattle Aquarium this week and you can see the trumpetfish . . .

(SFX: TRUMPET FANFARE.)

ANNCR: . . . the goatfish . . .

(SFX: GOAT BLEAT.)

ANNCR: . . . the damselfish . . .

1ST VOICE (WOMAN, SCREAMING IN DISTRESS.): Help. Save me. Please.

ANNCR: . . . the parrotfish . . .

(SFX: PARROT SQUAWK AND WHISTLE.)

ANNCR: . . . the triggerfish . . .

(SFX: GUN BEING COCKED, FIRED. CLICK. CLICK. BLAM.)

ANNCR: . . . the filefish . . .

2ND VOICE (MALE, BUSINESSLIKE.): Miss Finn, will you file this please?

ANNCR: . . . the rock crab . . .

(MUSIC: LOUD BLAST OF ROCK MUSIC.)

ANNCR: . . . the boxfish . . .

(SFX: FIGHT BELL RINGING REPEATEDLY.)

3RD VOICE (FIGHT ANNOUNCER, EXCITED.): Oh, what a punch. The champ is down.

ANNCR: . . . the thumbsplitter . . .

(SFX: TWO HAMMERWHACKS, THEN PERSON SCREAMING AS IF THEY'VE HAMMERED THEIR THUMB.)

ANNCR: . . . the sea star . . .

4TH VOICE (MALE.): No autographs, please. Miss Henderson's in a hurry.

ANNCR: . . . the wolf eel . . .

(SFX: WOLF HOWL.)

ANNCR: . . . the spiny dogfish . . .

(SFX: DOG BARKING.)

ANNCR: . . . the Spanish dancer gastropod . . .

(MUSIC: LIVELY FLAMENCO MUSIC.)

(SFX: FEET STAMPING ON FLOOR, LIKE IN FLAMENCO DANCE.)

ANNCR: . . . the sturgeon . . .

5TH VOICE (MALE.): Scalpel.

ANNCR: . . . the tiger rockfish . . .

(SFX: TIGER SNARL.)

ANNCR: . . . and the giant sea cucumber . . .

6TH VOICE (LAUGHS LIKE GREEN GIANT.): Ho. Ho. Ho.

ANNCR: . . . The Seattle Aquarium. See how the other two-thirds lives.

(SFX: SOUND EFFECTS, VOICES AND MUSIC THAT WE HEARD BEFORE ALL START AGAIN, REACH A CACOPHONY.)

ANNCR (SERIOUS SOUNDING.): If you visit the Seattle Aquarium this week, you can see the spearnose poacher . . .

VOICE 1 (SHOUTING.): Stop! Thief!

ANNCR: . . . the penpoint gunnel . . .

(SFX: CLICK OF BALL POINT PEN, THEN SCRIBBLING SOUNDS.)

VOICE 2 (TO HIMSELF.): Dear . . . mush for brains.

ANNCR: . . . the mosshead warbonnet . . .

(MUSIC: INDIAN WARDANCE MUSIC.)

ANNCR: . . . the brittle star . . .

(SFX: GLASS OR CHINA SHATTERING.)

ANNCR: . . . the Japanese oyster . . .

VOICE 3 (SAMURAI YELL.)

(SFX: SWORD SPLITTING WOOD.)

ANNCR: . . . the spiny lumpsucker . . .

(SFX: PERSON SUCKING ON STRAW IN EMPTY GLASS.)

VOICE 4 (GULPS AS IF HE SWALLOWED SOMETHING.): Ulp!

ANNCR: . . . the pencil urchin . . .

(SFX: SOUND OF PENCIL BEING SHARPENED.)

ANNCR: . . . the sponge . . .

VOICE 5: Hey, buddy. Could you loan me a fin?

ANNCR: . . . the sea lemon . . .

(SFX: SOUND OF CAR ENGINE TURNING OVER WHICH WON'T START.)

ANNCR: . . . the dire welk . . .

(SFX: LIKE LAWRENCE WELK.): Start the bubble machine, boys.

ANNCR: . . . the moon snail . . .

(SFX: REFRAIN FROM THE SONG, "BLUE MOON."): Bom Bom badom badom badom dom . . .

(UP TO THE WORDS "BLUE MOON.")

ANNCR: . . . the black-clawed crab . . .

VOICE 7 (SHOUTING.): Hey! Could you cut the racket!?

ANNCR: . . . and the hermit crab . . .

(SFX: WOMAN, A'LA GARBO.): I vant to be alone.

ANNCR: . . . The Seattle Aquarium. See how the other two-thirds lives.

ANNCR (SERIOUS SOUNDING.): This week at the Seattle Aquarium you can see the rabbit fish . . .

VOICE 1 (BUGS BUNNY IMITATION.): Eh, what's up, doc?

ANNCR: . . . the rosylip sculpin . . .

(SFX: LOUD, PRONOUNCED KISS.)

ANNCR: . . . the white-tip shark . . .

VOICE 2: Eight ball in the corner pocket.

(SFX: POOL BALLS HITTING.)

ANNCR: . . . the striped surf perch . . .

(MUSIC: BEACH BOYS SONG INTRO.)

ANNCR: . . . the cleaner wrasse . . .

VOICE 3 (WOMAN, DEJECTED.): This glass has spots.

ANNCR: . . . the Hawaiian cleaner wrasse . . .

(MUSIC: HAWAIIAN MELODY.)

VOICE 4 (HAWAIIAN WOMAN, DEJECTED.): This glass has spots.

ANNCR: . . . the reef coral . . .

(SFX: OPENING OF BARBER-SHOP-QUARTET SONG.)

ANNCR: . . . the buffalo sculpin . . .

(SFX: PRONOUNCED SOUND OF HERD STAMPEDING.)

ANNCR: . . . the saddleback gunnel . . .

(MUSIC: OPENING OF "WILLIAM TELL OVERTURE.")

ANNCR: . . . the manacled sculpin . . .

(SFX: SOUND OF HANDCUFFS CLICKING.)

VOICE 5: You have the right to remain silent . . .
(FADES.)

ANNCR: . . . and the unidentified shrimp . . .

VOICE 6 (A LA AMERICAN EXPRESS COMMERCIAL.): Do you know me? I've played some of the best-known watering holes in the Pacific . . .
(FADES.)

ANNCR: . . . The Seattle Aquarium. See how the other two-thirds lives.

(SFX: SOUND EFFECTS, VOICES AND MUSIC THAT WE HEARD BEFORE ALL STARTING AGAIN REACH A CACOPHONY.)

**Consumer Television
Over :30 (:45/:60/:90)
Single**

62 GOLD
ART DIRECTORS
Lee Clow
Gary Johns

WRITER
Jeff Gorman

CLIENT
Nike

DIRECTORS
Tim Newman
Mark Coppos

PRODUCTION COS.
Jenkins Covington Newman
Directors Consortium

AGENCY PRODUCER
Morty Baran

AGENCY
Chiat/Day-Los Angeles

63 SILVER
ART DIRECTOR
David Lamb

WRITER
Larry Simon

CLIENT
Anheuser-Busch/Bud Light

DIRECTOR
Joe Pytka

PRODUCTION CO.
Levine/Pytka & Associates

AGENCY PRODUCERS
Gary Conway
David Lamb

AGENCY
Needham Harper Worldwide/
Chicago

64 BRONZE
ART DIRECTOR
Harvey Hoffenberg

WRITERS
Phil Dusenberry
Ted Sann

CLIENT
Pepsi-Cola

DIRECTOR
Ridley Scott

PRODUCTION CO.
Fairbanks Films

AGENCY PRODUCER
Phyllis Landi

AGENCY
BBDO

62 GOLD

(MUSIC THROUGHOUT: "I Love L.A.")

RANDY NEWMAN: *Rollin' down Imperial Highway. A big nasty red-head at my side. Santa Ana winds blowin' hot from the north. We was born to ride. From the South Bay, to the Valley. From the West Side, to the East Side. Everybody's very happy 'cause the sun is shining all the time. It's like another perfect day. I love L.A.!*

CHORUS: *We love it!*

RANDY NEWMAN: *We love it!*

CHORUS: *Ah, ah, ah, ah . . .*

RANDY NEWMAN: *I love L.A.!*

CHORUS: *We love it!*

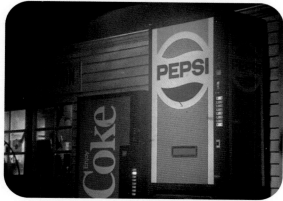

63 SILVER

(MUSIC INTRO)

1ST FARMER: Suppose that's them.

2ND FARMER: Don't know who else'd be out this early.

ANNCR: For the Caldwells, early morning's the best time to get things done. And times being what they are not much would make them shut down. Even for a few minutes.
But this summer of 1984 the Caldwells have shut down to see something they'll most likely never see again.

(SFX: FARMERS CLAPPING)

ANNCR: As we host the games this summer, let's hope we all learn that the true meaning of the Olympics is not in the winning but in discovering the best in all of us.

SINGERS: *Budweiser Light*

64 BRONZE

(OMINOUS MUSIC)

(SFX: SOUNDS OF BOY AND DOG PLAYING.)

BOY: Fetch boy

(DOG BARKS.)

(OMINOUS MUSIC GETS INCREASINGLY LOUDER.)

(SFX: WIND)

(SFX: LIGHT, COMPUTER-LIKE SOUNDS.)

(SOOTHING MUSIC)

V.O.: Pepsi. The Choice of a New Generation.

**Consumer Television
Over :30 (:45/:60/:90)
Campaign**

65 GOLD
ART DIRECTOR
Harvey Hoffenberg

WRITERS
Phil Dusenberry
Ted Sann

CLIENT
Pepsi-Cola

DIRECTORS
Bob Giraldi
Barry Meyers
Ridley Scott

PRODUCTION COS.
Giraldi Productions
Sunlight
Fairbanks Films

AGENCY PRODUCERS
Phyllis Landi
David Frankel

AGENCY
BBDO

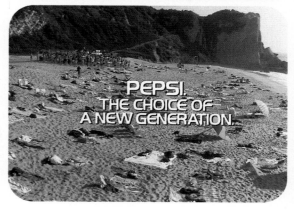

65 GOLD

(JACKSONS MUSIC)

JACKSONS: *You're a whole new generation
Dancing through the day
Grabbin' for the magic on the run
A whole new generation
You're loving what you do. Put a Pepsi . . .
into motion
The choice is up to you
Hey-Hey-Hey, You're the Pepsi generation
Guzzle down and taste the thrill of today, and
feel the Pepsi way.
Taste the thrill of today, and feel the Pepsi way.
You're a whole new generation, You're a whole
new generation,
You're a whole new generation.*

65 GOLD

(SFX: BEACH SOUNDS, I.E., WIND, WATER.)

(BACKGROUND SFX D.J. FROM RADIO.

SOUNDS OF SPEAKERS BEING RAISED ATOP TRUCK.

SOUNDS OF ICE CUBES BEING DROPPED INTO GLASS.

SOUND IS HEARD ACROSS BEACH.

SOUND OF POPPING TOP.

SOUND OF POPPING TOP ECHOES OVER BEACH.

SOUND OF POPPING CONTINUES.

SOUND OF FIZZING SODA.

SOUNDS OF FIZZING SODA ARE HEARD ACROSS BEACH.

SOUNDS OF FIZZING SODA CONTINUE.)

BOY: . . . Aah . . .

BOY: O.K. . . . who's first?

(SFX: CROWD NOISES.)

VO: Pepsi. The choice of a new generation.

65 GOLD

(OMINOUS MUSIC)

(SFX: SOUNDS OF BOY AND DOG PLAYING.)

BOY: "Fetch boy"

(OMINOUS MUSIC)

(SFX: DOG BARKS. OMINOUS MUSIC GETS INCREASINGLY
    LOUDER.

SFX: WIND

SFX: LIGHT, COMPUTER-LIKE SOUNDS.)

(SOOTHING MUSIC)

V.O.: "Pepsi. The choice of a new generation."

**Consumer Television
Over :30 (:45/:60/:90)
Campaign**

66 SILVER
ART DIRECTORS
Chris Blum
Leslie Caldwell
WRITER
Mike Koelker
CLIENT
Levi Strauss
DIRECTOR
Leslie Dektor
PRODUCTION CO.
Petermann/Dektor
AGENCY PRODUCER
Steve Neely
AGENCY
Foote Cone Belding/
San Francisco

66 SILVER

SINGER (VO): *Shrink to fit only you.*

SINGERS (VO): *501 Blues.*

SINGER: *Do the things that you do.*

GROUP: *501 Blues.*

SINGER: *Fit a personal way.*

GROUP: *501 Blues.*

SINGER: *Wear 'em every day.*

GROUP: *501 Blues.*

SINGER: *Nothin' like these jeans,
The coolest jeans I've seen,
501 Blues.*

*Levi's button-fly
501 Blues.*

66 SILVER

SINGER: *Ain't no body
Like my body
That's about the size of it
So I personalize my size
With Levi's 501 Blues
They shrink to fit
They're the blues that make me
feel good,
Levi's 501 Blues
Love them Blues!
Oh yeah!*

66 SILVER

SINGERS (VO): *Shrink to fit*
And a button fly, too
Aah-Ooh
Levi's 501 Blues
Shrink your own
Very personal pair
A little loose here
And a little tight there
We're so blue
We've got the blues
So blue
The 501 Blues
We're so blue
Levi's 501 Blues

LEAD SINGER: *Hahaha.*

Gold,
Silver
&
Bronze
Awards

**Consumer Television
:30 Single**

68 GOLD
ART DIRECTOR
Brent Thomas
WRITER
Brent Bouchez
CLIENT
Nike
DIRECTOR
Mark Coppos
PRODUCTION CO.
Directors Consortium
AGENCY PRODUCER
Richard O'Neill
AGENCY
Chiat/Day-Los Angeles

69 SILVER
ART DIRECTOR
Gary Johns
WRITER
Jeff Gorman
CLIENT
Nike
DIRECTOR
Mark Coppos
PRODUCTION CO.
Directors Consortium
AGENCY PRODUCER
Morty Baran
AGENCY
Chiat/Day-Los Angeles

70 BRONZE
ART DIRECTORS
Chris Blum
Leslie Caldwell
WRITER
Mike Koelker
CLIENT
Levi Strauss
DIRECTOR
Leslie Dektor
PRODUCTION CO.
Petermann/Dektor
AGENCY PRODUCER
Steve Neely
AGENCY
Foote Cone Belding/
San Francisco

68 GOLD

(MUSIC THROUGHOUT)

ANNCR (VO): At Nike we haven't forgotten why
they're called sweats.

69 SILVER

(SFX: CROWD. QUARTERBACK CALLING SIGNALS.)

HAYES (VO): By the time I hit the field, I've already worked overtime.
Studying films of the guy across the line.
Four hours a night.
Because I believe in doing my homework.

And people wonder how come I'm always in the right place . . .

(SFX: CRUNCH.)

HAYES (VO): . . . at the right time.

70 BRONZE

THE BLUES SINGER: *Ain't no body*
Like my body
That's about the size of it, Ummhhh.
So I personalize my size, with
Levi's 501 Blues . . .
They shrink to fit.
They're the Blues that make
me feel good.
Levi's 501 Blues . . .
Love them Blues, Oh Yeah!

**Consumer Television
:30 Campaign**

71 GOLD

ART DIRECTORS
Nick Gisonde
Dave Clark

WRITERS
Charlie Breen
Bob Tamburri

CLIENT
Miller Brewing/Lite Beer

DIRECTOR
Bob Giraldi

PRODUCTION CO.
Giraldi Productions

AGENCY PRODUCERS
Marc Mayhew
Andy Cornelius

AGENCY
Backer & Spielvogel

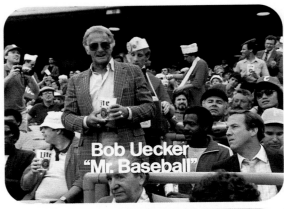

71 GOLD

(SFX: CROWD NOISE, CHEERING, ETC.)

BOB UECKER: Y'know one of the best things about being an ex-Big Leaguer is getting freebies to the game.
Called the front office . . . BINGO!

And once these fans recognize me, I probably won't even have to pay for my Lite Beer from Miller.

FAN VO (SHOUTING): Down in front!

BOB UECKER: Hah, I love 'em. These fans know I drink Lite, cuz it's less filling and it tastes great.

USHER: You're in the wrong seat buddy. C'mon . . .

UECKER: Oh, I must be in the front row!

USHER: C'mon, C'mon . . . C'mon

ANNCR: Lite Beer from Miller. Everything you always wanted in a beer. And less.

(SFX: CRACK OF A BASEBALL ON THE BAT. CROWD CHEERS AND GENERAL CROWD NOISE.)

BOB UECKER: Good seats, eh, Buddy?
(SHOUTING) He missed the tag!!! He missed the tag!!!

71 GOLD

L.C.: I crushed a lot of quarterbacks in my day. And I'm real sorry. So I wrote this letter. Dear Quarterbacks, I apologize for the way I've treated you. So please let me buy you a Lite Beer from Miller. Lite's my beer because it tastes great. I'm sure it's yours too because you little guys. . . . .

(CROWD: Oooh. LAUGHTER)

L.C.: . . . can't afford to get too filled up.

ANNCR. VO: Lite Beer from Miller. Everything you always wanted in a beer and less.

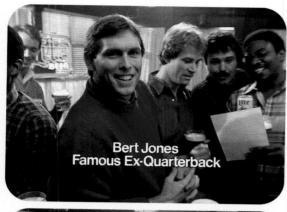

71 GOLD

JONES: I hear that L.C. Greenwood has invited QB's to join him for a Lite Beer from Miller. Here's my reply. Dear L.C., I accept your very gracious offer. A QB is far too intelligent to turn down a lite beer because it's less filling and it tastes great. Even you big clumsy linemen know that. Hope to see you soon. Sincerely, Bert Jones.

ANNCR. VO: Lite Beer from Miller. Everything you always wanted in a beer and less.

BERT: How did he do that?

Gold,
Silver
&
Bronze
Awards

**Consumer Television
:30 Campaign**

72 SILVER

ART DIRECTOR
Tony Angotti

WRITER
Tom Thomas

CLIENT
BMW of North America

DIRECTORS
Michael Seresin
Henry Sandbank

PRODUCTION COS.
Brooks Fulford Cramer
  Seresin
Sandbank Films

AGENCY PRODUCERS
Ozzie Spenningsby
Susan Shipman

AGENCY
Ammirati & Puris

72 SILVER

ANNCR (VO): Every day, BMW presents a
comprehensive report . . . on the state of
automotive technology.

Not through some dry dissertation . . . or the
theoretical vacuum of a laboratory . . . but
rather through a more appropriate vehicle.

The BMW 733i. The luxury sedan that translates
the intricacies of technology . . . into that very
elusive commodity . . .

. . . called fun.

BMW

72 SILVER

ANNCR (VO): In Germany . . .

The head of BMW's Personnel Department is an
engineer.

The Head of Corporate Planning . . .

is an engineer.

Even the Chairman . . . is an engineer.

So it's not surprising that BMW's leave the
factory with a very clear sense of priorities.

And that's crucial.

Because when you buy a car, what you're really
buying . . .

Is the company that built it.

BMW

72 SILVER

ANNCR (VO): For all those confrontations with the unpredictable . . .

. . . BMW introduces the ultimate defense.

The 535i.

With an amazingly agile suspension.

A computer controlled engine that constantly adjusts to changing driving conditions.

And an ingenious anti-lock braking system.

The BMW 535i.

It lets those who take driving seriously peacefully coexist . . .

. . . with those who don't.

BMW

**Consumer Television
:30 Campaign**

73 BRONZE
ART DIRECTOR
Tod Seisser
WRITER
Jay Taub
CLIENT
Citizen Watches
DIRECTOR
Henry Sandbank
PRODUCTION CO.
Sandbank Films
AGENCY PRODUCER
Rachel Novak
AGENCY
Levine Huntley Schmidt &
Beaver

73 BRONZE

ANNCR: This is the Atomic Clock in Boulder,
Colorado. Precise to within one second every
300,000 years, it's designed to be the world's
most accurate clock. Its cost—$500,000.

Which is astounding—when you consider that
$496,500 less buys you this Citizen. The world's
most accurate watch.

Citizen Watches. The smartest engineering ever
strapped to a wrist.

73 BRONZE

ANNCR: If there's one thing Germany is noted for,
it's engineering. It's a country where accuracy
and precision are everything.

Perhaps that's why in Germany, where they sell
over 350 different brands of watches, the watch
that sells most—is Citizen.

Citizen Watches. The smartest engineering ever
strapped to a wrist.

73 BRONZE

ANNCR: This is Big Ben. And this is the man who sets it. It's his job to keep this clock so accurate, you could set your watch by it. As millions of Londoners do.

The big question is, how does he check the accuracy of Big Ben? With a Citizen. The watch so accurate, you could set a clock by it.

Citizen Watches. The smartest engineering ever strapped to a wrist.

Gold,
Silver
&
Bronze
Awards

Consumer Television :10 Single

74 GOLD
ART DIRECTOR
Michael Tesch
WRITER
Patrick Kelly
CLIENT
Federal Express
DIRECTOR
Patrick Kelly
PRODUCTION CO.
Kelly Pictures
AGENCY PRODUCER
Jerry Haynes
AGENCY
Ally & Gargano

75 SILVER
ART DIRECTORS
Lee Clow
Brent Thomas
WRITERS
Steve Hayden
Penny Kapousouz
CLIENT
Apple Computer
DIRECTOR
Mark Coppos
PRODUCTION CO.
Directors Consortium
AGENCY PRODUCER
Morty Baran
AGENCY
Chiat/Day-Los Angeles

76 BRONZE
ART DIRECTOR
Barry Vetere
WRITER
Ron Berger
CLIENT
Dunkin' Donuts
DIRECTOR
Dick Loew
PRODUCTION CO.
Gomes-Loew
AGENCY PRODUCER
Beth Forman
AGENCY
Ally & Gargano

74 GOLD

MAN ON PHONE: Listen to me. I'm serious. I am desperate.

ANNCR: His job depended on getting a package somewhere overnight.

MAN ON PHONE: I need help.

ANNCR: Now he's got another job.

MAN: Fred's Weenies! Get your weenies! Red hot weenies.

ANNCR: Next time, send it Federal Express.

75 SILVER

ANNCR (VO): Using Apple's new Macintosh does require some technical skill.

Macintosh.

76 BRONZE

(MUSIC UNDER)

ANNCR (VO): Dunkin' Donuts introduces fresh baked croissants. France's great pastry chefs should find them interesting.

CHEF: They are brilliant.

(SFX: SHOUTING)

Gold,
Silver
&
Bronze
Awards

**Consumer Television
:10 Campaign**

77 GOLD
ART DIRECTOR
Michael Tesch

WRITER
Patrick Kelly

CLIENT
Federal Express

DIRECTOR
Patrick Kelly

PRODUCTION CO.
Kelly Pictures

AGENCY PRODUCER
Jerry Haynes

AGENCY
Ally & Gargano

77 GOLD

MAN ON PHONE: Listen to me. I'm serious. I am desperate.

ANNCR: His job depended on getting a package somewhere overnight.

MAN ON PHONE: I need help.

ANNCR: Now he's got another job.

MAN: Fred's Weenies! Get your weenies! Red hot weenies.

ANNCR: Next time, send it Federal Express.

77 GOLD

MAN YELLING LOUD ON THE PHONE: Hello, Federal Express . . . Listen . . . I'm expecting a large important package from Topeka early this morning and I just want to say . . .

(SFX: PLOP!)

(NORMAL VOICE). . . thank you very much.

77 GOLD

ANNCR: A lot of people think Federal Express
   carries only little packages. Our couriers would
   probably disagree with this.

(SFX: CRASH)

**Consumer Television
:10 Campaign**

78 SILVER
ART DIRECTORS
Lee Clow
Brent Thomas
WRITERS
Steve Hayden
Penny Kapousouz
CLIENT
Apple Computer
DIRECTOR
Mark Coppos
PRODUCTION CO.
Directors Consortium
AGENCY PRODUCER
Morty Baran
AGENCY
Chiat/Day-Los Angeles

78 SILVER

ANNCR (VO):With Macintosh from Apple . . . you can do all all of this . . . by simply doing this.

Macintosh.

78 SILVER

ANNCR (VO): Why learn all of this . . .

(SFX: THUD)

. . . when you can use Macintosh by simply learning this.

Macintosh.

ANNCR (VO): Using Apple's new Macintosh does require some technical skill.

Macintosh.

Gold,
Silver
&
Bronze
Awards

Public Service
Television Single

79 SILVER
ART DIRECTOR
Mike Moser

WRITER
Brian O'Neill

CLIENT
California Broadcasters
Association Against Drunk
Driving

DIRECTOR
Mike Cuesta

PRODUCTION CO.
Griner/Cuesta

AGENCY PRODUCER
Richard O'Neill

AGENCY
Chiat/Day-San Francisco

80 BRONZE
ART DIRECTOR
Michael Diliberto

WRITER
Jeff Millman

CLIENT
Maryland Council for
Developmental Disabilities

PRODUCTION CO.
Smith Burke & Azzam

AGENCY PRODUCER
Tom Trahan

AGENCY
Smith Burke & Azzam/
Baltimore

79 SILVER

ANNCR (VO): In the last year in California, 350,000
people were thrown in jail for drunk driving.
This year, the police are cracking down even
harder.

(SFX: JAIL DOOR SLAMS.)

But while you may be in jail for drunk driving . . .

(SFX: PRISONER OUTBURST.)

ANNCR (VO): they're not.

80 BRONZE

DEBBIE: I'm very proud to introduce . . . me. Ta-da!
My name's Debbie. I'm 17. I love Duran Duran.
I hate my hair. I'm real easy to talk to. I'm
basically adorable. So, if we happen to meet
remember—this is me. And this is just a chair.
Okay? Okay!

Gold,
Silver
&
Bronze
Awards

Public Service
Television Campaign

81 BRONZE
ART DIRECTOR
Doug Lew
WRITER
Bob Thacker
CLIENT
Minneapolis Institute of Arts
DIRECTOR
Steve Griak
PRODUCTION CO.
Wilson-Griak
AGENCY
Chuck Ruhr/Mpls.

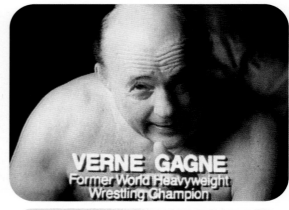

81 BRONZE

BOUZA: I want you to know about a very important bust here in Minneapolis. There have only been two others like it in the world. One back East. And one in Switzerland.

You might say, it began with a French Connection. A real master—Jean-Baptiste Lemoyne. The guy was an artist.

V.O.: The Bust of Louis XV. Of soft paste porcelain. Just one of Minnesota's new treasures at the Minneapolis Institute of Arts.

BOUZA: It's a crime if you don't go see it.

81 BRONZE

GAGNE: Anybody who knows Verne Gagne knows you gotta have real power to hold me. Well, the other day, right here in Minneapolis, I met my match. A Dutchman. World Heavyweight Class. Devastating.

ANNCR. V.O.: The River Landscape by Jan Van Goyen. Just one of Minnesota's newest treasures at the Minneapolis Institute of Arts.

GAGNE: The way this guy works on the canvas, I may have to retire, again.

81 BRONZE

HOLTZ: I wanna tell you about a couple of guards we just got here in Minnesota. Highly recruited. Everybody in the world wanted them. You say what about size? Six feet four. Over 300 pounds. They're awesome. No, they're not from Minnesota. They're from Japan.

ANNCR. V.O.: The Nio Guardian Statues from the Kamakura Period. Just two of Minnesota's newest treasures at the Minneapolis Institute of Arts.

HOLTZ: They are a little slow, but they do draw a crowd.

THE GOLD AWARD WINNERS ON THE GOLD AWARD WINNERS

The Gold Award Winners on The Gold Award Winners

**Consumer Newspaper
Over 600 Lines:
Single**

AGENCY: Scali, McCabe, Sloves
CLIENT: Perdue

So what if it was one of the first decent Saturdays of spring. And a major portion of the city's population was either in the park, on the street, or out of town.

We were fortunate enough to be working on a Perdue Oven Stuffer Roaster Parts campaign.

For about the third weekend in a row.

At the office.

Right across the hall from the agency bullpen which was fully staffed and in full swing. And evidently, every single member of the swing shift was under the impression that if they asked often enough, sooner or later someone would finally break down and show them where they were hiding the beef.

It took Clara Peller, Walter Mondale, and finally the studio crew, but we were the ones who ultimately broke down.

I went into a "Where's the beef?" chant.

Amy came back with a "Who cares?"

The planets aligned.

And down on paper went the idea.

On Monday morning, we went into Ed McCabe's office with our weekly collection of Roaster Parts comps. And when he saw Frank's retort, he told us it had nothing to do with the assignment. But who cares about that either. Let's do it.

Amy Schottenfels
Bruce Richter

1 GOLD

This ad goes back to the good old days in
advertising when being able to come up with an
interesting headline and visual was more important
than being able to write a good strategy statement.
    The client wanted to introduce a new shoe.
    The primary benefit: how light it was.
    We did the ad.
    They bought it.
    We produced it.
    They ran it.
    And, apparently, a lot of people liked it.

*Ron Berger
Dennis D'Amico*

See number 15 Gold

*Jeff Gorman
Gary Johns*

10 GOLD

7 GOLD

The Gold Award Winners on The Gold Award Winners

**Consumer Magazine
Black and White
Campaign Including
Magazine Supplements**

AGENCY: Levine, Huntley, Schmidt and Beaver
CLIENT: McCall's

This wasn't the first campaign we presented to the client. The first, despite all our efforts, got killed.
  Thank God.

Stephanie Arnold
Tana Klugherz

ONE OF THE DRAB HOMEBODIES WHO READS McCALL'S.

McCall's
MORE THAN THE EXPECTED.

13 GOLD

**Consumer Magazine
Color Campaign
Including Magazine
Supplements**

AGENCY: Chiat/Day, Los Angeles
CLIENT: Nike, Inc.

Words escape us.

Jeff Gorman
Gary Johns

15 GOLD

Trade
Black and White
Page or Spread

AGENCY: The Campaign Palace
CLIENT: The Campaign Palace

One of the supposed perks of this business is that it affords a nicer lifestyle.

You can, for instance, if you work hard enough, get to be part-owner of a gracious old 44-foot motor yacht upon which weekends can be spent recovering from the abrasions of advertising.

But if you're highly involved with what you do, reality is entirely different.

The boating weekend on which this ad was created was particularly glorious.

Broken Bay, just north of Sydney, was never more seductive: soothing sun, warm breeze, bronzed bodies (other people's) and ice boxes full of chilled Chablis.

This time it was a recruitment ad that had to be produced rather quickly.

All ads seem important, but none so much as the one destined to unearth a new Managing Director for your agency.

Nevertheless, it's times like this, when you occasionally lift your head from the work to gaze enviously at the real people innocently lazing about on the decks of passing boats, that you start to wonder whether it's really worth being in a business where you spend an entire holiday weekend writing a recruitment ad inside a boat in the midst of paradise.

Still, when you receive recognition for doing such idiotic things, it helps.

Real people may get to go bronze on a sun deck.

But they may never get to turn gold on a chart table.

Jack Vaughan
Rob Tomnay

Trade Color
Page or Spread

AGENCY: The Martin Agency
CLIENT: FMC Corporation

We spent a whole weekend under a 65-foot granite statue of a man on a horse, thinking about bugs. Perverse, but true.

Daniel Clay Russ
Diane Cook Tench

21 GOLD

18 GOLD

The Gold
Award
Winners on
The Gold
Award
Winners

**Trade
Any Size
B/W or Color
Campaign**

AGENCY: Fallon McElligott Rice
CLIENT: ITT Life Insurance Company

Obviously, the first step in creating a campaign to recruit insurance agents is to start thinking like an insurance agent.

So after a quick skim of the research, the three of us put on gaudy sport jackets and traded tired jokes in loud voices.

Then we did the ads.

*Dean Hanson
Rod Kilpatrick
Jarl Olsen*

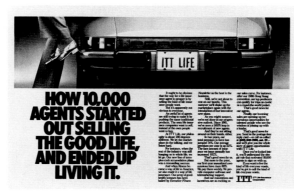

24 GOLD

**Collateral
Brochures
Other Than by Mail**

AGENCY: Lawler Ballard Advertising
CLIENT: Raleigh Cycle Company of America

We don't know how we came up with the concept, but here's a recipe for Mama Pink's Ice Box Pudding.

Cream together:
¼ lb. butter
¾ c. confectioners sugar
¼ tsp. almond flavoring
4 egg yolks
6 T cocoa

Fold in stiffly beaten egg whites. Line any pyrex dish with wax paper and stand lady fingers up around side of bowl. Fill dish with alternate layers of almond macaroons* and chocolate filling. Put in refrigerator till firm—serve with whipped cream.

*If macaroons seem stale—soak in water and squeeze out.

*Lloyd Wolfe
Marc Deschenes*

27 GOLD

**Collateral
Direct Mail**

AGENCY: Westbrook
CLIENT: Poplar Springs Hospital

We're more interested in the fact that this piece
helped fill up the hospital, of course, than the fact
that it won a gold medal in the One Show.
    But hey, let's have lunch anyway.

*Bill Westbrook
Robin Stanley
Carolyn Tye*

30 GOLD

**Collateral
P.O.P.**

AGENCY: Ammirati & Puris
CLIENT: BMW of North America, Inc.

We'd like to thank all those individuals whose
outstanding work on BMW over the last ten years
made this poster possible.
    After all, if the car and all it stands for were not
so thoroughly implanted, this idea would have sunk
like a rock.

*Mark Moffett
Mark Silveira*

33 GOLD

The Gold
Award
Winners on
The Gold
Award
Winners

**Outdoor
Single**

AGENCY: Livingston & Co.
CLIENT: Seattle Aquarium

It's nice to see words make a comeback in outdoor.

*Ron Sandilands
Bernie Hafeli*

SEE HOW THE OTHER TWO-THIRDS LIVES.

SEATTLE AQUARIUM

36 GOLD

**Outdoor
Campaign**

AGENCY: Chiat/Day
CLIENT: Nike, Inc.

What's left to say?

*Jeff Gorman
Gary Johns*

39 GOLD

Public Service
Newspaper or Magazine
Single

AGENCY: Wells Rich Greene/London
CLIENT: Down's Children's Association

If I could have got Evelyn to write this, she'd have given you no rationale, none of the strategic thinking behind giving the reader firsthand experience of the way Down's people think, no analysis of the way in which typography can play an important role in charity advertising.

What you would have got would have been a piece of writing capturing perfectly the unbridled joy of being recognized for this award, spelling errors, lousy punctuation, and all. Like the ad, in a better set of words than this writer could put together.

Mike Chapman

Public Service
Newspaper or Magazine
Campaign

AGENCY: Leonard Monahan Saabye
CLIENT: Volunteer Services for Animals

Where did the inspiration for these ads come from?

Maybe it hit us at the first client meeting, where we met people who were as psyched about doing terrific ads as we were.

Nah, that wasn't it.

Maybe it hit us after reading reams and reams of literature on animal laws and rights.

Nah, that wasn't it either.

Or maybe it hit us when we drove up to one of the local pounds and saw decomposing dog carcasses lying around on the front lawn.

Yeah. That was it.

David Lubars
Debbie Lucke
Bryan McPeak

My name is Evelyn. People call me a Mongol. I wrote this ad.

To help their childrens problems and feelings, I'm sure all Downsyndrome children in this world Like to stop The word Mongal becouse it hurts their feelings.

But They like To be normal and Treated normal. The Whole worlds peoples should help Down-syndrome children and play games with them, To feed Them and To give them Something to Drink.

I shall explain why. They have got 47 chromosomes and the world has got 46 chromosomes.

But we are Different and we can do more work although We are very slow.

But all of us can try to catch up. Downsyndrome children must work harder to keep up.

my name is EvELyn Also I used to go to school for 13 years at least, The Stress is powerful.

So They all call me mongal I dont Like that. But Teachers Dont say that at all and this is good on the Teachers part.

But all of us can try to catch up. I like Nena Weil she has The same problems in the television pro-gramme. Downsyndrome children must work harder to keep up.

I love holidays and staying at home But my father did not come when we went on holiday To morocco as he had some work to do and its very hard work, for the meeting in Bristol of Down-syndrome childrens Association.

We have to To Help Those Who have got Downs children or has got anything where They Have got problems.

We must Try To Help Them, The Lot. This is a very important and serious thing.

Its really needs to Be Done also get it Done and Done with.

I Like shopping also going to town. I Like playing my piano so I Love working very much indeed.

We can Breathe in the fresh air; so in the paradise on earth.

I Like Art also reading and writing also games. so I Like Tony Harts paintings.

I can cope on my own also I can run a House so I could Help my children if They got problems. now I do Typing for Scheidegger for A correspondence Course in Leicester. Its a Swiss School so I have a Tuter who comes every weekso I Like that.

Outside my front garden Theres A tree in Blossom and its white like there's A person Dressed up in Wedding Dress behind it.

I can get Dressed and Make my breakfast. In the Afternoon I do my typing. But when I get tired I Dont do it as much also I lay the table for all of us to eat then I write Letters to my friends.

This is my every daily Life and the Whole worlds childrens is the same as us.

We play Tennis all of us are no good but we need practice even our ice-skating so all of us needs more practice.

I Really enjoy Skiing very much indeed. We Like to go to the fair and Art gallery, also museums.

I go swimming its my favourite sport. I have got Three certificates The first one is my gold Award for proficiency in personal Survival at last September 1983.

Thats what we Believe so its Just works. It does work like its Just right, so thats The way To do it. I want To Help Those who have got Downsyndrome children so I Think Thats right to do. so it is a very serious Thing and should be Done.

The Down's Children's Association,
4 Oxford Street, London W1N 9FL.

We offer support and advice to parents and professionals living and working with Down's Syndrome children.
If you think there's anything wrong with the way Evelyn thinks, thanks for your time anyway.
If you think there's anything wrong with the way the rest of us think, we'd welcome your help.
☐ I would like to become a member.
☐ I enclose a donation or please debit credit card number:

The amount £ _____ Date _____
Sign here _____
Name _____
Address _____
_____ Postcode _____

Send to DCA, FREEPOST 32, London W1E 3YZ.

42 GOLD

It's not a dog.
It's a guinea pig.

There is a thriving black market in this country. A dreadful, despicable black market.

A black market where lost and stolen pets are sold to laboratories for experimentation.

And while its true that Rhode Island has passed legislation that makes selling pound animals for experimentation illegal here, it doesn't mean your pet is safe. Because it's a fact that thieves steal pets and smuggle them into states where selling animals for experimentation is legal.

What can you do?

Well, for your own dog, there are three things. One, don't let him run loose in the neighborhood. Keep him on a leash. Two, when you're not home, don't leave him alone in the backyard. And three, if you don't have ID tags, a license or a tattoo on him, get them immediately.

But there's something else you can do. You can join Volunteer Services for Animals.

We're a private, non-profit organization whose sole purpose is to improve the treatment and environment of animals in our state.

We also help municipalities provide humane services which they couldn't otherwise afford. For example, we have lost and found, adoption, veterinary care, population control, pet therapy and education programs.

So please call us at 273-0358. And help our animal operation prevent animal operations.

VOLUNTEER SERVICES FOR ANIMALS
401 Broadway, Providence, Rhode Island 02909

45 GOLD

The Gold
Award
Winners on
The Gold
Award
Winners

**Public Service
Outdoor Single**

AGENCY: Young & Rubicam
CLIENT: Young & Rubicam

The headline is nothing new. People have been
using it for years.

We just added pictures and gave them something
to think about.

Joe Lovering
Jerry Roach

48 GOLD

College Competition

CLIENT: NFL

Steve's Gold Medal Recipe

Ingredients:

2 Supportive parents.
1 Brother who won the previous year's One
Show.
1 Understanding fiancee.
3-5 Layout pads.
1 Award winning Advertising Program.
(East Texas State University)
3 (or more) Professional instructors.
(Rob Lawton, John Crawley and Bob
Marberry)
1 Good photographer. (Alan Cook)
1 Healthy spiritual life.
1 Big idea*.
*This will be the most difficult ingredient to
find.

To prepare:

Drain everything you can out of Ad Program
and instructors.
Fill all layout pads with lukewarm ideas.
Sift out big idea. (This should be done
approximately 3 days before deadline—no
sooner.)
Add type choice and designs to taste.
Blend with all other ingredients.
Ship overnight.
Pray.

Helpful hints:

Stay away from sharp objects and don't
operate heavy machinery until results are
obtained.
Nail-biting, crankiness and calling the One
Club everyday will not speed outcome.
Be sure to thank all who have been helpful and
supportive along the way.

Thank you

Steve Popp

50 GOLD

**Consumer Radio
Single**

AGENCY: Fallon McElligott Rice
CLIENT: New Orleans Breakers

The Breakers fired us immediately upon hearing this commercial. Is it a mere coincidence that they finished the season 8 and 10?

Jarl "Mojo Hand" Olsen

SEE GOLD AWARD WINNER 53

**Public Service
Radio Single**

AGENCY: Levine, Huntley, Schmidt and Beaver
CLIENT: Kronenbourg

This campaign not only helped the Kronenbourg people sell beer, it helped them sell their company.
  To Guinness.
  Who hates our campaign.

*Jay Taub
Tod Seisser*

SEE GOLD AWARD WINNER 59

**Public Service
Radio Campaign**

AGENCY: Livingston & Co.
CLIENT: Seattle Aquarium

I think it was Tom McElligott who wrote: "There are two times in life when you're totally alone. Just before you die. And just before you make a speech." I'd like to add a third: Just before you write a radio commercial. However, you're not alone for long. In short order, there are friendly people there to help. First-rate producers like Cindy Henderson. Brilliant sound engineers like Peter Lewis. Off-the-wall talent like Pat Fraley. This award is as much theirs as mine. Thanks.

Bernie Hafeli

SEE GOLD AWARD WINNER 61

**Consumer Television
60 Seconds Single**

AGENCY: Chiat/Day -Los Angeles
CLIENT: Nike, Inc.

Taking Randy Newman's video and turning it into Nike's salute to LA for the '84 Olympics was such an obviously good idea that while Jeff and Gary and I had the idea, so did Peter Moore and Rob Strasser at Nike, and even Gene Cameron, *our account supervisor!*, thought of it. (He still thinks it was his idea.)

Lee Clow

62 GOLD

**Consumer Television
30 Seconds Single**

AGENCY: Chiat/Day
CLIENT: Nike, Inc.

If you look real close at this commercial for Nike,
you'll notice the bearded face of Lee Clow.
   Which, I'm pretty sure, is the reason it won a
Gold medal.
Brent Bouchez

(You're still not getting a raise) *Lee Clow*

68 GOLD

**Consumer Television
30 Seconds Campaign**

AGENCY: Backer & Spielvogel
CLIENT: Lite Beer from Miller

We dedicate this to all those who never had a seat
in the front row.

Charlie Breen
Nick Gisonde
Bob Tamburri
Dave Clark

71 GOLD

PRINT FINALISTS

**Consumer Newspaper
Over 600 Lines: Single**

105
ART DIRECTOR
Harvey Baron
WRITER
Diane Rothschild
DESIGNER
Harvey Baron
PHOTOGRAPHER
Dennis Chalkin
CLIENT
CIGNA
AGENCY
Doyle Dane Bernbach

106
ART DIRECTOR
Mark Moffett
WRITER
Mark Silveira
PHOTOGRAPHER
Jack Couffer
CLIENT
Club Med
AGENCY
Ammirati & Puris

EVEN BUSY EXECUTIVES FIND A FEW MINUTES EVERY DAY TO THINK ABOUT THEIR MONEY.

It is one of life's ironies that the people most likely to accumulate a significant amount of money are the very people least likely to have the time to manage it.

Not many owners of successful businesses can take the time to coordinate the isolated planning of accountants, attorneys and investment advisors.

And few professional people have the time to map out personal financial strategies.

Not surprisingly, a great many successful people pay far more in taxes than they have to.

And spend years pouring money into investments that have little chance of taking them where they want to go.

Because financial planning isn't something that can be done on a part-time basis. It's a job that requires expertise, knowledge and constantly updated information.

And, at CIGNA Individual Financial Services,* that's exactly what we provide.

We analyze our clients' entire financial profiles. We come to understand their particular needs and financial goals. And, naturally, we draw on a variety of disciplines, from investment research to tax law, to develop customized financial strategies for each of our clients.

You'd expect that much from a financial planner.

What makes our service more valuable is that we go a step further.

We work with our clients' accountants. And attorneys. And other advisors. To help implement the strategies we recommend.

And as a result, we can provide our clients with a fully implemented, fully integrated financial program.

Which has often produced some very impressive results.

We've saved clients thousands of dollars in income taxes.

And sometimes even more in estate taxes.

And in case after case we've dramatically reduced the taxes associated with the transfer of a business within a family.

So if you'd like to talk with us about your financial needs, please call a local CIGNA Individual Financial Services office.

Or write CIGNA Corporation, Department RD, One Logan Square, Philadelphia, PA 19103.

Chances are we can save you more than just a night's sleep.

THERE MUST BE A MILLION REASONS TO TAKE YOUR SUMMER VACATION AT CLUB MED.

For one thing, there's the simple fact that for about what you'd pay for a week at any beach, you can come to Club Med and actually see the beach.

And, of course, with every Club Med vacation you get an entire village, not just a hotel room. So you can indulge yourself in

all sorts of fun things—waterskiing, sailing, windsurfing, snorkeling, tennis*—or do absolutely nothing. Your choice. No extra charge.

Then, there's the food. It's French. And the nightlife. And the people.

But best of all, there's the feeling. The very definite feeling that even though you've

only gone as far as the Caribbean or Mexico, the rest of civilization might as well be a million miles away.

CLUB MED
The antidote for civilization.℠
3 East 54th Street, NYC. 10022
Call 212-C·L·U·B·M·E·D (258-2633) or see your travel agent.

*Activities vary from village to village. ©1984 Club Med, Inc., 40 West 57th Street, New York, NY 10019

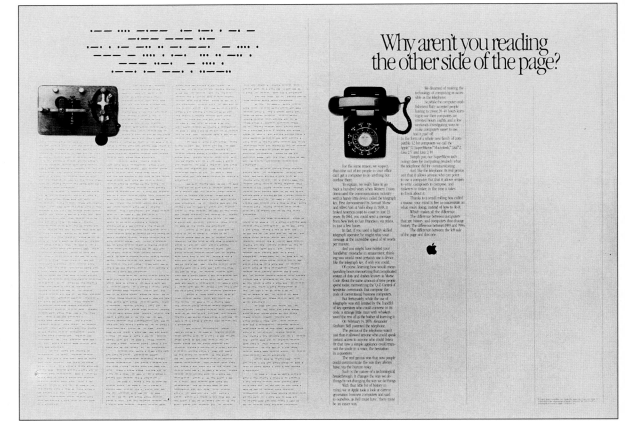

107

Parker Field echoes with four decades of baseball memories, from the early Vee teams of the 1950's to the championship Braves of recent years. While these memories may last forever, the stadium is showing its age. The stands are dangerously deteriorated. The seats are old and uncomfortable. Portions of the outfield have to be roped off to accommodate overflow crowds. Richmond needs a new ballpark. And you can help in several ways. With your time. With your money. You can even contribute to the effort by purchasing the designated Ballpark Specials being offered at participating retailers. For more information, call John D. Watt at 648-1234. It's your chance to help build a sparkling new setting for baseball in Richmond.

Let's Pitch In To Build A New Ballpark.

108

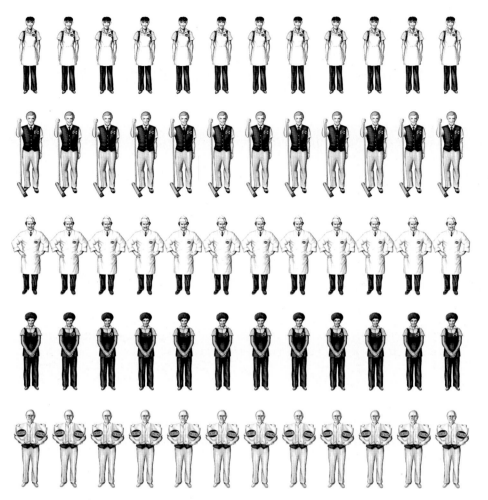

Ukrops has more of these hard to find items than any other supermarket.

At some supermarkets the hardest thing to find is help. Not at Ukrops.

What other stores spend on stamps, games and promotions, we spend on employees.

In fact, according to an independent survey, Ukrops has nearly twice as many employees per store than the average Richmond area supermarket.

That means if you have trouble finding something there's always someone close by to help you.

And we won't just point you in the general direction. We'll take you to it.

Having more people means a number of other things, too. For instance, there's always someone looking after the produce. Watering, trimming and restocking fresh fruits and vegetables.

Unlike many supermarkets, we don't trim the hours of our butchers. If we're open, there's always a butcher on duty to help you.

Even when we're not open people are working. Restocking shelves at night so you don't have to walk around boxes and cartons during the day.

And every Ukrops employee attends regular educational meetings. We believe the more you know about your business, the more you'll enjoy doing your job.

Perhaps all of this is why Richmond shoppers recently rated Ukrops as having the friendliest personnel, fastest checkout service, most attractive interiors, best meat and produce departments, cleanest stores and most orderly arrangement of items of any other supermarket in the area.

Visit Ukrops. It's hard to find a reason not to.

Ukrops

WHY BMW COUPES END UP IN MUSEUMS INSTEAD OF OBLIVION.

BMW coupes have appeared at the Louvre, the Whitney, and the Haus der Kunst in Munich.

They are on permanent display at the Los Angeles County Museum of Art and Germany's Deutsches Museum, as a sort of unofficial exhibit on Extremely Mobile Sculpture.

There's a simple reason BMW coupes end up in such ethereal resting places while others merely end up.

A BMW coupe is the automotive version of a bid for immortality—an admittedly audacious reason for being that requires a little help from destiny and all the attention

of the world's most obsessed engineers.

Which is why the engine components of the BMW 633CSi are controlled to tolerances of up to 4/100,000ths of an inch. And then pieced meticulously into a zealous fuel-injected engine that can trace its ancestry through generations of BMW grand touring machines.

Body panels and exterior surfaces are hand-fitted and hand-examined, and hand-inspected again between layers of multi-layered paint and primer. Cars are spot-checked with an incredibly picayune 38-page checklist.

Interior and exterior styling are free of

the 'model-year mentality' that freshly equips a car for obsolescence every November. At BMW, every design decision is governed by the science of ergonomics, a discipline far more enduring than automobile marketing.

"The creature comforts (and performance characteristics aren't met elsewhere," summed up AutoWeek. "The styling is only imitated elsewhere."

The BMW 633CSi. If your local museum is fresh out, we invite you to examine one at a BMW dealer near you.

THE ULTIMATE DRIVING MACHINE.

When it comes to birth control, our technology isn't exactly space age.

The country that has put men on the moon and given us cars that talk has not yet found the ideal birth control method.

Think about your own experience with contraceptives. Some of the memories would be funny, if they weren't so depressing.

Look at what's available. The diaphragm is what your great grandmother may have used. The Pill, which is effective, has a safety problem for older women. The IUD is a method from Biblical times, first used to prevent camels from getting pregnant on long desert treks. And for men, there's the condom — invented in the 17th century.

The problem is not just our lack of a perfect method, it's the lack of a concerted effort to find one. Last year the Federal Government allocated $8.5 million for new contraceptive research. In the 1965 budget, *four times* that amount is allocated for the costs of the U.S. Senate Sergeant-at-Arms and Door Keeper — and birth control is vital to everyone. Right now, promising research opportunities need public funding to make better birth control methods a reality.

Planned Parenthood is making the search for better contraception a high priority by fighting for legislation

and educating the public. It's part of our overall effort to make sure that every child born is a wanted child.

If you support our efforts, there are two ways you can show it.

First, you can give us your help with money that helps us reach others.

Second, you can make the political process work for your beliefs. Speak out. Tell public officials and candidates how you stand on these key birth control issues:

- I'm in favor of increased funds to find better birth control methods.
- I support public funding to make birth control available to all people who want it but can't afford it.
- I believe in a woman's right to safe, legal abortion.
- I'm in favor of sex education programs in the public schools.

Whatever you do, do it *now*. It's time our methods of contraception came out of the dark ages and into the space age.

**Consumer Newspaper
Over 600 Lines: Single**

113
ART DIRECTORS
Wayne Gibson
Carolyn Tye
WRITER
Kerry Feuerman
ARTIST
Reid Icard
CLIENT
Ukrop's Super Markets
AGENCY
Westbrook/Virginia

114
ART DIRECTORS
Lee Clow
Brent Thomas
WRITERS
Steve Hayden
Penny Kapousouz
PHOTOGRAPHER
Mark Coppos
CLIENT
Apple Computer
AGENCY
Chiat/Day - Los Angeles

Finally, a produce section with some meat to it.

Two years ago Ukrops made a decision to grow. Carrots, beans, nectarines, melons, artichokes, broccoli, oranges, avocados, even bamboo.

We wanted to have the largest selection of fresh produce in the area.

And we wanted more than choice, we wanted quality. Pineapples had to be field-ripened to the peak of sweetness and flown in twice a week from Hawaii.

Overgrown cucumbers wouldn't do. (Too many seeds.) So instead of just getting on the phone, we got on a plane.

We visited grape growers in California. We tasted grapefruits in Florida. We looked for the most flavorful fruits and vegetables in the country.

Today, over 175 different produce items are delivered fresh to Ukrops stores. And unlike many supermarkets, we make sure they stay fresh.

Our produce clerks are constantly watering, trimming and restocking items. We dig through the potatoes looking for bruises. And any bad apples are weeded out.

Ukrops also has a customer alert program to keep you informed on such things as the availability, flavor and nutritional value of particular items.

So if you want your pick of the finest fruits and vegetables available, come to us. If it's in season, chances are it's in Ukrops. **Ukrops**

Of the 235 million people in America, only a fraction can use a computer.

**Consumer Newspaper
Over 600 Lines: Single**

115
ART DIRECTOR
Carolyn Tye
WRITERS
Bill Westbrook
Kerry Feuerman
ARTIST
Reid Icard
CLIENT
Ukrop's Super Markets
AGENCY
Westbrook/Virginia

116
ART DIRECTORS
Carolyn Tye
Wayne Gibson
WRITERS
Bill Westbrook
Kerry Feuerman
ARTIST
Reid Icard
CLIENT
Ukrop's Super Markets
AGENCY
Westbrook/Virginia

117
ART DIRECTOR
Bob Barrie
WRITER
Rod Kilpatrick
PHOTOGRAPHER
Rick Dublin
CLIENT
MedCenters Health Plan
AGENCY
Fallon McElligott Rice/Mpls.

Supermarkets should wait on people, not vice versa.

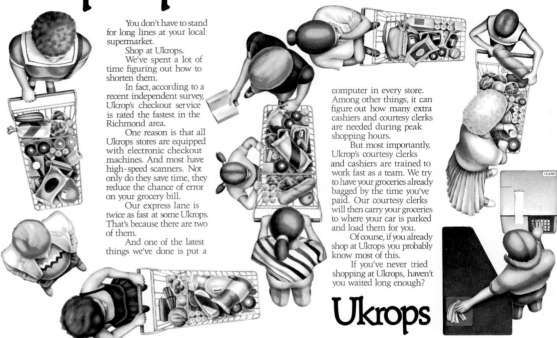

You don't have to stand for long lines at your local supermarket.

Shop at Ukrops.

We've spent a lot of time figuring out how to shorten them.

In fact, according to a recent independent survey, Ukrop's checkout service is rated the fastest in the Richmond area.

One reason is that all Ukrops stores are equipped with electronic checkout machines. And most have high-speed scanners. Not only do they save time, they reduce the chance of error on your grocery bill.

Our express lane is twice as fast at some Ukrops. That's because there are two of them.

And one of the latest things we've done is put a computer in every store. Among other things, it can figure out how many extra cashiers and courtesy clerks are needed during peak shopping hours.

But most importantly, Ukrop's courtesy clerks and cashiers are trained to work fast as a team. We try to have your groceries already bagged by the time you've paid. Our courtesy clerks will then carry your groceries to where your car is parked and load them for you.

Of course, if you already shop at Ukrops you probably know most of this.

If you've never tried shopping at Ukrops, haven't you waited long enough?

Ukrops

115

Don't buy cakes old enough to have birthdays.

When you blow out the candles and make a wish, it shouldn't be for a different cake.

Your cake should look fresh and moist. If it doesn't, it's past its prime.

At Dot's Pastry Shops in Ukrops, if we don't sell our cakes while they're fresh, we don't sell them.

The same goes for our pies, cookies, Danish, tarts and cupcakes.

In fact, the only thing that's old are our recipes. We use the same quality ingredients that Dot began using forty-four years ago.

Like rich fudge and pecans in our brownies. Fresh lemon juice in our famous lemon chess pies.

And you haven't lived until you've tasted one of Dot's delicious chocolate eclairs with creamy vanilla custard inside.

Another reason our desserts are so moist and fresh is because we don't overcook them. Actually, our cakes are taken out of the oven before they're quite done. (The heat that's still inside finishes baking them while they cool.)

In total, we bake 80 different desserts a day, five days a week. From scratch.

We'll even design, bake and decorate special order cakes for anniversaries, weddings, graduations, and, of course, birthdays.

And Dot's pastry chefs are fanatics. Each dessert has to look just as good as it tastes.

Our cakes are always decorated by hand, not machines. Our cookies have to be just the right size and shape. And if one of our gingerbread men loses his head, he's out the door.

Oh, there's one more thing. We don't add any preservatives to our desserts.

After all, they're never around long enough to need them.

Ukrops

116

The Average American Lives 73.7 Years. (Give Or Take A Few.)

Overweight. Subtract 5 Years.

Stress. Subtract 3 Years.

Excessive Drinking. Subtract 5 Years.

Lack Of Sleep. Subtract 2 Years.

Smoking. Subtract 6 Years.

Poor Diet. Subtract 4 Years.

Lack Of Exercise. Subtract 3 Years.

Your life expectancy isn't determined by statistics alone.

It's determined by the decisions you make every day. Decisions about things like smoking. Drinking. Exercise. Diet. Things that can have a profound impact on the length of your life—and on its quality.

At MedCenters, our goal is to keep you as healthy as we possibly can. So when you're sick, we provide you with doctors and medical facilities that are second to none.

More than 400 doctors, in fact, at 41 Twin Cities locations including the Park Nicollet Medical Center.

But we also have a lot to offer when you're not sick. We can help you make some important decisions about your health. And if you choose, we can help you conquer your bad health habits through information, classes, counseling—whatever it takes.

You see, our commitment to your health is more than a matter of thermometers, pills and stethoscopes. It's a matter of principle.

To find out more, ask your employer. Or write MedCenters Health Plan, 4951 Excelsior Boulevard, Minneapolis, MN 55416.

But don't put it off. Life's too short.

MEDCENTERS HEALTH PLAN

Life expectancy figures are for illustration purposes only and can vary widely. Consult your doctor.

118
ART DIRECTOR
Harvey Baron

WRITER
Diane Rothschild

DESIGNER
Harvey Baron

PHOTOGRAPHER
John Stewart

CLIENT
CIGNA

AGENCY
Doyle Dane Bernbach

119
ART DIRECTOR
Joseph Perz

WRITER
Neil Drossman

PHOTOGRAPHER
Howard Owen

CLIENT
Einstein Moomjy

AGENCY
Drossman Lehmann Marino

120
ART DIRECTOR
Peter Rauch

WRITER
Larry Spector

DESIGNER
Peter Rauch

PHOTOGRAPHER
Dick James

CLIENT
BMW of North America

AGENCY
Ammirati & Puris

WHERE THERE'S SMOKE, THERE'S LIABILITY.

No company can be held liable for non-polluting smoke.

Or clean waste disposal.

Or harmless emissions.

But any substance that does pollute carries with it not only the risk of liability but also the threat of extraordinary damages.

And these aren't levied only against corporations run by thoughtless or cynical polluters.

Many well-intentioned corporations have been held accountable for pollution.

Not because they didn't care.

But because laws, regulations and rulings in the area of environmental impairment have become so complex that even the best of intentions is no protection at all.

To protect itself today a corporation needs a staff of trained, experienced and sophisticated specialists in this field.

Which is exactly what we provide at CIGNA.

Our Environmental Health Laboratory is staffed with specialists who thoroughly assess a company's environmental impairment liability.

We assess the hazards associated with the materials a company uses.

With the processes it puts them through.

With their transport. With their storage. And their disposal.

We point out appropriate federal, state and local regulations.

We analyze the potential impact a facility is likely to have on the air, water, soil, and endangered species in its area.

Not to mention, on any human population.

We evaluate management systems for supervising and monitoring pollution control.

And, finally, we look at the emergency procedures a company has in place.

Or doesn't.

All in all, we seek to uncover every pollution exposure and vulnerability that a corporation might have. Then we follow up with specific recommendations to control them.

If you think this might be helpful to your company, write CIGNA Corporation, Dept. RF, One Logan Square, Phila., PA 19103 for more information.

After all, doesn't it make sense to have us look for the weaknesses in your pollution control procedures before somebody else does?

CIGNA

爱因斯坦
国地毯五折蒙
吉中大减价

(but only for the next two weeks).

In plain English, our entire collection of Oriental rugs from Mainland China (probably the most entire outside of Mainland China) is on sale.

Save on everything from ▪ to #, from Aubussons to French designs, Friendship designs and Florals, from Dragons to Pekings and Pandas, from colors of the past to colors of the pastel. All 100% wool, lustre washed, handmade, hand shaped, deeply hand carved and expertly hand picked by the Moomjys.

Stick in your thumb and pull out hand-tufted, hand-carved plum blossoms on a field of branches, a graceful design familiar to Chinese art, now artfully translated to Chinese rugs. In old ivory, black and blue, (A) 3'6"x5'6" was $650 is $199, 5'6"x8'6" was $1225 is $449, 8'3"x11'6" was $2200 is $799.

Deco a room with 70 line 4/8" hand-knotted florals in sandalwood beige and green tranquility. (B) 3'10"x6'2" was $750 is $345, 5'10"x9' was $1650 is $695, 8'3"x12' was $3000 is $1295, 9'10"x14' was $4200 is $1795, 4' octagon (or round) was $650 is $295, 2'3"x9' runner was $725 is $325.

Now you don't just have to know Chinese to read this ad, you have to know French. This hand-knotted 70 line 4/8" French Aubusson design has a center medallion of florals and leaves. There's a bouquet on every corner and nosegays that play the field. With a border of blossoms. It comes in silver beige and tea rose. (C) 3'10"x6'2" was $750, is $345, 5'10"x9' was $1650, is $695, 8'3"x12' was $3000, is $1295, 9'10'x14' was $4200, is $1795, 4' octagon was $650 is $295, 4' round was $650, is $325. 2'3"x9' runner was $725, is $325.

Legend has it (and you can have it too) that the Foo dog watches over Buddhist holy places. Here's what you'll see when you watch over our hand-knotted, hand-carved 90 line 5/8" super Chinese Foo dog. Chessboards, staffs and gourds, flower baskets, musical notes (no puppy dog tails) all appearing in a very tight, extra tufty rug from an ivory background with blue green and peach. And here's some more foo for thought: the prices. (D) 6'x9' was $2376 is $999, 8'x10' was $3520, is $1399, 9'x12' was $4752 is $1799.

What do you get when you cross flowers and geometrics? A striking hand-tufted floral with corner bouquets in ivory, antique copper and light blue that looks like it stepped right out of the roaring 20's. Here's what we get—(E) 3'10" x 6'2" was $650 is $295, 5'10"x9' was $1225 is $495, 8'3"x12' was $2200 is $895, 9'10'x14' was $3300 is $1495, 4' round (or octagon) was $595 is $245, 2'3"x9' runner was $650, run down to $295.

Nothing could be viner than the graceful leaves and stems that form the wandering vines of Albert Moomjy's private stock in 90 line 5/8"super Chinese. In old red, beige and blue green. From the Tang Dynasty (618– 907 AD) to the Moomjy Dynasty. The dragons mean power and masculinity, the center medallion means long life. What does it all mean? Who knows. (F) 3'x5' was $660, is $199. 6'x9' was $2376, is $999. 8'x10' was $3520 is $1399, 9'x12' was $4752 is $1799.

See ordinary, everyday articles of Chinese life, scenery and nature in a hand-tufted, hand-carved Peking that's anything but ordinary or everyday. A graduate of the traditional school of Chinese art, its design will make you say grace. And dignity. In heavenly blue and ivory pearl. (G) 3'10"x6'2" was $650 is $295, 5'10"x9' was $1225 is $495, 8'3"x12' was $2200 is $895, 9'10'x14' was $3300 is $1495, 4' round (or octagon) was $595 is $245, 2'3"x9' runner was $650, run down to $295.

These are just a few of the thousands of handmade Chinese rugs in all sizes, shapes and colors on sale at Einstein Moomjy for the next two weeks. If you miss the sale all we have to say is 家因斯坦哦蒙地中国地毯五折大减价 爱因斯坦哦蒙地中国地毯五折大减价.

Einstein Moomjy
The Carpet Department Store

WE INTERRUPT THE USUAL SCARCITY OF BMW'S TO BRING YOU A TEMPORARY ABUNDANCE.

The automobile metal workers' strike in Europe is over. Which now provides a rare opportunity on this side of the Atlantic.

BMW workers have foregone their vacations to assemble BMW's. As a result, BMW dealers now possess extensive selections of BMW's in extensive combinations of options and colors.

Which means instead of having to wait for the delivery of the pre-cise BMW you want, you're more likely to enjoy the instant gratification of driving one home. And experiencing for yourself the car whose "talents and heart are supreme" (Car and Driver).

A supremacy derived from such things as a computerized engine system so efficient, it powers a Grand Prix Champion race car. A suspension so advanced, it has earned international patents. And a production process so demanding, it requires 3 million operations for the assembly of the body alone.

However, this supremacy of BMW's on the road inevitably translates into a scarcity of BMW's in the showroom. So before the inevitable occurs, visit a BMW dealer. And enjoy the pleasures of purchasing a BMW. As well as the joy of driving one.

THE ULTIMATE DRIVING MACHINE.

This is what Dad looks like to some two year olds.

The price we pay for unwanted children is written on thousands of innocent faces, bodies and minds every year. The connection between the abused child and the unwanted child is clear. Too often, frustrated and trapped parents take out their despair on their children, both physically and emotionally.

The first priority is to protect the abused child and to help the troubled parents.

But *preventing* child abuse begins with making every child a wanted child, a child born by choice, not chance.

For that to happen, safe, effective birth control must be available to everyone. Abortion must be kept safe and legal for all women. And sex education in the schools and at home must help teens avoid parenthood before they are ready.

Today, most Americans share Planned Parenthood's commitment. If you do, there are two ways you

Planned Parenthood of New York City, Inc.
380 Second Ave., New York, N.Y. 10010 (212) 777-2002

☐ I believe in Planned Parenthood's objectives and I want to help. Here is my tax-deductible contribution of $_____
☐ I agree with your objectives and I'd like more facts. Please send your brochure.

Name

Address

City/State/Zip

Phone (H): _____ Phone (O):

This advertisement has been paid for with private contributions. A copy of our most recent financial report can be obtained from us or from the New York State Board of Social Welfare, Office Tower, Empire State Plaza, Albany, N.Y. 12223. © 1984 Planned Parenthood of New York City, Inc.

PLANNED PARENTHOOD
FOR THE LOVE OF CHILDREN

can show it.

First, you can give us your help, with money that helps us reach others.

Second, you can make the political process work for your beliefs. Speak out. Tell public officials and candidates how you stand on these key birth control issues:
• I'm in favor of sex education programs in the public schools.
• I support public funding to make birth control available to all people who want it but can't afford it.
• I believe in a woman's right to safe, legal abortion.
• I'm in favor of increased funds to find better birth control methods.

Your opinions count, so express them – in writing. Don't sit on the sidelines and then complain about the final score.

See how simple financing can be.

Now financing IBM equipment doesn't have to be a whole lot more complicated than signing on our dotted line.

To begin with, our master agreement is a mere four pages long. And you only need to sign it once.

Your signature will get you flexible financing. We offer a wide range of lease or installment purchase options to help you tailor a plan that suits your company's needs.

Your signature also gets you low rates. We're competitive.

And if you want to add or upgrade equipment down the road, a simple supplement to your original contract is all it takes.

So how do you go about getting IBM Credit Corporation financing?

Just call the same person who helps you choose the IBM computer or office equipment you need.

Your IBM marketing representative.

It's that simple.

IBM
Credit Corporation

122

Take Macintosh out for a test drive.

Since we introduced Macintosh,™ we've been telling you it's the first business computer anyone can learn to use overnight.

Now we're going to prove it.

By giving you a Macintosh to use overnight.

Right now anyone who qualifies can walk into a participating authorized Apple dealer, and walk out with a Macintosh Personal Computer.

No purchase necessary.

It's our way of letting you test drive a Macintosh in the comfort of your own office, home, RV, hotel room, dorm room or whatever.

And really experience, first-hand, how much your finger already knows about computing.

Now it should come at no surprise that Apple is the first major computer company ever to make such an offer.

When you think about it, we're the only computer company that could.

(If any other computer company were to lend you one of their computers for as long as it took you to learn to use it, they might never get it back.)

Simply put, in less time than it takes to get frustrated on an ordinary computer, you'll be doing real work on Macintosh.

Everything from writing memos to working with spreadsheets to creating charts to managing projects.

Because the hard part of test driving a Macintosh isn't figuring out how to use it.

The hard part is bringing it back.

123

IT SLICES, IT DICES, IT JULIENNES LIKE NO SMALL CHICKEN PART CAN.

It's a Perdue Oven Stuffer Roaster Part.

Since it's bigger and meatier than any ordinary chicken part, it's easier to work with.

So whether you're carving off big, even slices for sandwiches, large, plump cubes for kabobs, or long, tender strips for salads, you'll also be cutting down on the time and effort you usually put into your meals.

Try Perdue Oven Stuffer Roaster Parts. And get bigger, meatier pieces of chicken without working your fingers to the bone.

**PERDUE®
OVEN STUFFER.
ROASTER PARTS**

"I LOST 2000 POUNDS."

Over a lifetime, a person can lose thousands of pounds just dieting a few times a year.

Now there's a proven technique for breaking the diet/weight loss cycle. The Be Trim weight control program.

Offered only through hospitals, Be Trim teaches you not only how to lose weight, but how to keep it off once you've lost it.

In just six weeks, this course will help you get in control of your eating habits for the rest of your life.

To help you get started, we're offering the first session free. Get started on the last diet of your life by attending one of the sessions listed below.

METROPOLITAN MEDICAL CENTER

AFTER TWENTY YEARS, ANOTHER RECORD FROM MERSEYSIDE.

On October 19th, Shell's fab new refining plant opens at Stanlow. It is, we are proud to say, a record for Merseyside.

Construction of the plant was completed a full month ahead of schedule, and well under the £450 million plus budget. Relationships between the two hundred strong workforce and the management were excellent, and there were no strikes during the entire two and a half years the plant was being built.

In fact, here on Merseyside production was so impressive that we achieved higher than 1 on the Gulf Scale, the international measure first used in the Gulf of Mexico to gauge oil construction efficiency.

The Stanlow plant itself is also a new record for British technology. It is the most advanced of its kind in the world. The plant is known as a Platinum Reformer, or Platformer. It will use platinum as an extremely efficient catalyst in the production of high octane components for petrol, to enable Shell to comply with the new low lead legislation which comes into effect early in 1986.

The combined efforts of Shell, the contractors and the superb workforce have resulted in a record achievement for the Stanlow plant.

A new record for Merseyside. Or to put it another way, a platinum Number One!

YOU CAN BE SURE OF SHELL

**Consumer Newspaper
Over 600 Lines: Single**

127
ART DIRECTOR
Paul Jervis
WRITER
Jerry Brown
CLIENT
Red Lobster Inns
AGENCY
Backer & Spielvogel

128
ART DIRECTORS
Brian Kelly
Richard Kimmel
Jose Tapia
WRITER
Cathy Powless
PHOTOGRAPHER
Dave Jordano
CLIENT
Waste Management
AGENCY
Ogilvy & Mather/Chicago

How the bark improves the bite.

Generally considered a weed and a nuisance by farmers and ranchers, mesquite has found a home in our new grill at Red Lobster. Mesquite adds a slightly smoky flavor of its own, yet allows the character of the fish to come through.

The biggest seafood discovery we've made in years didn't even come from the ocean.

It comes from the desert.

Introducing the big new mesquite grill at Red Lobster.®

Mesquite has long been a favorite cooking wood in the Southwest.

And what it does to unlock the treasures of the deep is almost magical.

You've just never had seafood like this before.

Mesquite burns very, very hot. Sealing in the natural juices. Leaving fish (even steak and chicken) moist and tender. With just a hint of a smoky burnishing of flavor.

Mmmm. Come on in and try something hot and fresh off the grill.

Whether it's salmon, snapper, swordfish, halibut, or any number of fish we regularly feature.

We think you'll find it the best fish out of water.

Red Lobster.
There's a whole lot of good goin' on.™

127

WE'RE GOING TO TURN YOUR GARBAGE INTO SOMETHING USEFUL.

It might not be long before the trash you put out in the morning is returned to you that night.

As electricity.

Not generated by the power company. But made at a waste-to-energy plant like Waste Management will begin operating next June in Tampa, Florida.

There, the city's trash will be burned as fuel to make enough electricity to heat, air-condition and run every single appliance in 11,000 homes. Saving 275,000 barrels of oil a year.

The process is smokeless, odorless and has been proving itself in Europe and Japan for years. In fact, Denmark uses it to convert two-thirds of its waste into energy.

What's more, it destroys trash so completely, it significantly reduces the need for landfills. Which is particularly important in places like Tampa where new landfill sites are becoming scarce.

Little wonder, more and more cities in this country are deciding to turn their trash into electricity. Which is certainly better than just throwing it all away.

Waste Management, Inc.
Helping the world dispose of its problems.

IT COULD EXPLODE.
IT COULD BE FILLED WITH CYANIDE.
OR IT COULD BE NOTHING AT ALL.
NOW, HOW ARE YOU GOING TO FIND
OUT WITHOUT OPENING IT?

Logic says, open it up. See what you're faced with.

Fear says, leave it alone. Because you might find something dangerous. Even deadly. And then what can you do?

The answer is, plenty.

You can incinerate it. Neutralize it. Recycle it. Solidify it. Or otherwise make it safe for disposal.

Certainly these are far better solutions than just letting it sit there for who knows what to happen.

Yet there are millions of drums like this sitting in thousands of places around the country.

In many cases, because the very fear of hazardous waste has made people unable to act.

Waste Management has invested more of its resources in helping solve this problem than any other company.

In fact, we safely dispose of more hazardous waste than anyone else in our field.

But no one company can do more than a tiny fraction of the job to be done.

This is a problem that needs everyone's help. And perhaps more importantly, their understanding. Because the most hazardous thing we can do is nothing.

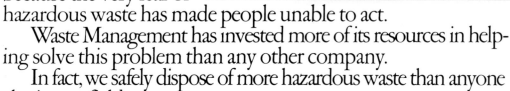

Waste Management, Inc.
Helping the world dispose of its problems.

This beer belly is brought to you by Pabst Light.

Pab Blue Ribbon LIGHT

Pabst Light. Just 96 great tasting calories* that won't fill you up. Or out.

*Per 12 oz. serving

© 1984 Pabst Brewing Co. Milwaukee, Wisconsin

Details, Details, Details.

One of the big things people notice about the Volvo 760 GLE are all the little things it has.

Dozens of thoughtful little touches that don't become apparent until you've owned the car awhile.

None of these details by itself is reason enough to buy a car.

But would you really want to buy a car from a company that decided to leave them out?

1. Volvo's front driver's seat automatically heats up when the temperature falls below 50°F. The passenger seat also warms up at the touch of a switch.

2. The rear shock absorbers automatically adjust themselves to provide a level ride even when the trunk is heavily loaded.

3. The overhead dome light in a Volvo has a delayed shut-off, so you still have light while you're buckling seatbelts and putting the key in the ignition. And speaking of lights, we have a lot: rear reading lights, map lights, a light in the trunk, and a light under the hood. There's even a little light that tells you when a headlight or taillight is out.

4. The remote-controlled outside rearview mirrors are heated to prevent the build up of ice and snow.

5. The rear window defogger is equipped with a timer. It turns itself off in case you forget to.

6. Tubular steel bars are built inside front and rear doors to help protect you in a collision. The inside edges of the doors have red warning lights so other drivers can see open doors at night.

7. A Volvo has six brakes. One power-assisted disc brake on each wheel. And a separate set of parking brakes. Our dual triangular split braking system gives you 80% of your stopping power even if one brake circuit should fail.

8. There are padded head restraints on rear as well as front seats.

9. In areas where the paint is most likely to get scratched, the zinc plating underneath "bleeds" to fill in the scratch and prevent rusting.

10. The doors open wide (to an angle of nearly 70°) to make getting in and out easier.

11. The engine's fuel injection system automatically adjusts for changes in barometric pressure, temperature and humidity.

12. The front bucket seats have adjustable lumbar supports to ease back strain.

13. The leather for the seats is supplied by the same renowned firm that supplies the leather for another luxury car. The Rolls Royce.

14. Fifteen separate vents inside the car assure the even distribution of air. The air is changed four times a minute even when the car is standing still.

15. Automatic Climate Control system. You dial the temperature, the system keeps it constant.

16. There are nine storage areas inside a Volvo 760 GLE, including one in the folding armrest in the center of the backseat.

17. Cruise control is standard. It's one more way Volvo makes highway driving less tiring.

18. Cross members inside the front seats prevent "submarining" (sliding under seatbelts) in the event of a crash.

19. The power-assisted steering system has fewer moving parts between you and the road. This lets you 'feel' more contact with the road than ordinary steering systems do.

20. The interior is ergonomically-designed so that 95% of America's adult population can reach all the controls without bending.

21. The hood swings up at a 90° angle to make servicing easier.

22. The fuel tank is located in front of the rear axle for added safety in a rear end collision.

23. The audio system has four speakers, two in front, two in back. There's an amplifier for each set of speakers. 25 watts-per-channel in the front. 40 watts-per-channel in the back. A graphic equalizer lets you balance the tone to your own taste.

24. The power sunroof tilts as well as slides.

25. Last, but not least, the most important detail of all. The little nameplate on the front that tells you the 760 GLE is built by a company that's been paying attention to details for over half a century.

The 700 Series by Volvo

**Consumer Newspaper
Over 600 Lines: Single**

132
ART DIRECTOR
Tom Shortlidge
WRITER
Mike Faems
PHOTOGRAPHER
JoAnn Carney
CLIENT
Pabst Light
AGENCY
Young & Rubicam/Chicago

133
ART DIRECTOR
Kathleen Lee
WRITER
Charles Bromley
DESIGNER
Kathleen Lee
PHOTOGRAPHER
Terry Niefield
CLIENT
Israel Government Tourist
Office
AGENCY
Biederman & Company

Last year, more Americans kept this resolution than ever before. Thank you.

Israel

134
ART DIRECTOR
Earl Cavanah
WRITERS
Ed McCabe
Larry Cadman
CLIENT
Scali McCabe Sloves
AGENCY
Scali McCabe Sloves

135
ART DIRECTOR
Felix Burgos
WRITER
Kathy Angotti
CLIENT
The New York Times
AGENCY
Bozell & Jacobs

TWO OUT OF THREE AIN'T BAD.

SAM SCALI
Inducted into the Art Director's
Hall of Fame, 1984

ED McCABE
Inducted into the Copy Hall of Fame,
1974

MARVIN SLOVES

All of us at Scali, McCabe, Sloves would like to congratulate Sam Scali on his induction into the Art Director's Hall of Fame.

We're very proud.

We're also proud of the fact that Sam is not alone. He joins his partner, Ed McCabe, who entered the Copy Hall of Fame in 1974.

And that makes Scali, McCabe, Sloves something very rare indeed: an advertising agency with two founding partners in the Hall of Fame.

Both of these men are advertising legends for good reason. Together, they have created some of the most renowned advertising of all time.

If you're interested in talking to a great art director or a great copywriter about your advertising, Sam and Ed aren't hard to find. They still come to work every day.

Or, if you'd like to talk to the person who does most of the talking for Sam and Ed, call Marvin.

There is, unfortunately, no such thing as a Management Hall of Fame.

But Marvin Sloves is a great reason for creating one.

SCALI, McCABE, SLOVES, INC.

800 Third Avenue, New York, N.Y. 10022 (212) 421-2050 Offices in: Houston, Melbourne, Montreal, Toronto, London, Dusseldorf, Mexico City
© 1984, Scali, McCabe, Sloves, Inc.

If we weren't so good, people wouldn't tear us apart.

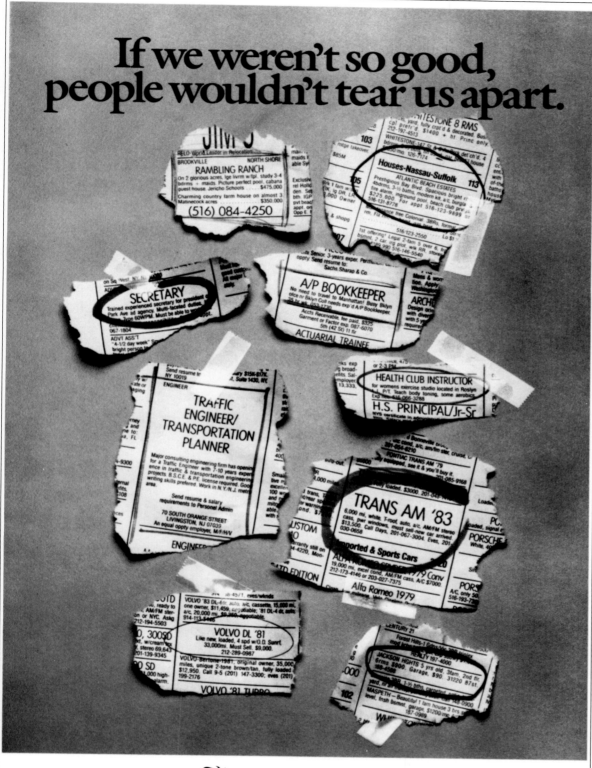

By the time most people have devoured The New York Times Classified, there's nothing left but bits and pieces. And the reason's simple.

There's nothing else like The Times when it comes to buying or selling anything.

The New York Times Classified

Our Classified pages have more listings for homes, cars and employment opportunities than any other newspaper.

We also have a full staff of professional Ad-Visors who can help even a beginner place an ad that really works.

We're a newspaper that delivers results. Not just replies.

It's The New York Times Classified. And if we weren't so good, people wouldn't tear us to pieces.

To place your ad, just call 1-800-AD-TIMES.

It's the #1 best seller.

THERE'S ANOTHER WAGON THAT COULD LAST UNTIL THE 21ST CENTURY. UNFORTUNATELY IT COULD TAKE THAT LONG TO PAY FOR IT.

$35,660 $16,642

We cannot tell a lie. Mercedes Benz builds a wagon that will last as long as a Volvo.

And that's no mean feat. The average life expectancy of a Volvo is over 16 years.*

But what Mercedes Benz doesn't do is build a wagon as well as we do for the price we do. A Volvo costs half what a Mercedes costs** without denying you the amenities you've come to expect in a truly luxurious automobile.

Like the Mercedes wagon, our Volvo GL wagon comes with alloy wheels, four wheel power disc brakes, air conditioning, tinted glass, power windows, a central locking system and a heated rear window.

But we also offer some features standard that the already expensive Mercedes makes you pay extra for.

Like orthopedically designed seats with adjustable lumbar support, and an electrically heated driver's seat. And you can't get rack and pinion steering on a Mercedes at any price.

So we invite you to test drive both a Mercedes and a Volvo.

When you do so, we think you'll find that while Mercedes claims to be "engineered like no other car in the world," the truth is it's simply priced like no other car in the world.

VOLVO
A car you can believe in.

136

ROUND AND ROUND SHE GOES...

Instead of the ordinary 5 digit odometer, a Volvo comes equipped with a 6 digit odometer. And for good reason. A Volvo is built to go a long way.

In fact, statistics show Volvos have an average life expectancy of 16.5 years.* So buy a Volvo and drive it around. Where she'll stop nobody knows. **VOLVO** A car you can believe in.

On January 24th, we're going to let the cat out of the bag. And the mouse, too.

We're much better at building computers than keeping secrets.
Probably just about every magazine in your dentist's office has something to say about Macintosh,™ from Apple.®
So you probably already know that it's powerful, portable, flexible, versatile. And not very expensive.
And that it has a "mouse"—a clever hand-held device that eliminates typed-in computer commands.
Maybe even the fact that your authorized Apple dealer will unveil this phenomenal machine to the world on January 24th.
But did you know Macintosh has its own bag?
See, we *can* keep a secret.

Soon there'll be just two kinds of people.
Those who use computers and those who use Apples.

Macintosh is a trademark licensed to Apple Computer Inc. © 1984 Apple Computer Inc.

139
ART DIRECTOR
Felix Burgos
WRITER
Kathy Angotti
CLIENT
The New York Times
AGENCY
Bozell & Jacobs

For the price of a few gallons of gas, we'll peddle your car all over town.

Car sales require fast movers, not fast talkers. Movers like The New York Times Classified. Not only can we create the kind of traffic needed to find a new owner for your car, we can do it faster than anyone else.

By showing your car to almost 3 million people a day, you'll be getting more exposure and visibility than with any other newspaper. As well as a staff of professional Ad-Visors who can help you place an ad that really works.

We've got everything from fully loaded creampuffs to the ultimate in pickups.

It's The New York Times Classified. Call us and we'll peddle your car to places you've never even heard of, all for the price of a few gallons of gas.

To place your ad, just call 1-800-AD-TIMES.

It's the #1 best seller.

Number 1 in the New York area.

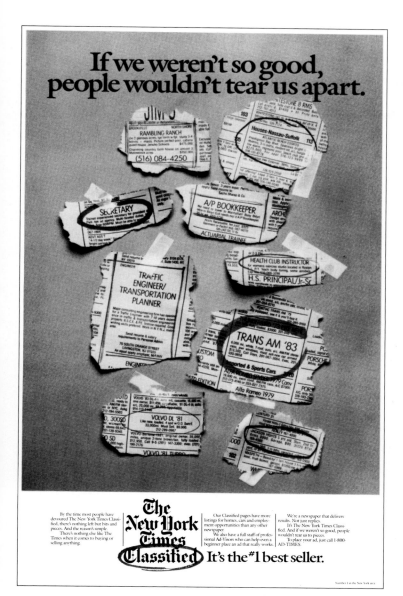

Don't buy cakes old enough to have birthdays.

When you blow out the candles and make a wish, it shouldn't be for a different cake.

Your cake should look fresh and moist. If it doesn't, it's past its prime.

At Dot's Pastry Shops in Ukrops, if we don't sell our cakes while they're fresh, we don't sell them.

The same goes for our pies, cookies, Danish, tarts and cupcakes.

In fact, the only thing that's old are our recipes. We use the same quality ingredients that Dot began using forty-four years ago.

Like rich fudge and pecans in our brownies. Fresh lemon juice in our famous lemon chess pies.

And you haven't lived until you've tasted one of Dot's delicious chocolate eclairs with creamy vanilla custard inside.

Another reason our desserts are so moist and fresh is because we don't overcook them. Actually, our cakes are taken out of the oven before they're quite done. (The heat that's still inside finishes baking them while they cool.)

In total, we bake 80 different desserts a day, five days a week. From scratch.

We'll even design, bake and decorate special order cakes for anniversaries, weddings, graduations, and, of course, birthdays.

And Dot's pastry chefs are fanatics. Each dessert has to look just as good as it tastes.

Our cakes are always decorated by hand, not machines. Our cookies have to be just the right size and shape. And if one of our gingerbread men loses his head, he's out the door.

Oh, there's one more thing. We don't add any preservatives to our desserts.

After all, they're never around long enough to need them.

Ukrops

When is a vegetable a lemon?

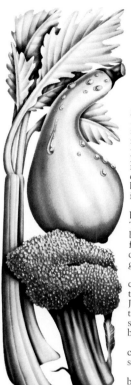

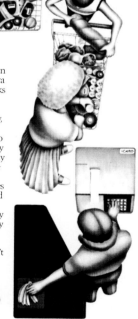

Buying a vegetable is a little like buying a car. If you aren't careful, you could end up with a lemon.

But how do you choose vegetables that aren't lemons? We suggest you look for the same things that Ukrops looks for.

Our produce personnel are very particular people. To them, an eggplant is a lemon if it's too big. Large, heavy eggplants usually have too many seeds. A good purple eggplant should be medium-sized and have a dark, satiny skin that doesn't bounce back when you press it with your thumb.

Buying large cucumbers is another big mistake. They're often tough with a bitter taste. Instead, we look for medium-sized, slender cucumbers that are dark green in color.

On the other hand, you can't buy asparagus that's too big. The fatter the better. Just make sure the tips are tight and pointed and the stalks are straight, round and bright green.

Fresh lettuce should be compact and heavy for its size. Not light and fluffy.

And when a head of broccoli changes from little green buds to pretty yellow flowers, it should be put in a vase. Not a pot.

At Ukrops, we're just as particular when we pick fruit. And you should be, too.

Look for green grapes that have a slight yellowish color to them. Grapes that are too green often have a sour taste. Don't buy them. We wouldn't.

And don't hold your breath waiting for a pineapple to ripen. If it isn't ripe when its picked, it never will be. (Ukrops' pineapples are picked at the peak of sweetness and flown in fresh from Hawaii twice a week.)

One way to tell the quality of a grapefruit is by its weight. The heavier a grapefruit is for its size the juicier and sweeter it will be. And, incidentally, the color makes no difference.

Unfortunately, there isn't enough room here to discuss every vegetable and fruit at length.

But no matter what you buy, there is one easy way to make sure it's the freshest and finest quality. Buy it at Ukrops.

Ukrops

Supermarkets should wait on people, not vice versa.

You don't have to stand for long lines at your local supermarket.

Shop at Ukrops.

We've spent a lot of time figuring out how to shorten them.

In fact, according to a recent independent survey, Ukrop's checkout service is rated the fastest in the Richmond area.

One reason is that all Ukrops stores are equipped with electronic checkout machines. And most have high-speed scanners. Not only do they save time, they reduce the chance of error on your grocery bill.

Our express lane is twice as fast at some Ukrops. That's because there are two of them.

And one of the latest things we've done is put a computer in every store. Among other things, it can figure out how many extra cashiers and courtesy clerks are needed during peak shopping hours.

But most importantly, Ukrop's courtesy clerks and cashiers are trained to work fast as a team. We try to have your groceries already bagged by the time you've paid. Our courtesy clerks will then carry your groceries to where your car is parked and load them for you.

Of course, if you already shop at Ukrops you probably know most of this.

If you've never tried shopping at Ukrops, haven't you waited long enough?

Ukrops

**Consumer Newspaper
Over 600 Lines:
Campaign**

141
ART DIRECTOR
Joe Del Vecchio
WRITER
Jeff Linder
DESIGNER
Joe Del Vecchio
PHOTOGRAPHER
Allan Luftig
CLIENT
CIGNA
AGENCY
Doyle Dane Bernbach

NO EXTRA CHARGE FOR DELIVERY.

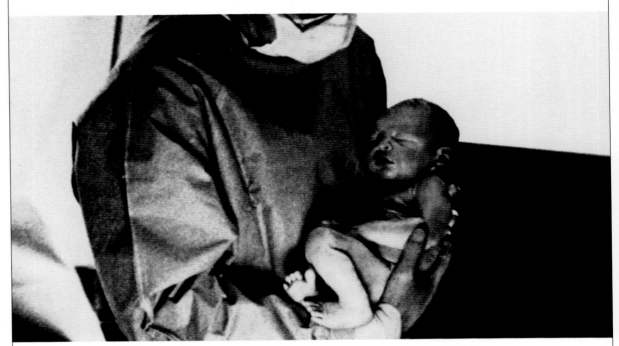

At CIGNA Healthplan every member pays a fixed monthly premium.

After that, they're covered for all authorized medical expenses, with just a small copayment.

When an expectant mother needs care, it's covered.

When her child has the mumps, it's covered.

When any eligible family member needs medical care, it's covered.

Your employees never pay an authorized bill from a doctor or a lab. Not even from a specialist.

With one single monthly premium, every one of your employees can easily budget their annual medical expenses. That way they know exactly what to expect.

And as one of the nation's leading health maintenance organizations, we understand the enormous financial pressures that medical expenses can put on a family.

We also realize that affordable health care has to be

quality health care. So we provide competent doctors, nurses, and support staff.

And we make sure they have the equipment and supplies they need. Either on premises or nearby.

We even make our medical director and senior physicians available for consultations.

Again, at no additional charge.

These are some of the ways we provide high quality health care.

And quality health care has always been important to CIGNA, our parent corporation, whose companies provide insurance and financial services around the world.

Call us collect at 214-934-4404. Or write to Vice President, Marketing, CIGNA Healthplan, Inc., 7616 LBJ Freeway, Suite 303, Dallas, TX 75251.

We'll answer any question. And there's no extra charge for that.

CIGNA Healthplan, Inc.
a CIGNA company

BEFORE THE DOCTOR EXAMINES THE PATIENT, WE EXAMINE THE DOCTOR.

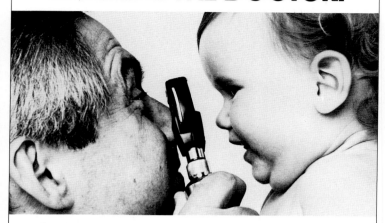

The quality of your employees' health care is determined by the quality of their doctors. Which is why employees choose the best doctors they can find.

Something most people do on the basis of a recommendation. Hopefully, a good one.

At CIGNA Healthplan, one of the nation's leading operators of health maintenance organizations, your employees will feel quite secure with the doctors we provide. Because our standards are so high.

We consider where the doctor has graduated from medical school. We consider whether the doctor has completed postgraduate training. Whether the doctor is Board Certified. Whether the doctor has had high caliber clinical experience. And we consider the quality of the doctor's bedside manner.

Once a physician is hired at CIGNA Healthplan, we appraise his or her performance after the first 3 months.
After the first 6 months.
After the first 12 months.

CIGNA Healthplan, Inc.
a CIGNA company

And every year after that.

We even make our medical director and senior physicians available for consultations. At our expense, not your employees'.

These are just some of the ways in which we're working to provide high quality health care. Of course, we also realize that quality health care is of no value unless your employees can afford it.

And making health care affordable has always been of prime importance to our parent, CIGNA Corporation, whose companies provide insurance and financial services around the world.

If you think your employees would be interested in CIGNA Healthplan, call us at 214-980-8925. Or write to Vice President, Marketing, CIGNA Healthplan, Inc., 7616 LBJ Freeway, Suite 303, Dallas, TX 75251.

We'll answer any questions you have about CIGNA Healthplan. That way you can examine us, before we examine you.

CIGNA

YOU'RE LOOKING AT A LUCKY MAN.

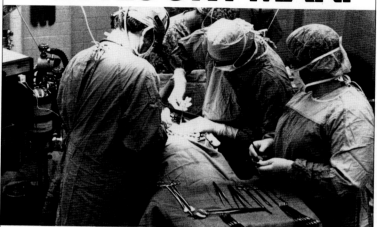

There's only one thing worse than having an operation you need.

Not having an operation you need.

At CIGNA Healthplan, a leading operator of health maintenance organizations, we've geared our operation to diagnosing and treating illness at the earliest possible moment. Whether it's a minor ailment or a major illness.

We accomplish this with a professional staff of extremely competent physicians, nurses, and medical technicians. With specialists, on staff or recommended. With testing facilities. With laboratories. With sophisticated diagnostic equipment, on premises or nearby. And with hospital facilities we make available, if need be.

And since our members are covered for all authorized medical expenses, with just a small copayment, they're more inclined to visit us at the first sign of illness.

CIGNA Healthplan, Inc.
a CIGNA company

For periodic checkups. And for particular problems.

We also work to reduce the incidence of serious illness in the first place. By approaching health care from a preventive point of view. We have our own health appraisal process, which not only includes testing, but also a comprehensive examination of health history and habits.

Of course, quality health care is of no value unless you and your employees can afford it.

And affordability has always been important to CIGNA, our parent corporation, whose companies provide insurance and financial services around the world.

Call us collect at 214-934-4404. Or write to Vice President, Marketing, CIGNA Healthplan, Inc., 7616 LBJ Freeway, Suite 303, Dallas, TX 75251.

If you offer CIGNA Healthplan to your employees, don't consider yourself lucky. Consider yourself smart.

CIGNA

THIS IS FOR WOMEN WHO ENJOY DRESSING DOWN AS MUCH AS DRESSING UP.

It's for women who feel as comfortable in an old pair of jeans, a polo shirt, and a crew neck, as they do in a linen skirt and a silk blouse.

It's for women who appreciate the statement made by a pair of khaki walking shorts and a button-down oxford as much as they do a tailored suit.

And it's for women who can make a simple T-shirt and draw string pants look as interesting as anything else.

You see, it's for women like these that we make Timberland® handsewns.

What will attract you at first is the softness and suppleness of the leathers. And how the genuine handsewn moccasin construction makes them comfortable instantly.

But what you won't discover instantly, but over time, is how Timberlands, like your favorite jeans and shorts, look and feel even better the longer you have them.

The ultimate result is something interesting.

Shoes you don't just wear with the most comfortable parts of your wardrobe but during the most relaxing parts of your life.

The Timberland Company, P.O. Box 370, Newmarket, New Hampshire 03857

IT'S ALWAYS SOMETHING.

A volcano here.
A typhoon there.
A shipment damaged in South America.
A ship damaged in the South Pacific.
When your business is international, so are your problems. And to make matters worse, sometimes the biggest problem a company faces is its insurance.
Because when things go wrong, many American businesses discover that the insurance they have isn't the insurance they thought they had.
Policies vary.
Customs vary.
And assumptions about coverage are very different from country to country. In Italy, for example, fire insurance covers all accidental fires.
Except those started by spontaneous combustion.
And in Great Britain, "World Wide" coverage covers England, Scotland, Guernsey and the Isle of Man. Period.
The point is, insuring international risks country by country can be something of a risk itself.

Which is why so many corporations depend on one global policy from CIGNA's international specialists.
At CIGNA, our companies provide American business with the coverage American business expects.
Without cultural gaps. Or quaint local peculiarities.
And without the difficulty of dealing with a stack of policies written in everything from Spanish to Swedish.
What's more, when something goes wrong we can also provide the kind of claims adjustment and responsiveness that American business demands.
In fact, we can provide a breadth of service unsurpassed by any other insurance company.
With local representatives in 130 countries.
If you think your company might benefit from the total protection we offer, please write CIGNA Corporation, Dept. RG, One Logan Square, Philadelphia, Pennsylvania 19103.
With all the things that can go wrong in this world, one of them shouldn't be your insurance.

See Dick run.

See Jane run.

See Jane burn 30% more calories.

Tests prove that running with Heavyhands not only increases aerobic capacity, but also burns between 30% and 100% more calories than running without Heavyhands.

At the same time, Heavyhands help tone and strengthen major muscle groups *throughout* the body, while decreasing the danger of injury.

Find out why more and more serious runners everywhere are using Heavyhands at your local running store. **Heavyhands™ from AMF.**

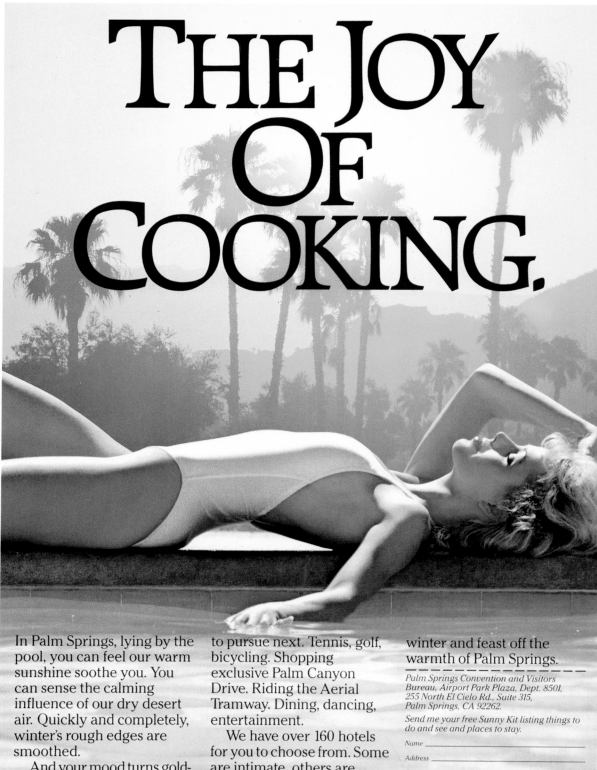

THE JOY OF COOKING.

In Palm Springs, lying by the pool, you can feel our warm sunshine soothe you. You can sense the calming influence of our dry desert air. Quickly and completely, winter's rough edges are smoothed.

And your mood turns golden right along with your tan.

Your most pressing decision will be what diversion to pursue next. Tennis, golf, bicycling. Shopping exclusive Palm Canyon Drive. Riding the Aerial Tramway. Dining, dancing, entertainment.

We have over 160 hotels for you to choose from. Some are intimate, others are grand. Some are economical, others quite luxurious.

So escape the gloom of winter and feast off the warmth of Palm Springs.

Palm Springs Convention and Visitors Bureau, Airport Park Plaza, Dept. 8501, 255 North El Cielo Rd., Suite 315, Palm Springs, CA 92262.

Send me your free Sunny Kit listing things to do and see and places to stay.

Name _____
Address _____
City _____
State _____ Zip _____

Palm Springs CALIFORNIA

147

148

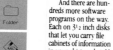
149

Consumer Magazine Color: 1 Page Or Spread Including Magazine Supplements

150
ART DIRECTOR
Rene Vidmer

WRITER
Ken Baron

PHOTOGRAPHER
Stanford Smilow

CLIENT
Gold Toe Socks

AGENCY
Baron & Zaretsky

151
ART DIRECTOR
Joost Hulsbosch

WRITER
Terry Murphy

DESIGNER
Joost Hulsbosch

PHOTOGRAPHER
Steve Cooper

CLIENT
Mercedes-Benz of South Africa

AGENCY
D'Arcy MacManus & Masius/
South Africa

152
ART DIRECTOR
Gary Johns

WRITER
Jeff Gorman

PHOTOGRAPHER
Mark Coppos

CLIENT
Nike

AGENCY
Chiat/Day - Los Angeles

It's time you changed your socks.

If you're like most men, your sock drawer is, to put it mildly, a disgrace. Ripped argyles snuggle next to dress socks growing heel holes of various sizes.

To top off these indignities, the tops refuse to remain much above your ankles. In short, you are long overdue for a change of socks.

If the toe on your sock is not gold, then the sock on your foot could be on its last leg.

As you go about restocking, don't go sticking your foot into yet another holey mistake.

To learn why Gold Toe is the best sock for your money (and not a lot of it), look at your awful-looking socks. Those sagging tops are due to too little (and inferior) elastic unable to survive the rigors of even routine washing. If you see your toes and heels *after* your socks are on, you're seeing a very obvious sign of unreinforced knitting.

Sadly, most socks are made in this mediocre way.

But there is only one Gold Toe, made by a small band of sock fanatics in Pennsylvania who—some for over 50 years—knit, dye, stitch, seam, loop, press, inspect, pair and just as carefully wrap the little band around each pair.

It's a shame the people who make Gold Toe Socks didn't make your car or office copier.

That gold thread in the Gold Toe toe isn't just your symbol

of quality. It's actually woven in as a double reinforcement to thwart a surprise appearance of your toe.

Both toe and heel are knitted in as pouches, so your foot needn't press and rub just to make room for itself. Slide your hand

into a Gold Toe top and feel how dozens of elastic rows gently yet firmly keep your socks up, for years.

You'll wear them for years, too, since they're made from the finest long-staple cotton, New Zealand wool and high-quality DuPont man-made fibers like Hi-Bulk Orlon.®

Simply the best socks money (from $3.00 and up, amazingly enough) can buy.

How many items do you own which let you say, "This is the best money can buy"?

So stop being humiliated by shabby socks. Go to a fine department store for Gold Toe socks (there were 162 colors and styles, at last count, from sweat socks to dress socks) to put in your drawer.

And, even better, to put on your feet.

From Cluett. © 1984

THE STANDARD OF QUALITY
GOLD TOE®

There are two cars here. The one you can see is a Mercedes-Benz.

Since a car is an amalgam of some 10 000 separate components, attention to little things can mean a lot.

No car manufacturer perceives this more clearly than Mercedes-Benz.

The tail light on a Mercedes car quite literally illuminates the Mercedes-Benz commitment to detail.

Ridges have been designed into the face to ensure the light is visible even in the most adverse circumstances.

With the car on the left above, enough dirt has splattered the rear lights to make the car virtually unseeable from the rear.

In the same conditions the recessed sections of the Mercedes-Benz rear light have remained dirt-free. The car remains visible.

A fact that increases the safety of the occupants and of those travelling behind it.

Closer inspection will show further evidence of Mercedes-Benz attention to detail.

Deflectors on the front roof pillars keep dirt and water away from side windows. A rain runnel above the rear window keeps the rear view clear.

Though seemingly unimportant, features such as these can have a major influence on safety.

To see, or be seen, in time is critically important on the road. The milliseconds of reaction time they can buy for the driver of a Mercedes-Benz could be the most important milliseconds of his life.

Mercedes-Benz. Engineered like no other car in the world.

A point of land
for people who can't
live without water.

If being close to the water makes you feel more alive, your life could go on forever at Sailfish Point.

Here, you are surrounded by the ocean you love. As well as the luxuries you demand. And because the entire peninsula is private, you can drink in its pleasures without taking in the rest of the world.

You can race with the wind just beyond the seawalled marina. Where ocean-going yachts can turn without cutting corners. You can drive down fairways that practically sail into the sea. On a par 72 golf course designed by Jack Nicklaus. You can even watch the waves unfold while you dine. Because the elegant Sailfish Point Country Club overlooks the ocean's edge.

For more information about Florida's most opulent private residence, or to arrange for a personal appointment, just write or call. Only a few will share this secluded point of land. And the endless supply of water that comes with it.

Sailfish Point.

Prices at Sailfish Point begin at $350,000. Dunes Realty Corporation is the Licensed Real Estate Broker and Exclusive Sales Agent. The address is 1755 S.E. Sailfish Point Boulevard, Suite 100B, Stuart, Florida 33494, (305) 225-6200. Broker participation invited.

The complete offering terms are in an offering plan available from sponsor. An offering statement filed with the New Jersey Real Estate Commission neither approves the offering nor in any way passes upon the merits and value of the property.(NJA No. D0984G-SAIL).Offer void in states where prohibited by law including Maine, Ohio and California. The Sailfish Point Golf Club is a private facility.

a Mobil company

154

155

156

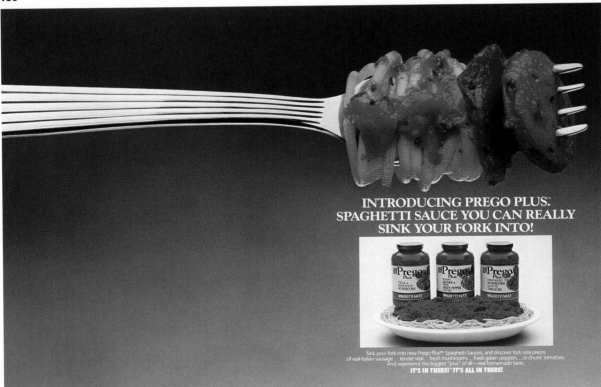

157

158

159

EVEN BUSY EXECUTIVES FIND A FEW MINUTES EVERY DAY TO THINK ABOUT THEIR MONEY.

It is one of life's ironies that the people most likely to accumulate a significant amount of money are the very people least likely to have the time to manage it.

Not many owners of successful businesses can take the time to coordinate the isolated planning of accountants, attorneys and investment advisors.

And few professional people have the time to map out personal financial strategies.

Not surprisingly, a great many successful people pay far more in taxes than they have to.

And spend years pouring money into investments that have little chance of taking them where they want to go.

Because financial planning can't be done on a part-time basis. It's a job that requires expertise, knowledge and constantly updated information.

And, at CIGNA Individual Financial Services, that's exactly what we provide.

We analyze our clients' entire financial profiles. We come to understand their particular needs and financial goals. And, naturally, we draw on a variety of disciplines, from investment research to tax law, to develop customized financial strategies for each of our clients.

Offering comprehensive financial planning and investment and insurance products through its affiliates.

You'd expect that much from a financial planner. What makes our service more valuable is that we go a step further.

We work with our clients' accountants. And attorneys. And other advisors. To help implement the strategies we recommend.

And as a result, we can provide our clients with a fully implemented, fully integrated financial program. Which has often produced some very impressive results.

We've saved clients thousands of dollars in income taxes.

And sometimes even more in estate taxes.

And in case after case we've dramatically reduced the taxes associated with the transfer of a business within a family.

So if you'd like to talk with us about your financial needs, please call a local CIGNA Individual Financial Services office or write CIGNA Corporation, Dept. RD, One Logan Square, Philadelphia, PA 19103.

Chances are we can save you more than just a night's sleep.

CIGNA

160

"I made it myself"

To a child these words are among the happiest in the English language.

Not too many toys encourage children to say them.

Ours can.

In fact, without imagination our toys would never run.

And we wouldn't want it any other way.

Give your child a Crayola® gift like the Crayon Carrousel or Draw N' Do Desk and you can watch creativity in progress. An eager young mind at work.

And does it really matter that there's no such thing as a green chicken?

Or that Uncle Fred looks like he doesn't have ears?

What matters is that it's something from the imagination.

And something from the heart.

We can't think of a better toy than that.

Our toys run on imagination.

161

See Dick run.

See Jane run.

See Jane burn 30% more calories.

Tests prove that running with Heavyhands not only increases aerobic capacity, but also burns between 30% and 100% more calories than running without Heavyhands.

At the same time, Heavyhands help strengthen and tone major muscle groups *throughout* the body, while decreasing the danger of injury.

Find out why more and more serious runners everywhere are using Heavyhands at your local running store.

Heavyhands™ from AMF.

Crayola

Stacy Dyer talks about her latest masterpiece.

This is the house my Uncle Sydney and Aunt Becky live in.

They gave me the Crayola Caddy® when I visited them last summer.

See here is their barn and right over here is where I fell down once.

I used red a lot because I like red. See in the background there's a small horse with black and white spots. I rode that horse around in a field.

Right next to the barn, that red thing is where I started to draw a wagon but I changed my mind so I made it into a fire hydrant instead.

In the corner on the right, see those little dots? That's Aunt Becky and Uncle Sydney.

I love them a lot.

Our toys run on imagination.

Why you should buy an Apple II-something instead of an IBM PC-anything.

Announcing a bloom of perfect color for your lips.
It's our rare lipstick formula drenched with natural
moisturizers, for color that stays very fresh. Very silky.
Imagine the pleasure of perfect, in 24 glorious shades.

Cutex Perfect Color

Pete Turner on
why he always shoots
with Nikon lenses:

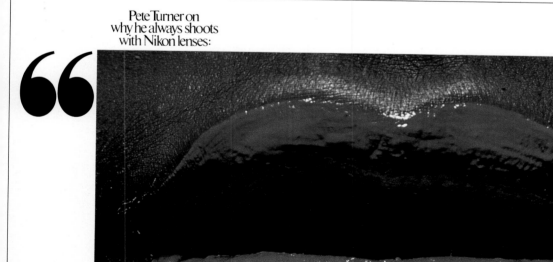

Pete Turner. "Hot Lips." 1967. Lens: 55mm f3.5 Micro-Nikkor.

Nikon
We take the world's
greatest pictures.

**Consumer Magazine
Color: Campaign
Including Magazine
Supplements**

175
ART DIRECTORS
Jeff Vogt
Tony Angotti
WRITER
Tom Thomas
DESIGNER
Jeff Vogt
PHOTOGRAPHER
Jere Cockerel
CLIENT
BMW of North America
AGENCY
Ammirati & Puris

IF LIFE IS A JOURNEY, THEN LIFE'S GREATEST TRAGEDY IS NOT HAVING ENJOYED THE TRIP.

You are looking at 3500 lbs. of "life goal fulfillment."

A car without which "you won't know where to go when the time comes that you can afford the very best."

Owners of the BMW coupe will have little difficulty recognizing their car in these characterizations of the 633CSi by Auto-Week magazine.

As for those who can "afford the very best" but drive something else, that suggests a fondness for self-denial. And that is one area where the new BMW 635CSi will be of no use at all.

HOW TO MAKE DESTINATIONS ANTICLIMACTIC.

The 635CSi is a luxury sports coupe that so far exceeds the requirements of basic transportation as to become its own destination, instead of simply a means to one.

Under its hood is a new 3.5-liter fuel-injected engine governed by a further refinement of BMW's Digital Motor Electronics—a system of sensors and microprocessors given the task of banishing imprecision from the engine. DME audits the engine hundreds of times a second, constantly adjusting fuel delivery and ignition timing for peak performance.

This in combination with a new rear axle ratio further boosts torque and acceleration. Result: the 635CSi will now do 0 to 60 mph in 7.8 seconds, a figure that would be impressive for cars sold on quickness alone.

But the 635CSi also excels at deceleration. A new anti-lock braking system applies brake pressure intermittently, in rapid, pulsating movements. This prevents locking and permits the car to be maneuvered even during emergency stops.

And control is very much the essence of this car.

Its fully-independent suspension system effortlessly subdues roads that many cars merely wrestle to a standoff.

Its graduated, power-assist steering system is uncannily precise and responsive, never blunting the driver's feel of the road.

In simpler terms, the car does everything it's instructed to do, and nothing that it isn't.

A CAR INTOLERANT OF DISCOMFORT.

A car of such technical and mechanical virtuosity might be forgiven an occasional lapse in luxury. The 635CSi asks and needs no such forgiveness.

Its leather seats are orthopedically designed, electrically operated and infinitely adjustable. It literally takes a conscious effort to be uncomfortable.

Push the directional signal and an on-board computer is activated, presenting you with such information as the outside temperature and the available driving range on remaining fuel.

Other controls report your actual mpg figures as you drive, and alert you when routine service is recommended. And the AM/FM stereo (with cassette) would satisfy the performance requirements of many living room sound systems.

All this is enclosed in a body whose design is pure functional elegance. (Not surprisingly, museums on two continents have chosen BMW coupes for display.)

At something between three and four times the cost of the average car, the price is predictably steep. But no decision to buy one will be made on that basis alone.

The 635CSi is for those who believe that no quantity of average cars add up to one "ultimate driving experience." (AutoWeek).

A test drive will vindicate that belief. And your BMW dealer will be happy to arrange one.

THE ULTIMATE DRIVING MACHINE.

©1984 BMW of North America, Inc. The BMW trademark and logo are registered. European Delivery can be arranged through your authorized U.S. BMW dealer.

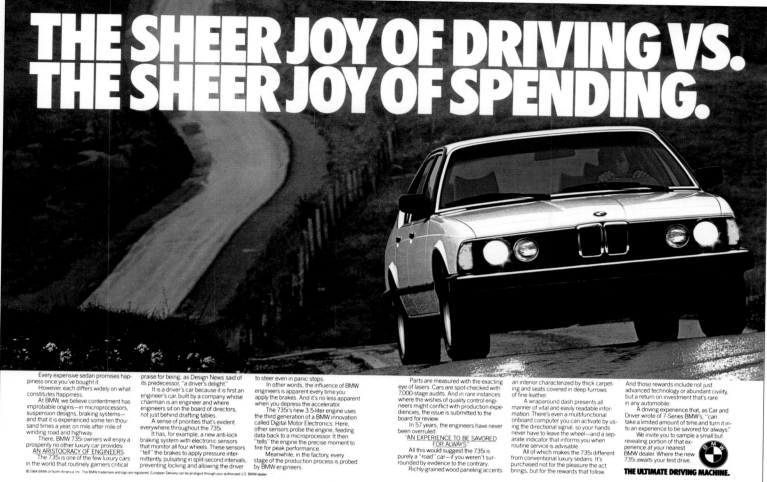

**Consumer Magazine
Color: Campaign
Including Magazine
Supplements**

176
ART DIRECTOR
Harvey Baron
WRITER
Diane Rothschild
CLIENT
CIGNA
AGENCY
Doyle Dane Bernbach

WHERE THERE'S SMOKE, THERE'S LIABILITY.

No company can be held liable for non-polluting smoke.

Or clean waste disposal.

Or harmless emissions.

But any substance that does pollute carries with it not only the risk of liability but also the threat of extraordinary damages.

And these aren't levied only against corporations run by thoughtless or cynical polluters.

Many well-intentioned corporations have been held accountable for pollution.

Not because they didn't care.

But because laws, regulations and rulings on environmental impairment have become so complex that the best of intentions is no protection at all.

To protect itself today a corporation needs a staff of trained, experienced and sophisticated specialists in this field.

Which is exactly what we provide at CIGNA.

Our Environmental Health Laboratory is staffed with specialists who thoroughly assess a company's environmental impairment liability.

We assess the hazards associated with the materials a company uses.

With the processes it puts them through.

With their transport. Their storage. And disposal.

We point out appropriate federal, state and local regulations.

We analyze the potential impact a facility is likely to have on the air, water, soil, and endangered species in its area.

Not to mention, on any human population at risk.

We evaluate management systems for supervising and monitoring pollution control.

And, finally, we look at the emergency procedures a company has in place.

Or doesn't.

All in all, we seek to uncover every pollution exposure and vulnerability that a corporation might have. Then we follow up with specific recommendations to control them.

If you think this might be helpful to your company, write CIGNA Corporation, Dept. RF, One Logan Square, Phila.,PA 19103 for more information.

After all, doesn't it make sense to have us look for the weakness in your pollution control before somebody else does?

IT'S ALWAYS SOMETHING.

A volcano here.

A typhoon there.

A shipment damaged in South America.

A ship damaged in the South Pacific.

When your business is international, so are your problems. And to make matters worse, sometimes the biggest problem a company faces is its insurance.

Because when things go wrong, many American businesses discover that the insurance they have isn't the insurance they thought they had.

Policies vary.

Customs vary.

And assumptions about coverage are very different from country to country. In Italy, for example, fire insurance covers all accidental fires.

Except those started by spontaneous combustion.

And in Great Britain, "World Wide" coverage covers England, Scotland, Guernsey and the Isle of Man. Period.

The point is, insuring international risks country by country can be something of a risk itself.

Which is why so many corporations depend on one global policy from CIGNA's international specialists.

At CIGNA, our companies provide American business with the coverage American business expects.

Without cultural gaps. Or quaint local peculiarities.

And without the difficulty of dealing with a stack of policies written in everything from Spanish to Swedish.

What's more, when something goes wrong we can also provide the kind of claims adjustment and responsiveness that American business demands.

In fact, we can provide a breadth of service unsurpassed by any other insurance company.

With local representatives in 130 countries.

If you think your company might benefit from the total protection we offer, please write CIGNA Corporation, Dept. RG, One Logan Square, Philadelphia, Pennsylvania 19103.

With all the things that can go wrong in this world, one of them shouldn't be your insurance.

CIGNA

WHO SAYS YOUR EMPLOYEES AREN'T PLANNING FOR THEIR RETIREMENT?

Most people realize there's not much security in Social Security.

And that few pensions can stand up to inflation.

Most people know perfectly well they should be saving for retirement. But they're still not doing it.

Not because they don't have the foresight.

But simply because they don't have the money. Or the discipline.

The truth is, short of winning a lottery, many people don't have a hope of accumulating enough savings, on their own, to see them comfortably through their retirement.

Which is why more and more employers are offering their employees the chance to save in the only way they realistically can.

Little by little. Week by week.

In fact, at Connecticut General, a CIGNA company, we're already administering more than two billion dollars of employee retirement savings for employees at over 2,000 corporations.

And we're helping those employees save in the most advantageous way.

Because we offer every major tax-advantaged savings plan that's currently available.

From 401Ks to IRAs to Voluntary Investment Plans for individual employee contributions.

But more than that, we also offer the kind of service that makes it feasible for a corporation to make these plans available.

Because we're prepared to help with everything from employee communication, to plan administration, to providing a range of investment alternatives.

And we're prepared to do it with one of the largest, most experienced staffs in the industry.

So if you're interested in discussing a savings plan designed for your corporation, please call your broker or your local Connecticut General representative. Or if you'd like more information on employee retirement savings plans write to CIGNA Corporation, Dept. RE, One Logan Square, Philadelphia, PA 19103.

We'll help you give your employees a means of retirement planning that's a little more secure than the one they're probably using now.

CIGNA

**Consumer Magazine
Color: Campaign
Including Magazine
Supplements**

177
ART DIRECTOR
Amy Levitan
WRITER
Richard Middendorf
ARTIST
Silverman
CLIENT
IBM
AGENCY
Doyle Dane Bernbach

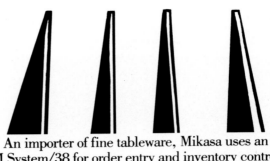

An importer of fine tableware, Mikasa uses an
IBM System/38 for order entry and inventory control to
make sure its customers get sterling service. Whatever business
you're in, an IBM Business Computer System is an invaluable tool.

177

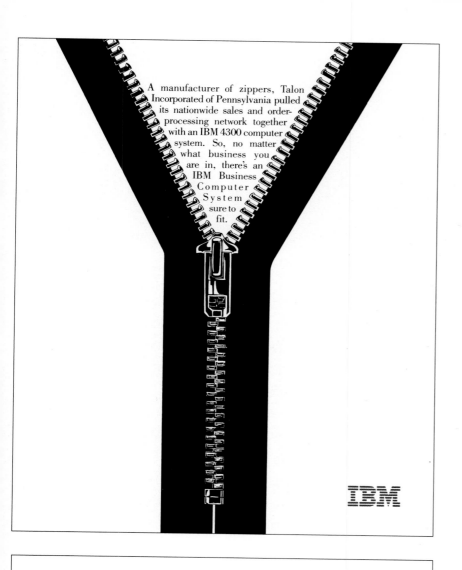

A manufacturer of zippers, Talon Incorporated of Pennsylvania pulled its nationwide sales and order-processing network together with an IBM 4300 computer system. So, no matter what business you are in, there's an IBM Business Computer System sure to fit.

IBM

A division of Ex-Cell-O Corporation, Cone Drive Operations of Traverse City, Michigan put production in high gear with a System/38 computer from IBM. Whatever business you are in, an IBM Business Computer System can help drive it.

IBM

**Consumer Magazine
Color: Campaign
Including Magazine
Supplements**

178
ART DIRECTOR
Wes Keebler
WRITER
Chuck Silverman
CLIENT
Tahiti Tourism Promotion
Board
AGENCY
Cunningham & Walsh/
California

WORKAHOLIC TREATMENT CENTER.

Career commitments are commendable. But not when they become a lifestyle. Then you need treatment. And Tahiti and her islands are just what the doctor ordered. Here you'll find the kind of beauty and tranquility necessary to put your priorities into proper perspective.

You see, in Tahiti work is never permitted to interfere with pleasure. People here only work to live. Never vice versa. And frankly, they're too busy enjoying life to feel guilty about it.

Why not force yourself to bask under clear blue skies? Swim in turquoise lagoons. Walk along secluded beaches. Explore lush rain forests. Feast on fresh fish and tropical fruit. Stroll through unusual shops and boutiques. Or, if you prefer, just relax and daydream for hours on end.

This unspoiled paradise will cure all your problems like nothing else in the world. Of course, there are telephones and conference rooms available for the truly terminal cases.

So visit Tahiti soon on UTA French Airlines. And give yourself the treatment you deserve.

TAHITI VIA UTA

For all the details and FREE color brochures write:
UTA French Airlines, P.O. Box 9000, Van Nuys,
California 91409. Or call your travel agent.

SORRY, NO McDONALD'S.

If fast-food and fast living are what you're looking for in a vacation, you'll probably be a bit disappointed with a visit to Tahiti and her islands.

Because taking life slow and easy is what Tahiti is all about. It's a philosophy that envelops you the moment you arrive.

You'll enjoy relaxed sunny days. Warm, crystal-clear lagoons. Cool, green foliage. Waterfalls. Flowers. Exotic scents. Bright blue skies. Secluded beaches. Graceful palms. Breathtaking sunsets. Soft evening breezes. And food that's simply outstanding.

Tahiti has everything you need to forget all of the pressures and problems of day-to-day living. And fully engross yourself in the fine art of doing absolutely nothing.

Granted, there are no towering high-rise hotels in Tahiti. No frantic freeways. No fancy cars or clothes. And alas, there are no Big Mac' or Quarter Pounder' sandwiches, either.

But most of the people who've been here seem to think that it's what Tahiti doesn't have that makes it what it is.

TAHITI via **UTA**

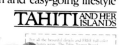

STAY IN A TAHITIAN HIGH-RISE.

In most tropical vacation locales, the original beauty and native way of life have long since given way to the growing pains and pressures of modern civilization. Towering hotels have replaced native huts. Hamburgers are on every menu. And crowds are on every beach.

But Tahiti and her islands offer no such compromises.

Here, nature is still as it was meant to be. Unspoiled and unaffected by the rigors of progress and profit.

In this tranquil paradise, you can trade everyday problems for a thatched-roof bungalow. And let the soft evening breezes and gentle ocean waves lull you to sleep each night.

You can stroll along secluded beaches. Swim in peaceful, crystal-clear lagoons. Enjoy exotic flowers and fauna. Smell the beautiful scents. Feast on the bountiful French and Polynesian cuisine. And just plain relax in a warm and easy-going lifestyle found nowhere else in the world.

Come visit Tahiti and her islands soon. You'll find a stay here to be the absolute height in low-key living.

TAHITI AND HER ISLANDS

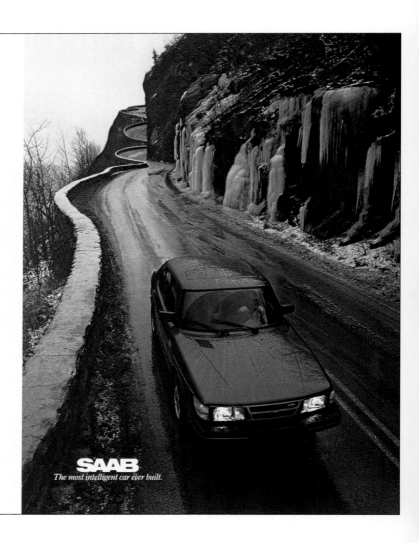

SAABS ARE ENGINEERED FOR THOSE WHO SEEK OUT THE THRILL OF DRIVING AS WELL AS THOSE WHO SEEK TO AVOID IT.

Consider your favorite twisty bit of road.

It's likely to contain a higher average number of curves per mile than the local interstate.

It probably snakes its way through or around an area of considerable scenic splendor.

This road is not without drama. An off-camber curve here, a patch of buckled pavement there. It is challenging enough to be a stimulating driving experience but not so hostile to be off-putting. And you know it like the back of your hand.

On a road such as this, you'd prefer your car to have attributes of a sporting nature. First and foremost among these is the ability to move along with a reasonable degree of speed, an ability which Saabs have in great abundance.

You'd want your car's steering to be linear, direct and highly accurate. And those are exactly the characteristics engineered into Saab's power-assisted rack-and-pinion steering system. With enough power assist to be very quick and enough feel to be exceptionally precise.

One thing you'd find indispensable is a firm but compliant union between your wheels and the road surface, regardless of the road surface's condition. This is something a Saab provides through the sheer traction of its 15″ Pirelli radial tires, the suppleness of its gas-filled shock absorbers* and the pull of its front-wheel drive.

In fact, Saab's front-wheel drive offers more than just traction. It offers the slight understeer essential for negotiating a series of bends in the quickest possible manner.

1984 SAAB PRICE LIST**	
900 3-door	$11,110
900 4-door	$11,420
900S 3-door	$13,850
900S 4-door	$14,310
900 Turbo 3-door	$16,940
900 Turbo 4-door	$17,400
Automatic transmission $390 additional.	

You'd be interested in seats that can hold you firmly but comfortably in place and controls that fall readily to hand as you keep your eyes fixed on the road, where they rightfully belong. And you'd get these things in a Saab.

But, of course, there are times when stimulation can go too far.

Consider the same stretch of road in a less favorable light. The curves you love so well are capped with ice or mud that's just as slippery. Visibility is limited to the point where not only the scenery is obscure but, at times, the course of the road itself is in question.

Perhaps, on this particular day, you are on this road out of necessity rather than choice. And interested in anything *but* driving stimulation.

A Saab is engineered for times like this as well.

The precision of its steering can help you avoid obstacles and negotiate slippery conditions while keeping you fully aware of your car's relationship to the direction of the road.

The slight understeer of a Saab's front-wheel drive will prove instrumental in helping prevent a change in your direction of travel when one isn't called for. And its front-wheel drive puts a Saab's power where it can do the most good in snow or mud or ice.

A Saab's heated driver's seat, the visibility provided by its wrap-around windshield and its high levels of interior efficiency can help you maintain a level of driving skill essential to a safe arrival at your destination.

In short, a Saab is really engineered for two entirely different kinds of driver.

Even when they happen to be the same person.

*900S and Turbo models only. **Manufacturer's suggested retail prices. Not including taxes, license, freight, dealer charges or options. There are a limited number of turbo models available with Saab's Exclusive Appointments Group, which includes: leather upholstery, fog lights, electronic cruise control and electric sunroof, at additional cost. Saab 900 5-speed APC Turbo 27 EPA estimated mpg, 34 estimated highway mpg. Use estimated mpg for comparison only. Mileage varies with speed, trip length and weather. Actual highway mileage will probably be less.*

SAAB
The most intelligent car ever built.

INTRODUCING THE 16-VALVE, INTERCOOLED SAAB TURBO. IN ANY OTHER CAR, THIS MUCH POWER WOULD BE IRRESPONSIBLE.

Remember muscle cars? "Getting rubber"? "Slam shifting"? "Blowing someone's doors off"?

Screech. Graunch. Whoosh. The golden songs of a golden era. Tributes to the prodigality of power in the hands of impetuous youth. Redolent of nostalgia. And like many things nostalgic, out of place in the present.

Now that gas is back, so is muscle. Only today, you have a choice. You can once again buy a car that uses it frivolously.

Or you can buy the Saab 900 Turbo.

The new 16-valve, intercooled Saab Turbo engine is fuel-efficient, like the first and second generation Saab turbocharged engines that preceded it. While being considerably more powerful at the same time.

Having four valves per cylinder (with dual-overhead camshafts) helps the new Saab Turbo engine inhale and exhale easier. It enables the spark plug to be located at the center of the hemispherical combustion chamber.

In strictly practical terms, this means combustion is more complete and efficient. So compression can be raised without raising the octane of the fuel needed to achieve it.

Increased compression means better throttle response. With no penalty in fuel economy. Both mean greatly increased driving enjoyment.

Intercooling lowers the temperature of the air mass compressed by the turbocharger. Which means boost can be increased (it has) and, along with it, power (it has too).

The intercooling and 16-valve head combine to produce the kind of mid-range torque you may remember from the halcyon days of the muscle car.

1985 SAAB PRICE LIST*	
900 3-door	$11,850
900 4-door	$12,170
900S 3-door	$15,040
900S 4-door	$15,510
Turbo 3-door	$18,150
Turbo 4-door	$18,620
Automatic transmission $400 additional.	

But, unlike the power of yesteryear, the power of the Saab Turbo has been harnessed to be of maximum practical advantage in a real world.

How to put power to its best use.

Making a car go faster used to entail nothing more complex than squeezing into it the largest engine and carburetors that would fit.

With steering that was often, to be charitable, a bit vague. Tiny drum brakes. A chassis that was nothing if not flexible.

And a body that had little crashworthiness going for it other than sheer mass.

Saab thinks other things should precede power before it can be put to responsible uses.

First, you should build a body that is not only rigid, but safe.

Under that, you should put the best shock absorbers available (gas filled) so the power can be transmitted to the road no matter what kind of road it's transmitted to.

The brakes should be more than equal to the power they're meant to hold in check. Four-wheel disc brakes.

These brakes should ride within wheels and tires capable of resolute traction. Light-alloy, 15" wheels with low profile, high-performance radials.

Steering should be precise, channeling power towards its proper course.

And power should be transmitted through the front wheels, where it can do the most practical good.

All these things make a Saab the perfect environment for an engine like the intercooled, 16-valve Turbo engine being introduced in 1985.

Of course, if you look for them, you will find more powerful cars on the market.

But none that use their power so wisely or as well.

Manufacturer's suggested retail prices. Not including taxes, license, freight, dealer charges or options. There are a limited number of turbo models available with Saab's Exclusive Appointments group, which includes: leather upholstery, fog lights, and electric sunroof, at additional cost.

⊚SAAB
The most intelligent car ever built.

IT ISN'T ESSENTIAL THAT ONE EXPERIENCE OTHER CARS BEFORE BUYING A SAAB. BUT IT CAN BE VERY CONVINCING.

The road to a Saab is littered with the hulks of cars you thought would be just what you wanted, but weren't.

When you wanted style, that's just what you got. You got tail fins, two-tones and flash. You got mundane engineering clothed in futuristic dazzle. A truck in a tuxedo.

When you wanted performance, you went out and bought it. You bought twice as many cylinders as necessary. Twice as many carburetor barrels. Twice as many exhaust pipes. You had to: you had to move around twice as much weight.

When you wanted economy or utility, you knew where to get it. You got it in a plain brown wrapper. No frills. No unpleasant surprises. No pleasant ones, either.

Whenever you wanted any of these things, you never had trouble getting them in a car. The trouble was, you could never get them all in the same car.

The ideal car should do everything well.

It probably isn't possible to make the ideal car. For one thing, especially in a big car company, it's often impossible to get everybody to agree on what the ideal car is.

Fortunately, Saab is a small car company. And all parties involved in the creation of Saab automobiles have come to the general agreement that, for their part, the ideal car is one that does everything well.

You can tell how close a carmaker has come to making the ideal car by examining that car's strong points.

Paradoxically, there really shouldn't be any.

In a Saab, for example, you'd be pressed to point out a single feature that is demonstrably superior to another.

1985 SAAB PRICE LIST*	
900 3-door	$11,850
900 4-door	$12,170
900S 3-door	$15,040
900S 4-door	$15,510
Turbo 3-door	$18,150
Turbo 4-door	$18,620
Automatic transmission $400 additional.	

Saabs are generally acknowledged to be fine-handling cars. This is the result of front-wheel drive, rack-and-pinion steering, low-profile radial tires and excellent shock absorbers.

Yet a Saab's handling complements, rather than overshadows, its performance, which is equally impressive. That performance, in the case of the Saab 900 Turbo, is derived from the use of turbocharging, intercooling, 16 valves and dual-overhead camshafts.

Since there is no compelling reason why a Saab's performance and handling should not be perfectly compatible with comfort, room and utility, a Saab has those things too.

Is the ideal car, then, one that handles well, performs well and does many other things well besides? Well, ask yourself—why shouldn't a car do all this?

A Saab could never be your first car.

No one at Saab would be rash enough to claim they've made the ideal car.

On the other hand, no one at Saab would disagree that making the ideal car is their common goal. To understand this, is to begin to understand what a Saab is.

And many car buyers have begun to understand. Because, for the past four years, demand for Saabs has exceeded an ever-increasing supply.

Every year, for the past four, an increasing number of drivers have discovered that a Saab is close to their personal ideal of what the ideal car should be: fun to drive, practical, comfortable and durable.

But it's doubtful they would have ever recognized all these Saab virtues without having lived through other cars' shortcomings.

Which is why it's a relatively safe assumption that a Saab could never be your first car.

Although it is highly likely it could be your last.

⊚SAAB
The most intelligent car ever built.

Manufacturer's suggested retail prices. Not including taxes, license, freight, dealer charges or options. There are a limited number of turbo models available with Saab's Exclusive Appointments group, which includes: leather upholstery, fog lights, and electric sunroof, at additional cost.

**Consumer Magazine
Color: Campaign
Including Magazine
Supplements**

180
ART DIRECTOR
Tom Schwartz

WRITER
Richard Middendorf

PHOTOGRAPHER
Jerry Friedman

CLIENT
IBM

AGENCY
Doyle Dane Bernbach

One financing arrangement simpler than ours.

If you're looking for a way to simplify the process of financing IBM equipment, consider the IBM Credit Corporation.

Our term lease master contract, which you need to sign only once, is a mere four pages. A little longer than an IOU, but look what it gets you.

Flexibility. We'll tailor lease financing to meet your company's needs.

Upgradability. If your business grows or you want to add equipment, a simple supplement to your original contract is all it takes.

Competitive rates.

We not only reduce your paperwork, we reduce your peoplework.

The same person who helps you choose the IBM equipment your business needs can also arrange to finance it.

Call your IBM representative to get more information about the IBM Credit Corporation. Or call 1 800 IBM-2468 Ext. 171, code AG.

You owe it to yourself.

See how simple financing can be.

IBM
Credit Corporation

See how simple financing can be.

Now financing IBM equipment doesn't have to be a whole lot more complicated than signing on our dotted line.

To begin with, our master agreement is a mere four pages long. And you only need to sign it once.

Your signature will get you flexible financing. We offer a wide range of lease or installment purchase options to help you tailor a plan that suits your company's needs.

Your signature also gets you low rates. We're competitive.

And if you want to add or upgrade equipment down the road, a simple supplement to your original contract is all it takes.

So how do you go about getting IBM Credit Corporation financing?

Just call the same person who helps you choose the IBM computer or office equipment you need.

Your IBM marketing representative.

It's that simple.

IBM
Credit Corporation

Compared with some financing documents

ours is only a little boring.

An IBM Credit Corporation master agreement is a mere four pages long. What's missing?

Mostly the same thing that's missing from our whole financing process: unnecessary work.

To begin with, you don't need to deal with a lot of people to get the IBM computer you want.

The same IBM marketing representative you see for your IBM equipment can arrange financing for it, too.

But don't think that less work means less flexibility. You can choose the financing that's best for your company from our wide range of lease or installment purchase options.

You don't have to give up low rates either. We're competitive.

We've even made sure financing that starts simple, stays simple. A supplement to your original contract is all it takes to add or upgrade equipment.

If a financing process that's less of a process interests you, call your IBM marketing representative and ask about the IBM Credit Corporation. Or call 1 800 IBM-2468 Ext. 90, code AL.

See how simple financing can be.

IBM
Credit Corporation

**Consumer Magazine
Color: Campaign
Including Magazine
Supplements**

181
ART DIRECTOR
Paul Boley

WRITER
Richard Rand

PHOTOGRAPHERS
Joe Baraban
Joel Baldwin
Gil Core

CLIENT
Schenley

AGENCY
Leo Burnett USA/Chicago

The trophies are few and the purses small,
but the reason to run in the Glendevon
sheepdog trials is as old as the
Scottish hills themselves. Sooner or later,
every dog has his day.
The good things in life stay that way.

DEWAR'S
White Label.
never varies.

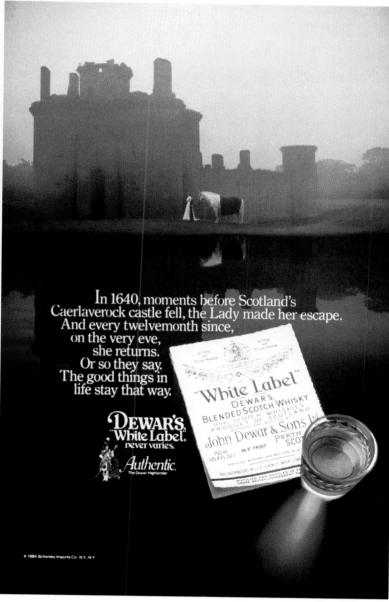

In 1640, moments before Scotland's
Caerlaverock castle fell, the Lady made her escape.
And every twelvemonth since,
on the very eve,
she returns.
Or so they say.
The good things in
life stay that way.

DEWAR'S
White Label.
never varies.

Authentic
The Dewar Highlander

Consumer Magazine
Color: Campaign
Including Magazine
Supplements

182
ART DIRECTOR
Mark Moffett
WRITER
Richard Pels
DESIGNER
Mark Moffett
CLIENT
Club Med
AGENCY
Ammirati & Puris

HOW TO GO TO THE ISLANDS ALONE WITHOUT FEELING MAROONED.

There's freedom in traveling on your own. There's privacy. There's a great deal of self-satisfaction.

There's also a great deal of work. Enough day-to-day planning to tax the most rugged individual. And often, there's more privacy than you care to have.

Which is why there's Club Med.

For one all-inclusive price Club Med makes your reservations, confirms your flights, provides transportation to and from the airport and gives you a truly remarkable variety of things to do. As well as 96 distinct vacation villages worldwide to do them in.

There's waterskiing, board sailing, scuba diving, sailing and tennis. Art classes, French language labs, classical music concerts—each just a barefoot walk from the other so you'll never need a map of the island to pinpoint their location.

And in addition to making all the activities accessible, Club Med does the same for people. Instead of the pomp and ceremony typical of resort hotels, the atmosphere of a Club Med village is comfortable and casual. An atmosphere in which meeting your fellow vacationers becomes effortless.

Not meeting them, you may be interested to know, is equally effortless. For there are miles of serene, sandy beaches that allow vacationers to take a vacation from each other.

All of which makes Club Med one of the few places on earth where you can travel solo and still have someone else do all the work. And not come back feeling like you've spent a week in solitary.

For more information, call your travel agent or Club Med at 1-800-528-3100 and ask for Ms. McNally.

CLUB MED®
The antidote for civilization.℠
© 1984 Club Med, Inc., 40 W. 57th St., NY, NY 10019.

HOTELS OFFER YOU A ROOM. CLUB MED OFFERS YOU AN ENTIRE VILLAGE.

Picture yourself vacationing in a tropical village nestled alongside the sea.

A place of flowering gardens and palm-studded pathways. Unspoiled by the beep of a horn, the ring of a phone, or even the chime of a clock.

By day, your hosts take you waterskiing or, perhaps, teach you how to catch the breeze on a windsurfer. They refuse to be thanked with anything more costly than a smile.

In the evening, they undergo a seemingly magical transformation. Turning from sports instructors into mimes, musicians, dancers and comedians. You're lavishly entertained and even more lavishly wined and dined.

A dream? No, a Club Med Vacation Village.

A resort that, in scope and spirit alike, goes far beyond the confines of a hotel.

The first Club Med Village was created in 1950 on the shores of Alcudia, Spain. Today, there are more than 90 in 26 countries throughout the world. From the distant coast of Malaysia to the nearer shores of the Bahamas, the Caribbean Islands, Mexico and Tahiti.

Activities abound at all of them. Waterskiing, windsurfing, scuba diving, snorkeling, tennis, aerobics. Each just a barefoot walk from the other.

Inactivity abounds as well. Along miles of serene beaches that offer vacationers the inalienable right to take a barefoot walk away from each other.

Leave most of your money behind. For virtually everything is included for what most hotels charge for a mere room.

Leave your formal wear behind too. Here, bathing suits, casual slacks, sport shirts and sundresses will do perfectly.

Life, in short, is more relaxed here. The atmosphere is warmer. The people are friendlier. And your vacation is all the more fulfilling because of it.

We'll be glad to tell you about any of our villages throughout the four corners of the earth.

Each of which you'll find infinitely more intriguing than the four walls of a hotel room.

Call your travel agent or Club Med at 1-800-528-3100 and ask for Ms. O'Neill.

CLUB MED
The antidote for civilization.™

A CLUB MED VACATION MUST BE TERRIFIC. TAHITIANS HAVE BEEN ON ONE FOR 10,000 YEARS.

Tahiti is a place sheltered from the hustle and bustle of civilization. One where the natives are relaxed, friendly and carefree. And where the most difficult decision one has to make is whether to sail, windsurf or just bask in the sun on the white-sand beach.

Club Med is also such a place. And the similarities between the two are purely deliberate. Because in the 1950's, on the theory that the Tahitians' way of life is the best way to relax, Club Med designed a vacation the rest of the world could take advantage of.

We even went so far as to put the first Club Med village offered to America in Tahiti itself: Club Med Moorea.

It's a magical realm that fills your senses with the exquisite scent of Tiare gardenias and frangipani flowers, with the soothing rhythm of the surf on a pink coral reef. And with the soft caress of the island Trade Winds. As well as filling your days with leisurely activities, exotic meals, nightly entertainment—everything just a barefoot stroll from your thatched-roof beachfront cottage.

And virtually everything is included in one reasonable, prepaid price. The Tahitians taught us that hassling with money is no way to live, let alone a way to vacation. Tipping is out of the question, too—it's simply bad manners in Tahiti, or Club Med.

If all this seems appealing to you, there's a good reason. After all, it's taken the people of Tahiti since the Bronze Age just to perfect a vacation such as this.

So join us in Tahiti at Club Med Moorea. The village has just been completely refurbished, and is reopening in its full splendor in March 1985. For reservations or more information about Club Med, simply call your travel agent or Club Med at 1-800-528-3100 and ask for Ms. Moffett.

CLUB MED
The antidote for civilization.™

Consumer Magazine Color: Campaign Including Magazine Supplements

183
ART DIRECTOR
Jerry Whitley
WRITER
Joe O'Neill
DESIGNER
Jerry Whitley
PHOTOGRAPHERS
Mark Coppos
Robert Cohen
CLIENT
BMW of North America
AGENCY
Ammirati & Puris

Over nine feet of hand-welding goes into every BMW frame.

Connecting rods are individually weighed to achieve optimum balance.

Hand-grinding removes imperfections that machines miss.

BMW still believes in hand-pinstriping, not pasting on decals.

Flaws aren't covered by paint; they're sanded out by hand.

Every BMW is individually test-ridden at speeds of up to 85 mph.

SPEED LIMITS SHOULD BE OBSERVED BY THE PEOPLE WHO BUILD MOTORCYCLES. NOT JUST THE PEOPLE WHO RIDE THEM.

There are no radar traps for motorcycle manufacturers. No cops lurking behind billboards ready to pull us over for building bikes too fast.

We are expected to use self-control. Something BMW seems more capable of than any other manufacturer.

Some might find our production rate downright laughable. After all, for each motorcycle BMW builds, Suzuki whisks out 46. Yamaha, 77. And Honda a hair-raising 98.

You, however, should find it reassuring that each and every BMW frame is welded entirely by hand, instead of machine. Then aligned and scrutinized by a craftsman who takes full responsibility by stamping the metal with his own seal.

Onto this steady foundation are mounted some of the most precisely-tooled components ever to grace a motorcycle. Tolerances off by as little as one-tenth of a millimeter are not tolerated.

As a BMW inches along the assembly line, it is inspected an average of once every 72 seconds. Single-part components such as pistons receive 22 separate inspections and are individually X-rayed to determine their stress value. Even the inspectors are, themselves, inspected by inspectors.

To make certain that the whole performs as soundly as its parts, each and every BMW is then individually test-ridden at speeds of up to 85 mph. A final and, to us, a crucial examination for which high-volume manufacturers simply don't find time.

But one well worth your taking time to consider.

For it means the difference between becoming a motorcycle's owner. Or its test rider.

© 1984 BMW of North America, Inc. The BMW trademark and logo are registered.

THE LEGENDARY MOTORCYCLES OF GERMANY.

A BIG BORE BIKE THAT DOESN'T CONFINE YOU TO BIG BORING ROADS.

There is a vast array of coastal routes, winding canyon roads and country one-laners beyond the reach of America's highways.

Unfortunately, they're also beyond the reach of most riders of large cc bikes. The BMW R80ST will change all that.

Enter a series of twisties on the ST and you'll experience a sensation rare in its category: exhilaration instead of exhaustion.

The bike can literally be flicked through turn after turn. The reason? The ST is among the lightest 800cc motorcycles ever built. And what little weight it has is slung remarkably low. Thanks to its horizontally-opposed, twin-cylinder engine.

"No engine configuration known to man is better at aiding the low 'cg' required in a flick-left, flick-right bike than the opposed twin" (Cycle Guide).

This handling is enhanced by another device not known to man until BMW invented it in 1981: the Monolever™ single-rear swing arm. A revolutionary suspension that subtracts pounds and adds 50% more torsional stiffness than conventional swing arms. And also allows the rear wheel to be removed faster and easier than a conventional motorcycle.

The R80ST will let you revisit roads you probably haven't enjoyed since you outgrew your 550.

In fact, there's only one road that it is not likely to take you down very quickly, the one to the repair shop. For its limited warranty protects you against defects in workmanship and materials for 3 years and for an unlimited number of miles.* Or, in other words, for as long as the warranties offered by Honda, Suzuki and Yamaha. Put together.

The BMW R80ST. The one 800cc machine engineered to take you from the straightaway to the every-which-way.

*Warranty applies to motorcycles purchased from authorized U.S. dealers and BMW European Delivery only and is transferable within the period specified. See your BMW dealer for details. © 1984 BMW of North America, Inc. The BMW trademark and logo are registered.

BMW believes top-heavy motorcycles should be avoided at all costs. Hence, the opposed twin with the lowest cg in the world today.

THE LEGENDARY MOTORCYCLES OF GERMANY.

BMW

PATRICK WHITE 230,689 MILES

JIM KLAS 273,884 MILES

LARRY WATSON 274,607 MILES

ELWIN RUSSELL 355,700 MILES

MIGUEL A'LLERIO 385,000 MILES

FRED TAUSCH 232,943 MILES

CARL GOLDSBY 303,400 MILES

WILLIAM STOKES 239,177 MILES

BMW. A MOTORCYCLE ENGINEERED TO PUT MORE DISTANCE BETWEEN YOU AND YOUR NEXT MOTORCYCLE.

"Most motorcycle riders like to think of turning their next quarter-mile. I like to think of turning my next quarter-million."

Those words came from Jim Klas, a man who has ridden the equivalent of from here to the moon on a single motorcycle.

The motorcycle, of course, came from BMW. And as you can see from the surrounding photos, it's not an oddity. Quite the opposite, in fact. It's a trend. A trend that owes its existence to the creation of one ingeniously simple engine: the horizontally-opposed twin.

Here is a motorcycle engine whose limited number of moving parts provides it with an innate ability to keep on moving.

And whose capacity for providing ample torque at significantly low rpm's results in "The kind of engine speeds that make for a long and trouble-free life" (Touring Bike).

How long a life? Surely, no one can promise you a motorcycle Methuselah. But at a time when the average motorcycle lasts just 17,000 miles, BMW can point to a 200,000-Mile Motorcycle Club with an ever-expanding membership.

And we can point to something else as well. Namely, a limited warranty that protects you against any defects in workmanship and materials for 3 years and for an unlimited number of miles.*

Or, in other words, for as long as Honda's, Yamaha's and Suzuki's. Put together.

The kind of warranty a rider like Jim Klas, for one, can put to good use.

Jim has logged over 50,000 miles on his BMW in the last 6 months alone.

*Warranty applies to motorcycles purchased from authorized U.S. dealers and BMW European Delivery only and is transferable within the period specified. See your BMW dealer for details. © 1984 BMW of North America, Inc. The BMW trademark and logo are registered.

THE LEGENDARY MOTORCYCLES OF GERMANY.

BMW

184
ART DIRECTOR
Gary Goldsmith
WRITER
Irwin Warren
DESIGNER & ARTIST
Gary Goldsmith
CLIENT
IBM
AGENCY
Doyle Dane Bernbach

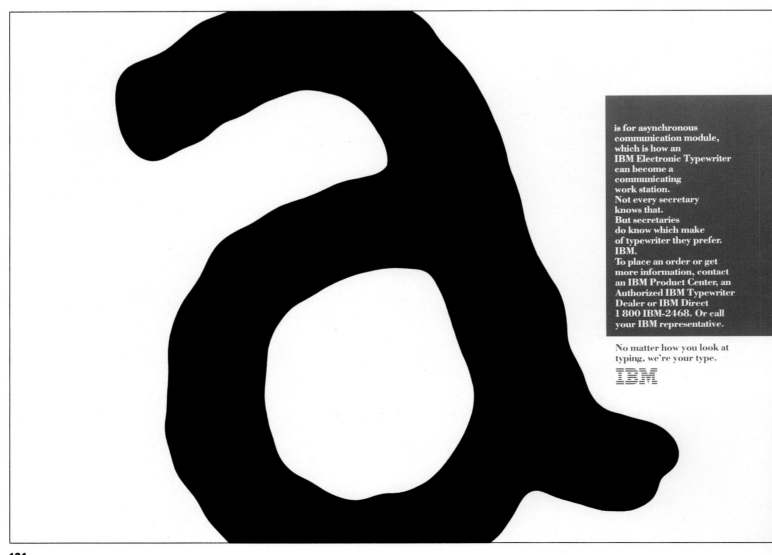

is for asynchronous
communication module,
which is how an
IBM Electronic Typewriter
can become a
communicating
work station.
Not every secretary
knows that.
But secretaries
do know which make
of typewriter they prefer.
IBM.
To place an order or get
more information, contact
an IBM Product Center, an
Authorized IBM Typewriter
Dealer or IBM Direct
1 800 IBM-2468. Or call
your IBM representative.

No matter how you look at
typing, we're your type.

IBM

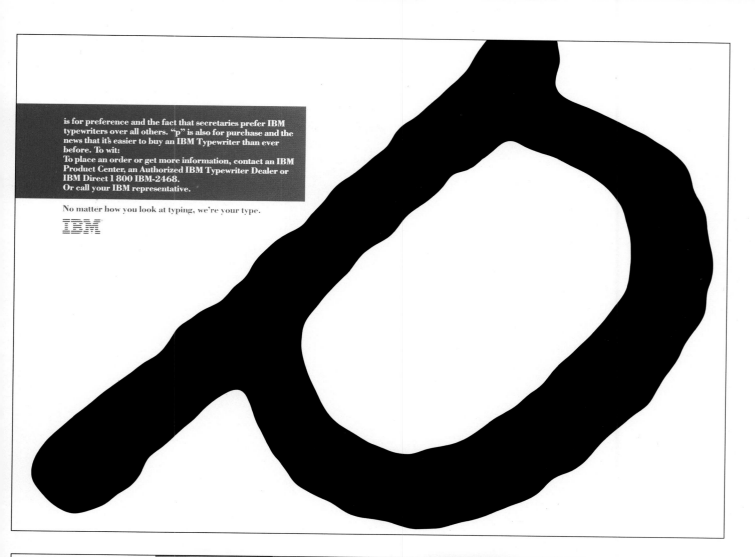

is for preference and the fact that secretaries prefer IBM typewriters over all others. "p" is also for purchase and the news that it's easier to buy an IBM Typewriter than ever before. To wit:
To place an order or get more information, contact an IBM Product Center, an Authorized IBM Typewriter Dealer or IBM Direct 1 800 IBM-2468.
Or call your IBM representative.

No matter how you look at typing, we're your type.

IBM

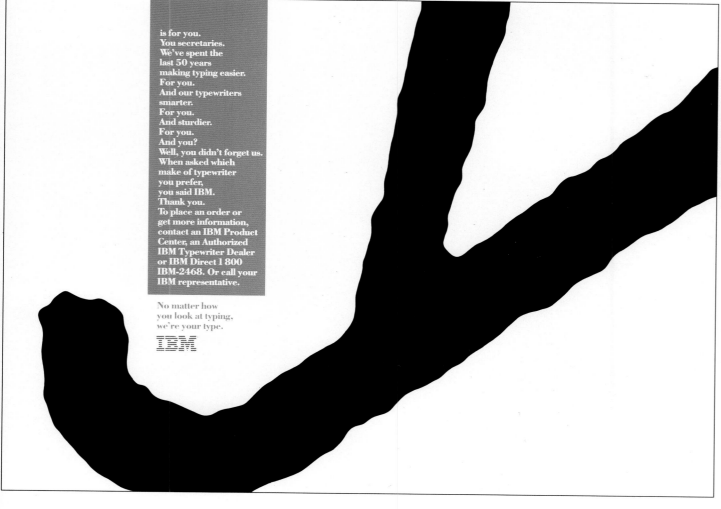

is for you.
You secretaries.
We've spent the
last 50 years
making typing easier.
For you.
And our typewriters
smarter.
For you.
And sturdier.
For you.
And you?
Well, you didn't forget us.
When asked which
make of typewriter
you prefer,
you said IBM.
Thank you.
To place an order or
get more information,
contact an IBM Product
Center, an Authorized
IBM Typewriter Dealer
or IBM Direct 1 800
IBM-2468. Or call your
IBM representative.

No matter how
you look at typing,
we're your type.

IBM

185

ART DIRECTORS
Dom Farrell
Barbara Dube

WRITER
Margaret Wilcox

PHOTOGRAPHERS
Myron
Bruno Joachim

CLIENT
Ocean Spray

AGENCY
Ingalls/Boston

WHY THE
CRANBERRY
IS BIGGER THAN
THE PINEAPPLE.

Ocean Spray® is the number one brand of canned and bottled juices and juice drinks in America.

We're the one that outsells all brands of tomato juice combined. We're the one that outsells grape. And pineapple juice. We're the one that outsells grapefruit.

In fact, outside the canned and bottled category, Ocean Spray is second *only* to leading brands of orange juice.

In the American home today, when over 75 million people reach for a juice or juice drink, the brand they reach for is Ocean Spray.

And if it's their choice at home, it'll be their choice outside the home.

If you menu it, they'll ask for it. Again. And again. Because they'll know you're serving the best.

In addition, Ocean Spray will spend over $17 million this year in national advertising letting people know the Ocean Spray quality story.

So stock the one brand that's the biggest around. Stock the littlest berry around. Ocean Spray.

®Ocean Spray is a registered trademark of Ocean Spray Cranberries, Inc.

Ocean Spray
WE'RE THE ONE.

WHY THE CRANBERRY IS BIGGER THAN THE TOMATO.

Ocean Spray® is the number one brand of canned and bottled juices and juice drinks in America.

We're the one that outsells all brands of tomato juice combined. We're the one that outsells grapefruit and pineapple. In fact, outside the canned and bottled category Ocean Spray is second *only* to leading brands of orange juice.

In the American home today, when over 75 million people reach for a juice or juice drink, the brand they reach for is Ocean Spray.

And if it's their choice at home it will be their choice outside the home.

If you menu it, they'll ask for it. Again. And again. Because they'll know you're serving the best.

In addition, Ocean Spray will spend over $13 million this year in national advertising letting people know the Ocean Spray quality story.

So stock the one brand that's the biggest around. Stock the littlest berry around. Ocean Spray.

Ocean Spray
WE'RE THE ONE.

*Ocean Spray is a registered trademark of Ocean Spray Cranberries, Inc.

WHY THE CRANBERRY IS BIGGER THAN THE TOMATO, PINEAPPLE, GRAPE, APPLE OR GRAPEFRUIT.

Ocean Spray® is the number one brand of canned and bottled juices and juice drinks in America.

We're the one that outsells all individual brands of apple juice. And when it comes to tomato juice, we outsell all brands combined. The same is true of grape. Pineapple. And grapefruit juice.

In fact, outside the canned and bottled category, Ocean Spray is second *only* to leading brands of orange juice.

In the American home today, when over 75 million people reach for a juice or juice drink, the brand they reach for is Ocean Spray.

And if it's their choice at home, it'll be their choice outside the home.

If you menu it, they'll ask for it. Again. And again. Because they'll know you're serving the best.

In addition, Ocean Spray will spend over $17 million this year in national advertising letting people know the Ocean Spray quality story.

So stock the one brand that's the biggest around. Stock the littlest berry around. Ocean Spray.

Ocean Spray
WE'RE THE ONE.

®Ocean Spray is a registered trademark of Ocean Spray Cranberries, Inc.

186
ART DIRECTOR
Mike Withers

WRITER
Charlie Ewell

DESIGNER
Mike Withers

PHOTOGRAPHERS
Steve Bronstein
Dave Langley

CLIENT
The Travelers

AGENCY
Ally & Gargano

Blue chip customers like these don't stay with you for forty years
unless you treat them fairly.

Forty years is a long time to keep the most demanding customers satisfied. It's proof of the importance The Travelers places on maintaining long-term relationships. (More than half a million of our customers have been with us more than 25 years.)

For a track record like that, you need to know how to deal fairly. And that's not as easy as it was in simpler times when fairness was mostly a matter of knowing your business inside out, and staying honest and evenhanded.

In today's complex business environment, a company also has to stay on its toes to give customers the fair treatment they expect and deserve. That means constantly adjusting to changing circumstances and attitudes. Anticipating a myriad of legal and regulatory developments. Understanding and identifying new technologies and cost-saving opportunities that affect relationships with customers. Keeping an open mind to different ways of thinking and doing things.

That's our measure of what it takes to be fair. We think that any company that isn't up to it can't stay fair. And any company that can't stay fair can't last long.

The Travelers
Fairness is good business.

In the last 30 years Bill Enright has had 3 jobs, 3 homes, 8 cars, but just one insurance company.

Since Mr. Enright went with The Travelers back in '54, he's become one of more than half a million people who have stayed with The Travelers for more than 25 years.

That's a long time for so many customers to stay satisfied. It says a great deal about how fairly The Travelers treats their customers.

Being fair wasn't too complicated when The Travelers started 120 years ago. Merely a matter of simple, well-defined decency. But in the complex world of today, you have to be more than decent to be fair. You have to be responsive.

That means constantly adjusting to ever changing circumstances and attitudes. Keeping current with economic developments and the swirl of social and political events that affect relationships with customers. Being able to keep an open mind. Being willing to change the most time-honored customs and the most ingrained habits.

Any company that isn't up to it, can't stay fair. And any company that can't stay fair can't last long.

TheTravelers
Fairness is good business.

How do we treat small business? With the knowledge that every large business was once a small one.

Some of our biggest customers weren't so big when they came to us. But since we dealt with them fairly, understood how to meet their differing needs at different stages of their growth, they're still with us today. Like more than half a million of our customers who have been with us for more than 25 years. Because we're always looking for new ways to stay fair.

Like The Travelers group life and health plans for companies with as few as two employees. And our money management plan especially designed for businesses grossing less than $10 million annually. Or our customized insurance for the specialized needs of many small businesses.

Small businesses are the backbone of America's economy. They deserve a fair shake. To give it to them, you have to stay responsive to their changing needs. Any company that can't, can't stay fair. And any company that can't stay fair can't last long.

To find out how your independent Travelers agent can help you, look for the listing in the Yellow Pages.

TheTravelers
Fairness is good business.

How Amtrol helped a herd of Holsteins solve a serious drinking problem.

When Wisconsin dairy farmer, Bob Beier's, 60-odd head of cattle get down to serious drinking, Bob's entire water system gets banged with serious water hammer problems.

Bossie's automatic drinking cup is the culprit. When she drinks, water flows into her cup from a 20 gallon per minute main. When she stops, the flow stops. And the resulting shock wave is akin to slamming the pipeline with a 20 lb. sledge hammer.

Multiply this by 60 head of hard-drinking Holsteins and you can see why Bob Beier never quite got used to the water hammer noise and damage throughout his entire water system.

Bob's contractor, Glen Redeker, of Redeker Dairy Equipment, finally solved the problem. By using a small Well-X-Trol™ Model 102 as a shock absorber.

He installed it in the barn on the main line servicing the automatic drinking cups. It absorbs dangerous shock waves caused by the quickly closing cups, and prevents water hammer from banging on system mains, pumps, and fittings.

Says Redeker, "Amtrol's got more than 45 Well-X-Trol models to use, and they tell me how to use them to solve many different kinds of problems."

Says Beier, "Now my cows are quiet drinkers."

Well-X-Trols by Amtrol. They work dependably in more ways than any other tank line in the industry.

Amtrol Inc., West Warwick, RI 02893.

AMTROL

187

Everyone in favor of office automation, raise your hand.

Automation is an outmoded concept, a leftover. It belongs to the mentality of the Industrial Revolution. This is the Information Age.

Office Humanation™ goes beyond the centuries-old concept of replacing human labor with machine labor. It sees people as an investment whose growth can compound dramatically over time, given the proper leverage. And CXC's products are designed to provide that leverage.

CXC has created for your office a single central nervous system that relates to the way humans work. The Rose™ Office Humanation System™ is the first communications system able to support all the functions of the office of the future in one integrated network.

Its distributed node architecture, with simultaneous voice and data switching, gives it features and capabilities far beyond even third generation PBX systems.

It is dedicated to the proposition that technology should extend your sense of mastery, not your sense that you've been mastered. That a system should challenge your ability to grow—instead of the other way around.

We have also created the Rose Personal Teleterminal™ bringing voice and data to your desk in a single compact unit. You can use it to access your entire company information base. And you can use its RS-232 port to attach a printer, a terminal, or even a personal computer—if you still need one.

While office automation clutters your desk, the Personal Teleterminal clears it for you. The day of the automated telephone, with its bewildering array of unuseable features, is over. The Personal Teleterminal is a computer so advanced, you may never have to think of it as more than a simple phone.

Of course, systems that make this much "people sense" will make the most business sense in the long run. But with Office Humanation there's an added bonus. Its very simplicity makes it your least-cost route right now.

And anything else would be purchased at the expense of your employees.

The Office Humanation Company. CXC

CXC Corporation. 2852 Alton, Irvine, CA 92714 (714) 760-7171. Personal Teleterminal,™ Office Humanation,™ Office Humanation Company™ and Rose™ are registered trademarks of CXC Corporation.

188

THE FURADAN GUARANTEE. ROOTWORMS WILL EXPIRE LONG BEFORE IT DOES.

Rootworms. They're the number one corn pest facing farmers today. And they can devastate your crop. But Furadan® insecticide provides excellent rootworm control. We're so sure of it, we're willing to back it with a guarantee.

If Furadan doesn't control rootworms, then we'll refund your choice of the purchase price or product, equal to the amount on the acres in question.

Remember that only Furadan will control rootworms while reducing first generation corn borers.

See your farm chemical dealer for information on the Furadan rootworm guarantee. Furadan from FMC.

FMC

FMC Corporation, Agricultural Chemical Group, 2000 Market Street, Philadelphia, PA 19103. Furadan and FMC are registered trademarks of FMC Corporation. Read and follow label directions. © 1985 FMC Corporation.

189

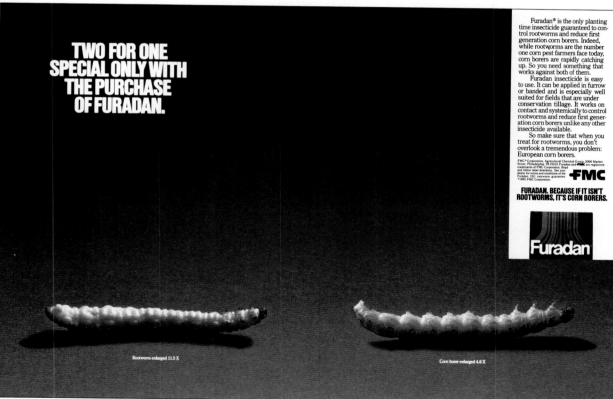

TWO FOR ONE SPECIAL ONLY WITH THE PURCHASE OF FURADAN.

Furadan® is the only planting time insecticide guaranteed to control rootworms and reduce first generation corn borers. Indeed, while rootworms are the number one corn pest farmers face today, corn borers are rapidly catching up. So you need something that works against both of them.

Furadan insecticide is easy to use. It can be applied in furrow or banded and is especially well suited for fields that are under conservation tillage. It works on contact and systemically to control rootworms and reduce first generation corn borers unlike any other insecticide available.

So make sure that when you treat for rootworms, you don't overlook a tremendous problem: European corn borers.

FMC® Corporation, Agricultural Chemical Group, 2000 Market Street, Philadelphia, PA 19103. Furadan and FMC are registered trademarks of FMC Corporation. Read and follow label directions. See your dealer for terms and conditions of the Furadan 15G rootworm guarantee. © 1985 FMC Corporation.

FMC

FURADAN. BECAUSE IF IT ISN'T ROOTWORMS, IT'S CORN BORERS.

Furadan

Rootworm enlarged 11.5 X

Corn borer enlarged 4.6 X

190

Trade
Color:
1 Page Or Spread

191
ART DIRECTOR
Joe Del Vecchio
WRITER
Jim Walsh
PHOTOGRAPHER
Allan Luftig
CLIENT
Jameson Irish Coffee
AGENCY
Doyle Dane Bernbach

192
ART DIRECTORS
Jeff Vogt
Craig Joslin
WRITER
David Tessler
DESIGNER
Craig Joslin
PHOTOGRAPHER
Dennis Chalkin
CLIENT
Sony
AGENCY
Ammirati & Puris

193
ART DIRECTOR
Gordon Bennett
WRITER
Rav Freidel
DESIGNER
Brandt Wilkins
PHOTOGRAPHERS
Big City Productions
Steve Steigman
CLIENT
Sony
AGENCY
Ammirati & Puris

Jameson Irish Coffee is the last thing you should suggest to your customers.
Just before you add up your customers' bill, why not add one last suggestion?
Jameson Irish Coffee.
It's the perfect way to end a meal. Because it begins with delicious Jameson Irish Whiskey.
Jameson has a delicate, distinctive flavor that's remarkably soft and smooth.
Served straight, over ice or with a splash, it's been a favorite of whiskey drinkers for over 200 years.
Served in Irish Coffee after dinner, it has a delightfully satisfying flavor all its own.
So be sure you get your customers to enjoy Jameson Irish Coffee before they get up to leave.
It'll be an enriching experience for them. And for you.
JAMESON
IRISH WHISKEY
80 PROOF • CALVERT DISTILLERS CO., NYC

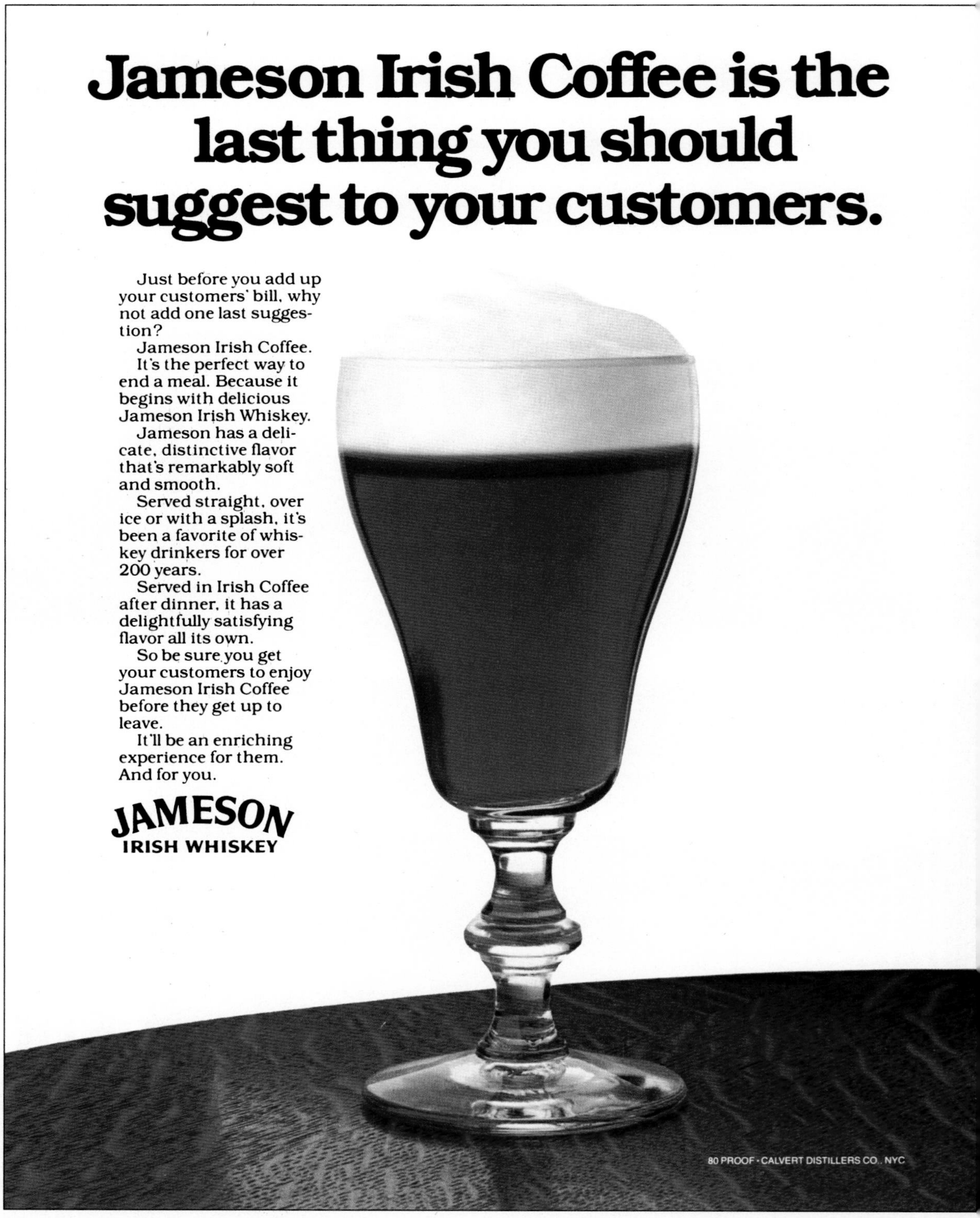

191

NOW YOU CAN LOOK TERRIFIC FOR GENERATIONS.

1ST GENERATION SONY K-SERIES

5TH GENERATION SONY K-SERIES

You can search the tape manufacturing facilities from Toledo to Transylvania and you'll go bats trying to find a ¾″ videotape that'll render pictures like the new Sony K-Series.

In the deep recesses of the Sony labs, our scientists have discovered the secret to long life. No longer will multigenerations draw the color out of your production. This is due in part to Sony's exclusive signal retention binder. It keeps the signal on the tape under the most demanding uses, even extreme temperature fluctuations.

The tape formulation is equally unique. Sony K-Series features Vivax™ magnetic particles, which are smaller than chrome oxide particles, and give you more information on the tape than ever before. So you start out with more vivid, lifelike pictures. Demons like dropouts, which have a nasty habit of puncturing holes in your video, have been dramatically reduced. As is the case for modulation noise. And the Sony K-Series has the highest color

signal-to-noise ratio in the industry. This new Sony U-matic* tape is also distinguished by a smoother tape surface. It reduces headwear. So you not only increase your tapes' usability, but your tape recorder's as well.

And there's one other significant factor to consider. After close examination of videotape, we've discovered one thing is consistent: the inconsistency of tape. This is a problem you won't have to face with Sony K-Series. The millionth one you buy will be a mirror image of the first.

So if you're looking for a U-matic tape that gives you better pictures that last longer, look for the one designed for the run and rerun and rerun and rerun. New K-Series from Sony.

SONY
The Tape Measure In Video.

Sony Tape Sales Company, Sony Drive, Park Ridge, New Jersey 07656. © 1984 Sony Corp. of America. Sony and U-matic are registered trademarks and Vivax is a trademark of Sony Corp.

THE MACHINE INSPIRED BY BILLIONS OF DOLLARS WORTH OF COMMERCIAL FAILURES.

What you see above is yet another installment of TV's longest-running horror series: "The Lost Commercial."

The villain is the antiquated 2-inch cart machine—notorious for making valuable commercial air time vanish into thin air. And its appetite for destruction seems endless. Statistics show it's not unusual for a station to squander upwards of $15 million yearly on makegoods alone.

But the nightmare is ending. Because Sony announces the first real advance in cart machine technology in over a decade. The new Betacart™ multicassette system.

THE CART MACHINE VS. THE SMART MACHINE.

What the old cart machine tried to do by mechanical means, the Sony Betacart achieves through superior intelligence.

Microprocessors keep constant track of 40 cassettes. They maintain the alignment of the system's four BVW-11 decks and its elevator. They run self-check diagnostic routines.

And, in the belief that an ounce of prevention is worth many times its weight in makegoods, they solve problems before they occur—such as warning a technician that he's about to remove a cassette that's due to air shortly.

The Betacart is communicative in other ways, too. It's smart enough to guide your technicians through its operation, and will even interface directly with your station's main computer.

MAINTAINING MACHINERY VS. MAINTAINING PROFITS.

The end result of all this electronic

sophistication is the kind of mechanical simplicity that virtually eliminates breakdowns—not to mention the makegoods, excessive downtime and high maintenance costs that are generally part of the package.

And, as its name implies, the Sony Betacart uses Betacam cassettes—which cost less than a third of what 2-inch cartridges cost. Its format also makes the system ideal for ENG use during newscasts—thanks to its compatibility with the Betacam™ camera/recorder, along with its multiple video and audio outputs and freeze/instant-start capabilities.

All these advantages, plus its low initial cost make the Sony

Betacart multicassette an investment that will pay for itself quickly. And it will keep paying off in new ways. Its stereo capability, for example, will allow you to capitalize on the coming introduction of stereo TV broadcasting.

For more information, call in New York/New Jersey (201) 833-5350; in the Northeast/Mid-Atlantic (201) 833-5375; in the Midwest (312) 773-6045; in the Southeast (404) 451-7671; in the Southwest (214) 659-3600; in the West (213) 841-8711.

After all, to err may be human. But there's nothing divine about having to forgive a machine.

SONY
Broadcast

Sony Broadcast Products Co., 1600 Queen Anne Rd., Teaneck, NJ 07666. © 1984 Sony Corp. of America. Sony is a registered trademark and Betacart and Betacam are trademarks of the Sony Corp.

**Trade
Any Size
B/W Or Color
Campaign**

194
ART DIRECTOR
Ken Sausville
WRITER
Maryanne Renz
PHOTOGRAPHER
Joe Standart
CLIENT
KitchenAid
AGENCY
NW Ayer

To introduce our new built-in ovens, we came up with a really hot idea: Retained Heat* cooking.

This exclusive feature lets you roast a turkey to juicy perfection. In half the time. With the fuel turned *off*.

Just start about 100° higher than normal, to brown the meat. Then your

THE KITCHENAID OVEN. TURN IT OFF AND WATCH IT COOK.

KitchenAid oven turns itself off. Automatically. And continues cooking with heat stored in the oven.

The new KitchenAid Superba ovens have everything you want. High styling. High-performance insulation. Self-cleaning (electric only). A constant-cool door. A meat probe. A rotisserie.

With our Variable Broiling, you can control the cooking temperature. And broil Dover sole at 350°; medium rare T-bone steaks at 550°

The first line of ovens and cooktops (electric and gas) good enough to be called KitchenAid is at your dealer now. Look into it.

KitchenAid
For the way it's made.™

THE KITCHENAID® SOLID STATE DISHWASHER. IT HAS A MEMORY LIKE AN ELEPHANT AND A BODY LIKE A TANK.

Just tell it what you want. Decide *how* you want your dishes washed. And *when*.

And the new KitchenAid® solid state dishwasher will remember. Until you tell it to forget.

Meanwhile, it can tell you a thing or two. Like what's going on inside. Which cycles save energy.

It even tells you if there's a problem. (Maybe its door isn't closed all the way.)

Although our new solid state has a mind of its own, we didn't forget the body that got us where we are today.

Our steel wash tank and inner door have two coats of porcelain plus an overglaze. To resist scratches and stains.

Our motor is the strongest in the industry. (A stronger motor strains less, so it's less likely to wear out.)

And we put our warranties where our mouth is. With a 1-Year Full Warranty on the complete dishwasher. A 5-Year Limited Warranty on both the fnotor and the touch controls. And a 10-Year Limited Warranty on the tank and inner door.

Check out the new KitchenAid solid state dishwasher. It's not only very solid. It's very smart.

KitchenAid®
For the way it's made.™

WE'RE NOT IN THE REAL ESTATE BUSINESS. BUT WE HELP SELL A LOT OF HOUSES.

For most people, the kitchen is the most important room in the house. And for builders, the kitchen can make or break the sale.

Which is why your homes should have KitchenAid® appliances. Your customers know our reputation for quality and durability.

So our name in your home says a lot of good things about you. It says you use the finest materials, with quality construction. (Even in places they *can't* see.)

And now, with our cooking equipment, we can offer a complete line of premium appliances: dishwashers, built-in ovens, cooktops, trash compactors, disposers and hot water dispensers.

Our dishwashers have a new triple filtration system, so they clean better than any other leading brand.

Our new built-in ovens and cooktops come in gas and electric, in a full range of sizes. And be sure to check out our Retained Heat® Cooking. It's an exclusive feature on our Superba ovens.

Our trash compactors have enough muscle to zap four bags of ugly trash into one tidy little bundle.

Our disposer works quickly, yet quietly. And at 190°, our Instant-Hot® water dispenser gives your customers *really* instant coffee, soup or hot chocolate. The instant they want it.

Why are more and more builders using our appliances? Because they know KitchenAid helps sell a lot of houses.

KitchenAid®
For the way it's made.™

Trade
Any Size
B/W Or Color
Campaign

195
ART DIRECTOR
Vincent Picardi
WRITER
Alison Grant
CLIENT
Frank Picardi & Sons
AGENCY
Alison Grant &
Vincent Picardi

Eating this page
can be healthier than eating some meat.

Meat is an excellent source of protein for the body. But when chemicals like red dye #3, riboflavin and ammonium chloride are used in meat it can actually do you more harm than good.

It's always been my policy never to use any chemical additives or preservatives in my meat. I make very sure that the meat I choose to sell meets with my standards or I won't sell it.

Frank Picardi and Sons.

I'll only sell you the meat I serve my family.

When they say 100% beef it's 100% bull.

A lot of people claim to sell 100% beef. But 100% can mean 100% bull beef. And even though bull beef isn't the most tender you can buy, the government says it's acceptable to sell it.

I don't agree. All my cuts of choice and prime are 100% steer beef 100% of the time. And that's no bull.

Frank Picardi and Sons.

I'll only sell you the meat I serve my family.

Aged beef isn't old meat.

Like wine, fine beef is aged. That's why I keep all my cuts of choice and prime beef in 8-inch maple wood insulated coolers. They're designed with special ventilation systems to keep moisture out and put tenderness in. And beef that's tenderized naturally is much better for you than beef that's treated with artificial tenderizers. You can tell the difference just by tasting.

Frank Picardi and Sons.

I'll only sell you the meat I serve my family.

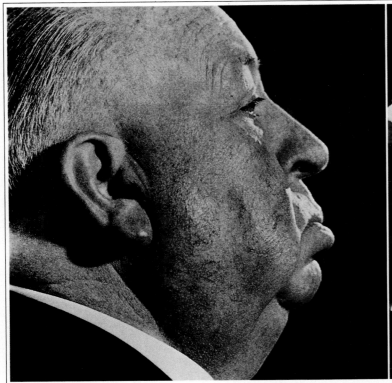 

CRIME AND PUNISHMENT.

At USA, crime does pay. It pays because here you can cash in on some of the most popular shows on television.

For instance, we've added a mystery guest to our schedule, the ever thrilling Alfred Hitchcock. We've also added "Crimebusters"—an arresting series of cops-and-robbers favorites that's capturing viewers of all ages.

And then, in this corner, is our Friday night prime time boxing. And if that doesn't knock you out, we've also got a terrific tennis schedule line up as well. In fact, USA has exclusive coverage of the

U.S. Open. With 8 nights of prime time coverage all the way through the quarter finals.

What's more, we've gone to the movies with big new packages that are better than ever. Plus, there's "Alive and Well" for women, as well as "Cartoon Express" expressly for kids.

So if you thought we were just another sports network, now you know we're really sporting a whole new entertainment concept for the whole family.

And when you see all the entertainment on USA, you'll realize why it'd be a crime not to give us a look.

USA
NETWORK

AMERICA'S ALL ENTERTAINMENT NETWORK

197

ART DIRECTOR
John Morrison

WRITER
Jarl Olsen

PHOTOGRAPHER
Steve Umland

CLIENT
Shade Information Systems

AGENCY
Fallon McElligott Rice/Mpls.

You can't control something if you don't know where it comes from.

Computer diskettes are a monster for the corporate purchasing agent. With everyone from office managers to word processors buying them, it's almost impossible to keep track of where they're coming from—or where they're going. Which makes it difficult when you're the one who's supposed to be accounting for what they cost.

In addition to offering a high quality product, Shade can assist you to centralize diskette buying and incur the least possible expense to your company.

Using a system proven successful with our computer stock forms, Shade's National Account program can provide you with comprehensive management reports of diskette usage. So you can easily manage inventories within your company.

For more information on the Shade National Account Program, call 1-800-742-3475. And get control of a monster.

The entire Eastern Seaboard was just wiped out by a single cup of coffee.

It can take hundreds of hours to fill up the memory on a computer diskette. And just a second to erase it.

That's why Shade offers their high-quality diskettes in a rigid plastic carton.

For just a little more, you get a permanent storage library for ten 5¼" diskettes.

When your precious memories are in the carton, they aren't being bashed with notebooks. Or drowned with coffee. Or scorched with cigarette ashes. And they aren't being lost.

Call us at 1-800-742-3475 and we'll tell you how you can order Shade diskettes in the plastic carton. Do it today.

Before you're wiped out by a paperweight.

1984 SHADE INFORMATION SYSTEMS, INC. GREEN BAY, WI

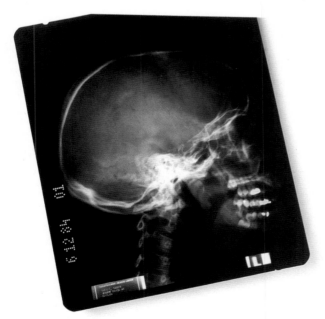

Nature had the right idea when she put your memory in a hard container.

It isn't surprising that it doesn't take much to affect the memory on a floppy disk: if your skull were only .004" thick, a slight bump might make you forget things, too.

After Shade diskettes are manufactured to the highest specifications, they're enclosed in a plastic jacket which is 33% thicker than the industry standard. To better protect them from fingerprints, dust and the occasional brush with a blunt instrument.

For just a little more, you can buy Shade disks in a rigid plastic box. Which not only keeps your precious memories from having coffee spilled on them, but makes a convenient storage place to file away disks which could get lost or mislaid.

Call us at 1-800-742-3475 for further information on Shade diskettes. We'd love to sell you on the advantages of a well-protected memory.

Even if we can't take credit for the idea.

We knew of only one more way we could improve our tape.

And we finally pulled it off.

For years, people have been sticking with our Scotch® Brand Magic Transparent Tape. After all, it's virtually invisible and it stays put.

But sometimes, what goes down must come up. So we set out to create a tape that comes off as easily as it goes on. And we finally pulled it off. Introducing Scotch® Brand Magic Plus™ Removable Transparent Tape.

It's perfect for taping things temporarily for photocopying. Leaving notes and

memos. Practically any use where you want to stick something down for now without getting stuck with it for good.

Stop in at your local stationer for a free sample. Or write Commercial Tape Division/3M, 3M Center, Bldg. 223-3S, St. Paul, MN 55144, and we'll send you one.

Scotch Magic Plus Removable Transparent Tape. Of course, you'll still want regular Magic Tape for permanent uses. But once you try Magic Plus, we think you'll make temporary tape a permanent fixture.

Commercial Office Supply Division/3M

3M hears you...

3M

Nobody's Perfect.

That's why we created our new Scotch® Brand Magic Plus™ Removable Transparent Tape. It's perfect for people who aren't.

Just like our regular Scotch® Brand Magic Transparent Tape, it's practically invisible on the job. But Magic Plus also comes off as easily as it goes on. So if you don't get things quite right the first time, you won't be in a sticky situation.

It's perfect for assembling multiple pieces. Taping things temporarily for photocopying. Virtually any use where you want to stick something down without getting stuck with the results.

Stop in at your local stationer for a free sample. Or write Commercial Tape Division/3M, 3M Center, Building 223-3S, St. Paul, MN 55144, and we'll send you one.

Scotch Magic Plus Removable Transparent Tape. Now you can pull anything off. No matter how many tries it takes.

Scotch
Magic Plus™
Removable
Transparent Tape
811
3M

Commercial Office Supply Division/3M

3M hears you...

3M

Rip Off.

You've just demonstrated the incredible feature of our new Scotch® Brand Magic Plus™ Removable Transparent Tape. It comes off. As easily as it goes on.

Now stop in at your local stationer and rip us off for a free roll.

Magic Plus is perfect for any time you want to stick something down without getting stuck with it for good. Like taping things together temporarily for photocopying. Leaving notes and memos. Or, if you're assembling pieces and don't get things lined up straight, Magic Plus give you a second chance.

Stop in and get your free sample roll today.

Scotch Magic Plus Removable Transparent Tape. We finally pulled it off.

Scotch
Magic Plus™
Removable
Transparent Tape
811
3M

Commercial Tape Division/3M

3M hears you...

3M

SELL MORE BATTERIES.

Offer your customers prints on Kodak paper. This can help you sell more toothpaste, more magazines, more batteries—greater quantities of the high-margin "impulse items" you stock.

Only Kodak paper is nationally advertised. It has achieved the highest level of awareness ever among photofinishing customers. Our research shows significant percentages of amateur picture-takers *prefer* prints on Kodak paper, and will actually *switch retailers* if Kodak paper is not available.

So if you're not dealing with a photofinisher who uses Kodak paper, you could be missing out twice: first, on additional photofinishing sales generated by new customers who insist on having their prints on Kodak paper, and then on the high-profit "impulse purchases" those customers traditionally make when they drop off film and return to pick up prints. Tap into this potential profit by contacting a photofinisher who offers Kodak color paper.

Use the Kodak paper symbol in your advertising, and display Kodak's "Good Look" signs, so customers know you have what they're looking for.

For more information, write on your letterhead to: "The Good Look," Dept. 412L-226, Eastman Kodak Company, Rochester, NY 14650.

COLOR PAPER BY KODAK

© Eastman Kodak Company, 1984   *EVEREADY and ENERGIZER are registered trademarks of Union Carbide Corporation.*

199

SELL MORE TOOTHPASTE.

Offer your customers prints on Kodak paper. This can help you sell more toothpaste, more magazines, more batteries—greater quantities of all the high-margin "impulse items" you stock.

Only Kodak paper is nationally advertised. It has achieved the highest level of awareness ever among photofinishing customers.

Our research shows significant percentages of amateur picture-takers *prefer* prints on Kodak paper, and will actually *switch retailers* if Kodak paper is not available.

So if you're not dealing with a photofinisher who uses Kodak paper, you could be missing out twice: first, on additional photofinishing sales generated by new customers who insist on having their prints on Kodak paper, and

then on the high-profit "impulse purchases" those customers traditionally make when they drop off film and return to pick up prints.

Tap into this potential profit by contacting a photofinisher who offers Kodak color paper.

Use the Kodak paper symbol in your advertising, and display Kodak's "Good Look" signs, so customers know you have what they're looking for.

For more information, write on your letterhead to: "The Good Look," Dept. 412L-224, Eastman Kodak Company, Rochester, NY 14650.

 COLOR PAPER BY KODAK

© Eastman Kodak Company, 1984

SELL MORE MAGAZINES.

Offer your customers prints on Kodak paper. This can help you sell more toothpaste, more magazines, more batteries—greater quantities of the high-margin "impulse items" you stock.

Only Kodak paper is nationally advertised. It has achieved the highest level of awareness ever among photofinishing customers. Our research shows significant percentages of amateur picture-takers

prefer prints on Kodak paper, and will actually *switch retailers* if Kodak paper is not available.

So if you're not dealing with a photofinisher who uses Kodak paper, you could be missing out twice: first, on additional photofinishing sales generated by new customers who insist on having their prints on Kodak paper, and then on the high-profit "impulse purchases" those

customers traditionally make when they drop off film and return to pick up prints.

Tap into this potential profit by contacting a photofinisher who offers Kodak color paper.

Use the Kodak paper symbol in your advertising, and display Kodak's "Good Look" signs, so customers know you have what they're looking for.

For more information, write on your letterhead to: "The Good Look," Dept. 412L-225, Eastman Kodak Company, Rochester, NY 14650.

 COLOR PAPER BY KODAK

© Eastman Kodak Company, 1984

One financing arrangement simpler than ours.

If you're looking for a way to simplify the process of financing IBM equipment, consider the IBM Credit Corporation.

Our term lease master contract, which you need to sign only once, is a mere four pages. A little longer than an IOU, but look what it gets you.

Flexibility. We'll tailor lease financing to meet your company's needs.

Upgradability. If your business grows or you want to add equipment, a simple supplement to your original contract is all it takes.

Competitive rates.

We not only reduce your paperwork, we reduce your peoplework.

The same person who helps you choose the IBM equipment your business needs can also arrange to finance it.

Call your IBM representative to get more information about the IBM Credit Corporation. Or call 1 800 IBM-2468 Ext. 90, code AG.

You owe it to yourself.

See how simple financing can be.

Credit Corporation

See how simple financing can be.

Now financing IBM equipment doesn't have to be a whole lot more complicated than signing on our dotted line.

To begin with, our master agreement is a mere four pages long. And you only need to sign it once.

Your signature will get you flexible financing. We offer a wide range of lease or installment purchase options to help you tailor a plan that suits your company's needs.

Your signature also gets you low rates. We're competitive.

And if you want to add or upgrade equipment down the road, a simple supplement to your original contract is all it takes.

So how do you go about getting IBM Credit Corporation financing?

Just call the same person who helps you choose the IBM computer or office equipment you need.

Your IBM marketing representative.
It's that simple.

IBM
Credit Corporation

Compared with some financing documents

ours is only a little boring.

An IBM Credit Corporation master agreement is a mere four pages long. What's missing?

Mostly the same thing that's missing from our whole financing process: unnecessary work.

To begin with, you don't need to deal with a lot of people to get the IBM computer you want.

The same IBM marketing representative you see for your IBM equipment can arrange financing for it, too.

But don't think that less work means less flexibility. You can choose the financing that's best for your company from our wide range of lease or installment purchase options.

You don't have to give up low rates either. We're competitive.

We've even made sure financing that starts simple, stays simple. A supplement to your original contract is all it takes to add or upgrade equipment.

If a financing process that's less of a process interests you, call your IBM marketing representative and ask about the IBM Credit Corporation. Or call 1 800 IBM-2468 Ext. 90, code AL.

See how simple financing can be.

IBM
Credit Corporation

201
ART DIRECTOR
Woody Pirtle Design
WRITER
Maxwell Arnold
DESIGNER
Woody Pirtle Design
CLIENT
Simpson Paper Company
AGENCY
Maxwell Arnold Jackson/
San Francisco

202
ART DIRECTORS
Mike Tesch
Herb Levitt
WRITERS
Tom Nathan
Bill Pitts
Jim Durfee
Julian Koenig
Bob Levenson
Phyllis Robinson
Alan Peckolick
DESIGNERS
Mike Tesch
Herb Levitt
ARTIST
Nick Fasciano
PHOTOGRAPHER
Dennis Chalkin
CLIENT
The One Club for Art & Copy
AGENCY
Ally & Gargano

203
ART DIRECTORS
Roger Cook
Don Shanosky
WRITER
Dave Eynon
DESIGNERS
Roger Cook
Don Shanosky
PHOTOGRAPHER
Jay Maisel
CLIENT
American Bell
AGENCY
Cook & Shanosky/New Jersey

201

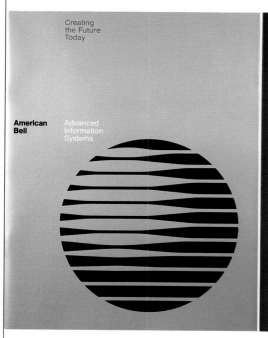

Creating
the Future
Today

American Bell   Advanced
Information
Systems

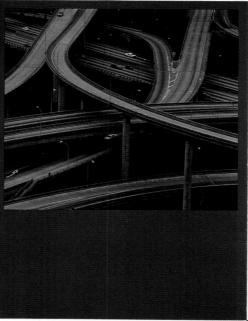

"All I ask,
the heaven above
me/And the
road below me."
Robert Louis Stevenson

> *Call Detail Reporting.* This gives
the customer detailed records of
outgoing and incoming calls to help
manage cost control and allocation.

DIMENSION® AIS™/System 85

Another of our offerings, System
85, will have dramatic, long-term
impact on information management
markets. This system is a completely integrated voice, data,
office, building, and network information system designed to dovetail
with our DIMENSION product line.
Among its features and
benefits are:

> *Uniform numbering.* This elimi-
nates wasted time by allowing
employees to dial a standardized,
uniform number regardless of
calling location.

> *Simultaneous voice and data
communications.* This enables
salespeople, for example, to talk to
customers and access their
records at the same time over a
single communications line.

> *Electronic document communi-
cations.* This provides an efficient
means of transmitting information
around the office or around the
country.

> *Building management.* This can
schedule energy usage in a 366-
day clock. Each day can be identi-
fied as a workday, Saturday, Sunday, or holiday so that power may
be allocated according to building
occupancy.

> *Networking* capabilities can
bring together an organization's
people, functions, terminals, and
transmission facilities into a single,
integrated system. System 85 can
also serve as the gateway to other
local and national networks—for
example, Net 1000.

Com Key® and Horizon® Systems

Among the products we offer to
small business customers are the
Com Key and *Horizon* communication systems. These products bring
the benefits of advanced technology to a wide range of businesses
—from restaurants and real estate

Collateral Brochures: Other Than By Mail

204
ART DIRECTORS
Ted McNeil
Richard Ostroff
WRITERS
Paul Levett
Patti Goldberg
PHOTOGRAPHER
Bob Huntzinger
CLIENT
Alfa Romeo
AGENCY
HCM

205
ART DIRECTORS
David Edelstein
Nancy Edelstein
Lanny French
WRITER
David Edelstein
DESIGNERS
David Edelstein
Nancy Edelstein
Lanny French
Norman Hathaway
D. Thom Bissett
ARTISTS
Norman Hathaway
David Edelstein
PHOTOGRAPHERS
Jim Cummins
Peter Gravelle
Karl Bischoff
CLIENT
Generra Sportswear
AGENCY
Edelstein Associates/Seattle

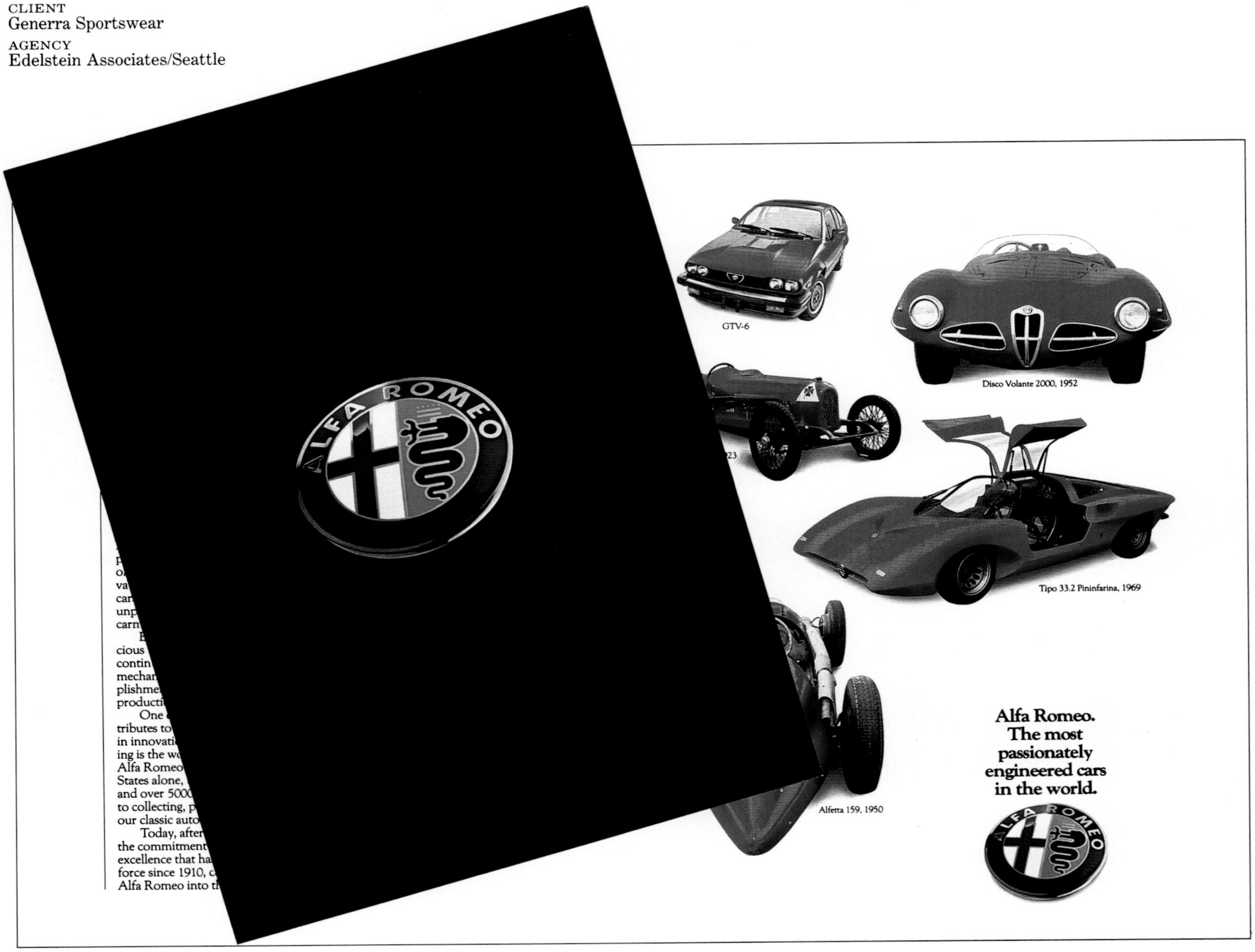

ALFA ROMEO
GTV-6
Disco Volante 2000, 1952
Tipo 33.2 Pininfarina, 1969
Alfetta 159, 1950
Alfa Romeo.
The most
passionately
engineered cars
in the world.
ALFA ROMEO

GENERRA
WPROJECTEN

Laß Blumen sprechen

GENERRA
PROJECT

strong lines, designs
for living, for fun in
movement and creating
romance

86
GENERRA

Collateral
Direct Mail

206
ART DIRECTOR
Fabian Melgar
WRITER
Bruce Novograd
DESIGNER
Fabian Melgar
PHOTOGRAPHER
Fabian Melgar
CLIENT
Melgar Nordlinger
AGENCY
Melgar Nordlinger

207
ART DIRECTOR
Bill Hoo
WRITER
Jon Goward
ARTIST
Jim Thomas
CLIENT
Deck House
AGENCY
ClarkeGowardFitts/Boston

208
ART DIRECTOR
Mark Ashley
WRITER
Ken Lewis
DESIGNER
Mark Ashley
CLIENT
J. Walter Thompson
AGENCY
J. Walter Thompson/Atlanta

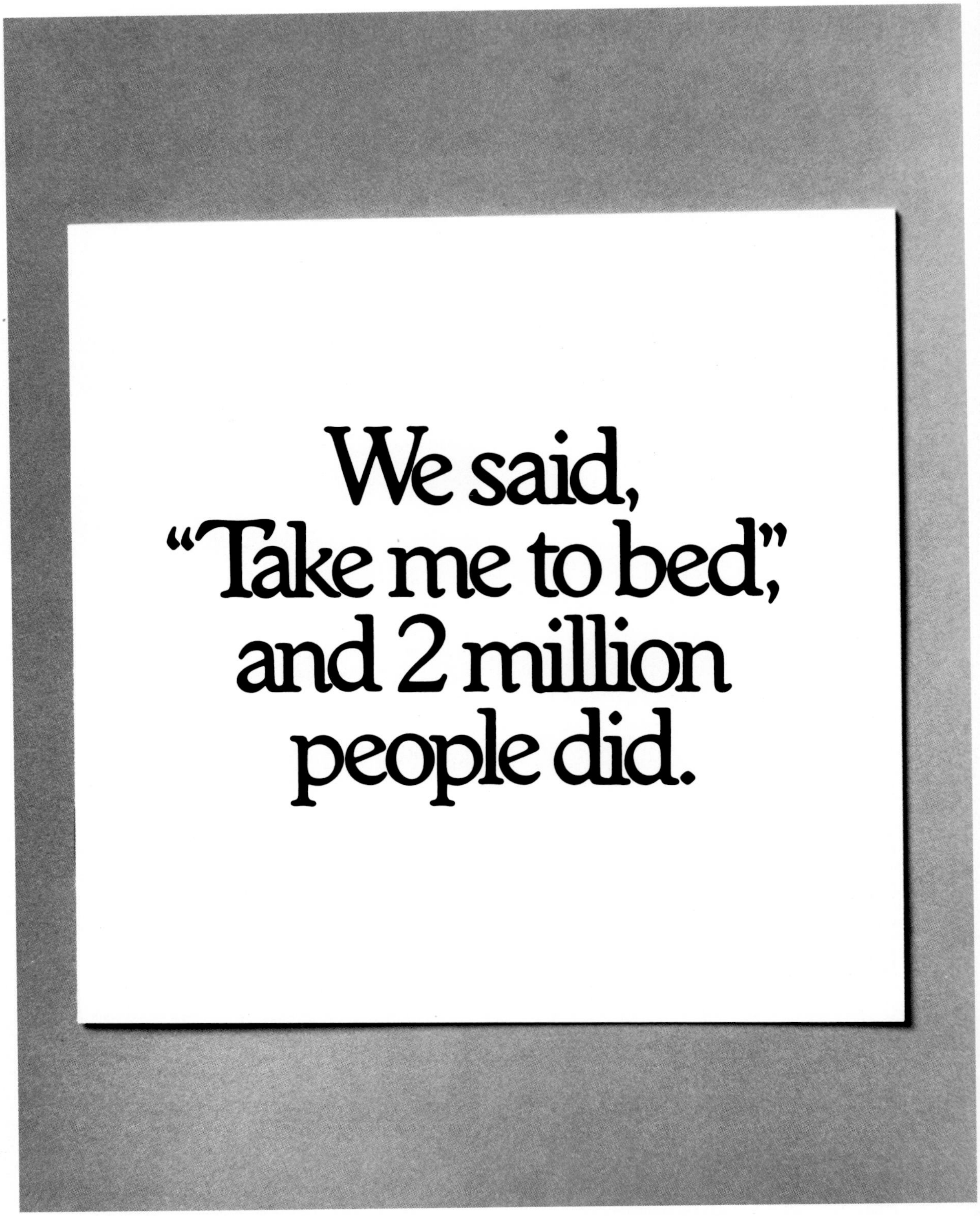
We said,
"Take me to bed,"
and 2 million
people did.

206

How to tell ripe from wrong.

Look for it in the produce section of your bookstore.

TWINKLE, TWINKLE LITTLE STAR.

We know not everyone who wears Converse is a great athlete. Yet.  CONVERSE

210

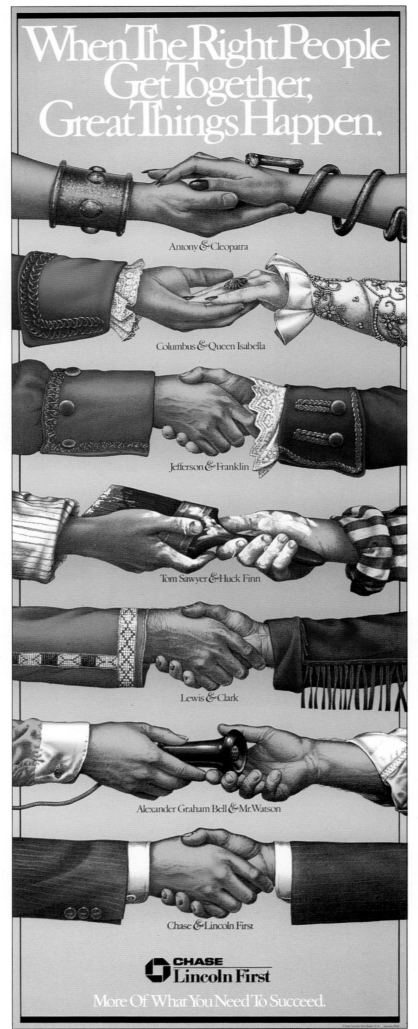

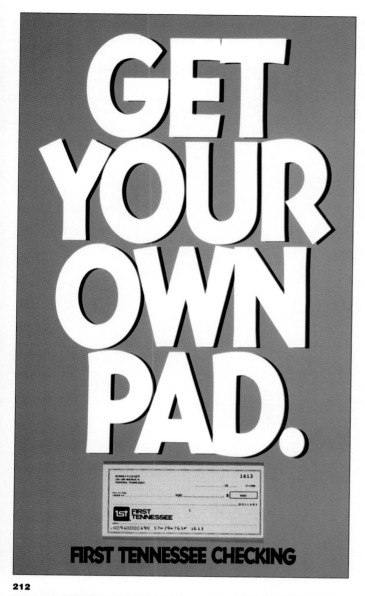

FIRST TENNESSEE CHECKING

212

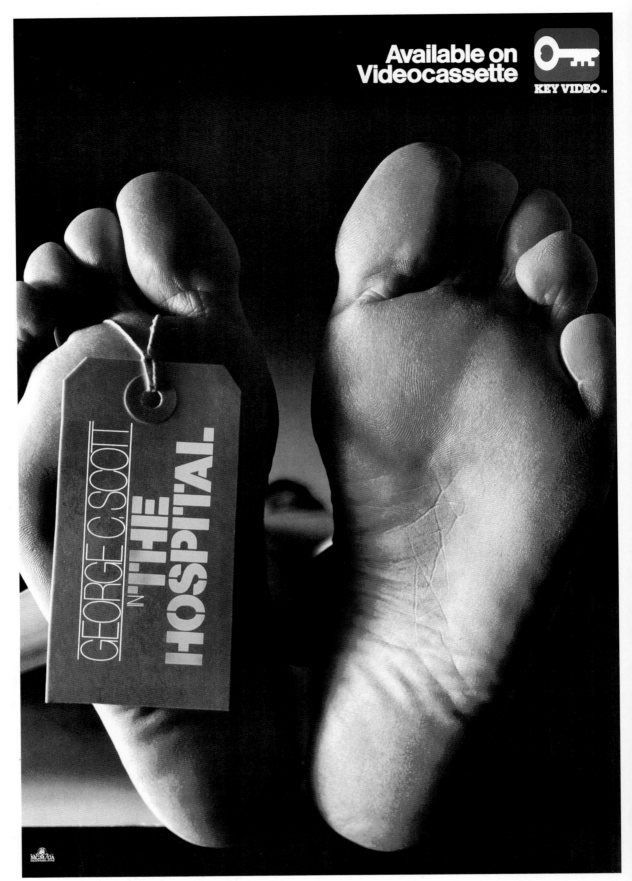

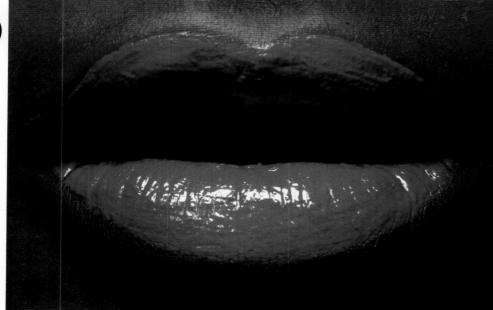

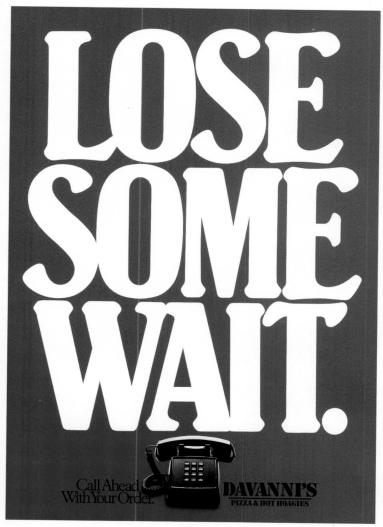

Call Ahead With Your Order.

DAVANNI'S
PIZZA & HOT HOAGIES

218

HOW TO TELL A GENUINE BMW PART FROM AN IMITATION BEFORE YOUR BMW DOES.

12-MONTH/12,000-MILE LIMITED WARRANTY.*   0-MONTH/0-MILE LIMITED WARRANTY.

It's next to impossible for the human eye to distinguish between a genuine and an imitation BMW part. But one absolutely infallible way of telling the difference is by looking at the warranty.

The part on the left, for example, like all Genuine BMW Parts, has been built to the same exacting tolerances and with the same inspired engineering as the part it will be replacing. Consequently, it's equipped with a warranty that reflects that fact.

The part on the right is merely an imitation. And it's accompanied by a warranty equal in value.

So, given the choice between a genuine and an imitation BMW part, the decision is not only obvious, it's warranted.

GENUINE BMW PARTS

219

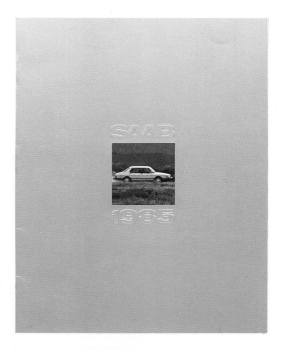

220

ONE OF THE DRAB HOMEBODIES
WHO READS McCALL'S.

McCall's
MORE THAN THE EXPECTED.

16rocksongsinarowwithnointerruption.

WNEW-FM
102.7

THAT'S A MUSIC MARATHON WHERE ROCK LIVES

223
ART DIRECTOR
Bob Barrie

WRITER
Phil Hanft

ARTIST
Leland Klanderman

CLIENT
The Minnesota Zoo

AGENCY
Fallon McElligott Rice/Mpls.

224
ART DIRECTOR
Bob Akers

WRITER
Richard Rand

CLIENT
Schenley

AGENCY
Leo Burnett USA/Chicago

225
ART DIRECTOR
André Morkel

WRITER
Brian Quennell

ARTIST
Lou Normandeau

PHOTOGRAPHERS
Bruce Horn
Ray Avery

CLIENT
Apple Computer/Canada

AGENCY
Scali McCabe Sloves/Canada

223

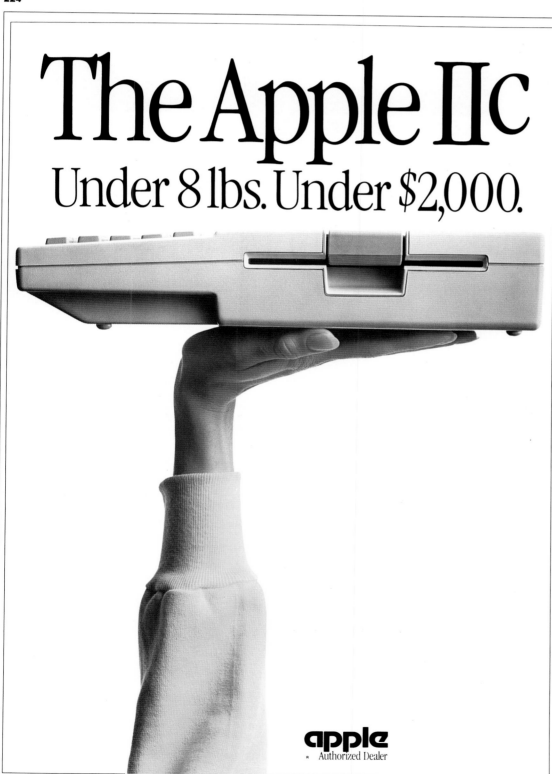

The Apple IIc
Under 8 lbs. Under $2,000.

apple
Authorized Dealer

226
ART DIRECTOR
Mark Fuller
WRITER
Mac Calhoun
PHOTOGRAPHER
Bob Jones, Jr.
CLIENT
Richmond Metropolitan
Authority
AGENCY
Finnegan & Agee/Virginia

227
ART DIRECTOR
Tana Klugherz
WRITER
Stephanie Arnold
PHOTOGRAPHER
Francesco Scavullo
CLIENT
McCall's Magazine
AGENCY
Levine Huntley Schmidt &
Beaver

228
ART DIRECTOR
Scott Frederick
WRITER
Craig Jackson
DESIGNER
Scott Frederick
PHOTOGRAPHER
Mike Caporale
CLIENT
Kroger
AGENCY
Northlich Stolley/Cincinnati

229
ART DIRECTORS
Allen Cohn
Bill Hesterberg
WRITER
Allen Cohn
CLIENT
Illinois Bell
AGENCY
NW Ayer/Chicago

Parker Field echoes with four decades of baseball memories, from the early Vee teams of the 1950's to the championship Braves of recent years. While these memories may last forever, the stadium is showing its age. The stands are dangerously deteriorated. The seats are old and uncomfortable. Portions of the outfield have to be roped off to accommodate overflow crowds. Richmond needs a new ballpark. And you can help in several ways. With your time. With your money. You can even contribute to the effort by purchasing the designated Ballpark Specials being offered at participating retailers. For more information, call John D. Watt at 648-1234. It's your chance to help build a sparkling new setting for baseball in Richmond.

226

227

NO SIDE EFFECTS.

ONE HALF GALLON 1.89L

LACTOSE REDUCED LOWFAT MILK

VIT. A & D · 2% MILKFAT

Enjoy

Specially Digestible Milk

NEW ENJOY. SPECIALLY DIGESTIBLE MILK.

Before you go to the jeweler's, give him a ring.

Phone first.

 Illinois Bell

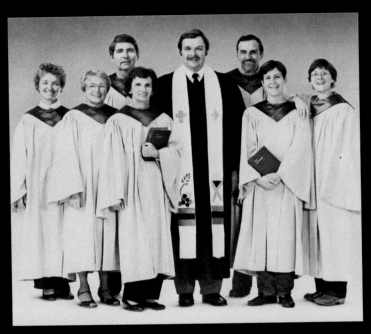

We're looking for an organ donor.

We're the First Presbyterian Church of Duncanville. And to put it bluntly, our organ has been diagnosed as terminal.

The sharp notes have gone flat. And the flat notes have gone sour. And some keys don't strike any notes at all.

The last time the repairman was out, he suggested that we shoot it and put it out of its misery. So when it strikes a final chord, it won't really come as any big surprise.

In fact, every year for the last several years, we've put a new organ in our budget. And every year, it gets cut. Because we end up needing the money for missionary work, for community projects, or to help needy families in our neighborhood.

Then it dawned on us that someone might have an organ they would be willing to donate.

If you have such an organ, please give us a call at (214) 298-3043. We'll be more than happy to transplant it for you.

Or if you would like to make a contribution to our Organ Fund, send it to: First Presbyterian Church of Duncanville, E. Wheatland at Freeman St., P.O. Box 61, Duncanville, TX 75116. A contribution in any amount will be greatly appreciated. And it's tax deductible.

But if you're like most people, you probably don't have an organ to donate. And maybe you can't afford to donate any money right now. Well, there's still a way you can help us improve the harmony in our congregation. Join us in worship next Sunday.

We have a choir that sings a cappella beautifully. But if we don't get a new organ soon, the whole congregation will be singing a cappella. And when that happens, we're going to need all the help we can get.

First Presbyterian Church

230

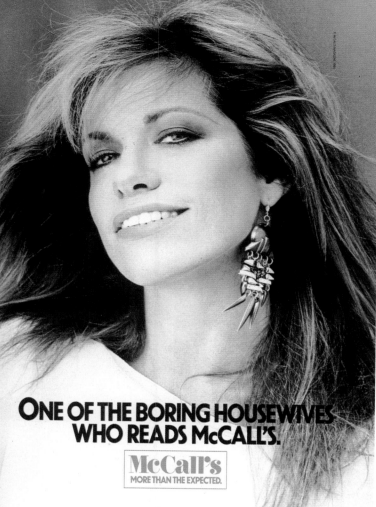

ONE OF THE DRAB HOMEBODIES WHO READS McCALL'S.

McCall's
MORE THAN THE EXPECTED.

ONE OF THE BORING HOUSEWIVES WHO READS McCALL'S.

McCall's
MORE THAN THE EXPECTED.

Don't waste your time going to Buffalo.

Take the Eastern Express from the Air-Shuttle Terminal
and save time with our on-board ticketing.

EASTERN
We earn our wings every day℠

233

234

Wise men phone first.

Illinois Bell

© Illinois Bell, 1984

235

236

237
ART DIRECTOR
Dean Hanson
WRITER
Jarl Olsen
CLIENT
7 South 8th for Hair
AGENCY
Fallon McElligott Rice/Mpls.

238
ART DIRECTOR
Harvey Baron
WRITER
Diane Rothschild
DESIGNER
Harvey Baron
PHOTOGRAPHER
Michael O'Neill
CLIENT
CIGNA
AGENCY
Doyle Dane Bernbach

237

IT'S ALWAYS SOMETHING.

A volcano here.

A typhoon there.

A shipment damaged in South America.

A ship damaged in the South Pacific.

When your business is international, so are your problems. And to make matters worse, sometimes the biggest problem a company faces is its insurance.

Because when things go wrong, many American businesses discover that the insurance they have isn't the insurance they thought they had.

Policies vary.

Customs vary.

And assumptions about coverage are very different from country to country. In Italy, for example, fire insurance covers all accidental fires.

Except those started by spontaneous combustion.

And in Great Britain, "World Wide" coverage covers England, Scotland, Guernsey and the Isle of Man. Period.

The point is, insuring international risks country by country can be something of a risk itself.

Which is why so many corporations depend on one global policy from CIGNA's international specialists.

At CIGNA, our companies provide American business with the coverage American business expects.

Without cultural gaps. Or quaint local peculiarities.

And without the difficulty of dealing with a stack of policies written in everything from Spanish to Swedish.

What's more, when something goes wrong we can also provide the kind of claims adjustment and responsiveness that American business demands.

In fact, we can provide a breadth of service unsurpassed by any other insurance company.

With local representatives in 130 countries.

If you think your company might benefit from the total protection we offer, please write CIGNA Corporation, Dept. RG, One Logan Square, Philadelphia, Pennsylvania 19103.

With all the things that can go wrong in this world, one of them shouldn't be your insurance.

**Public Service
Newspaper Or
Magazine: Single**

239
ART DIRECTOR
Mike Moser

WRITER
Brian O'Neill

PHOTOGRAPHER
Bob Mizono

CLIENT
Univ. of CA Berkeley
Foundation

AGENCY
Chiat/Day - San Francisco

240
ART DIRECTOR
Debbie Lucke

WRITER
David Lubars

DESIGNER
Debbie Lucke

ARTIST
Dom Denardo

PHOTOGRAPHER
John Holt

CLIENT
Volunteer Services for
Animals

AGENCY
Leonard Monahan Saabye/
Rhode Island

THIS BUILDING IS FILLED WITH MAD SCIENTISTS.

They're some of the most respected scientific minds in the country.

They're also mad.

You would be too if you had to teach and conduct critical research in Cal's Life Sciences building.

There are cracks in the ceilings and cracks in the walls.

And leaks in all the cracks.

Because of the rotten plumbing.

Which may be what's causing those terrible odors.

The ones that won't go away, on account of all the ventilation problems.

And it won't be long before we'll have to put laboratories in the lavatories. (We've just about filled up the halls.)

Despite these and other hardships, our Biosciences departments continue to achieve world acclaim for breakthrough research in cancer prevention, brain development, and many other areas.

But the fact remains, Nobel Prize winners and Guggenheim Fellows don't grow on trees. In order to hang on to those we have—and continue to attract top faculty—we need more than a few new beakers and Bunsen burners.

We need your support.

Because largely through private contributions, we hope to begin building a Biological Sciences facility befitting a world class university.

So please call the number below.

And help us put a stop to this madness.

U.C. BERKELEY
It's not the same without you.

U.C. Berkeley Foundation, 2440 Bancroft Way, Rm. 301, Berkeley, California 94720.
Call the Donor Line, collect, Mon.-Fri., 9-5: (415) 642-4379.

It's not a dog.
It's a guinea pig.

There is a thriving black market in this country. A dreadful, despicable black market.

A black market where lost and stolen pets are sold to laboratories for experimentation.

And while it's true that Rhode Island has passed legislation that makes selling pound animals for experimentation illegal here, it doesn't mean your pet is safe. Because it's a fact that thieves steal pets and smuggle them into states where selling animals for experimentation is legal.

What can you do?

Well, for your own dog, there are three things. One, don't let him run loose in the neighborhood. Keep him on a leash. Two, when you're not home, don't leave him alone in the backyard. And three, if you don't have ID tags, a license or a tattoo on him, get them immediately.

But there's something else you can do. You can join Volunteer Services for Animals.

We're a private, non-profit organization whose sole purpose is to improve the treatment and environment of animals in our state.

We also help municipalities provide humane services which they couldn't otherwise afford. For example, we have lost and found, adoption, veterinary care, population control, pet therapy and education programs.

So please call us at 273-0358.

And help our animal operation prevent animal   operations.

VOLUNTEER SERVICES for ANIMALS
401 Broadway, Providence, Rhode Island 02909

**Public Service
Newspaper Or
Magazine: Single**

241
ART DIRECTOR
Jerry Roach
WRITER
Joe Lovering
CLIENT
Young & Rubicam
AGENCY
Young & Rubicam

242
ART DIRECTOR
Mike Moser
WRITER
Brian O'Neill
ARTIST
Mike Bull
CLIENT
Univ. of CA Berkeley
Foundation
AGENCY
Chiat/Day - San Francisco

243
ART DIRECTOR
Michael Ranallo
WRITER
Derek Hansen
CLIENT
Royal Prince Alfred Hospital
AGENCY
Forbes MacFie Hansen/
Australia

241

BERKELEY THREATENS RUSSIA.

NOBEL PRIZES

U.C. Berkeley (14)	U.S.S.R. (15)

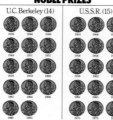

It's true, Cal's faculty has won almost as many Nobel Prizes as the entire Soviet Union.

Fourteen, to be exact.

That's four more than all of Italy. Five more than Japan and Canada combined.

But hey, who's counting?

Certainly not our professors, they've been too busy.

Discovering plutonium.

Pioneering the first laser beam.

Isolating the virus that would play a key role in conquering polio.

These and other prize-winning achievements reflect an overall academic standard that has for over half a century been consistently phenomenal.

And for that, *you* deserve a medal.

Your contributions have provided our great minds with the resources needed to do great work.

However, now is not the time to rest on our Laureates.

Just ask our latest Nobel winner, economist Gerard Debreu. Upon receiving his award, he had this to say: "The magnificent research environment I have known at this university during the past 20 years ... is threatened by very lean budgets."

So please, contribute all you can. Our professors will gladly repay you. In gold.

U.C. BERKELEY
It's not the same without you.

U.C. Berkeley Foundation, 2440 Bancroft Way, Rm. 301, Berkeley, California 94720.
Call the Donor Line, collect, Mon. - Fri., 9am-5pm: (415) 642-4379.

There are three popular misconceptions about kidney disease.

The first is that it couldn't happen to you.

The second is that, if it did, all you do is go on a kidney machine or have a kidney transplant and everything is back to normal.

The third is that kidney disease only affects the aged, and 'neurotic housewives' who overdose on analgesics.

The truth is, no matter how old you are or how well you look after yourself, the risk of kidney disease is third only to cancer and heart disease.

Yes, it could happen to you.

To put things into perspective, one in five Australians will suffer from some form of kidney or urinary disease during their lifetime.

However, only one in about five hundred will lose all their kidney function.

Of these, one in ten will be somebody's child.

Four in ten will be under thirty-five.

Now what happens to those who suffer total kidney failure depends on a number of factors.

Firstly, age.

One of the more unfair aspects of kidney failure is that children suffer most.

Kidney machines can keep children alive, but unfortunately they also keep them child-like.

They neither grow nor mature.

(Can you imagine how daunting school can be when you're fifteen but only look about eight?)

Of course, they could get lucky and have a kidney transplant.

Luck should not be, but unfortunately is, another of the key factors in rehabilitation.

Today you have to be lucky to get a transplant.

Consider this.

In Australia last year, there were 1,800 men, women and children on kidney machines awaiting the chance of a kidney transplant.

Each year 600 more people start on kidney machines.

Yet last year, only 360 patients received transplants.

To catch up on the backlog, we would need to do five transplants a day for a year, and three transplants per day thereafter.

Unthinkable now, but possible if there were enough kidney donors.

So another factor is the willingness of people like yourself to carry donor cards.

Unquestionably, the best treatment for kidney failure is transplantation.

Only 40% of patients on kidney machines are able to work compared to 80% of those who receive a transplant.

Some transplant recipients go on to lead more energetic lives than most Australians.

The irony is, while most people support transplantation, very few carry donor cards.

As a result, in the event of their unexpected or accidental death, their kidneys, which are so desperately needed, go with them to the grave.

It's not just a shame, to those on kidney machines it's a tragedy.

Each potential kidney donor lost, deprives two patients of a second chance.

There are two ways you can help.

The first is, to apply for and carry a kidney donor card.

Some people think of it as a shot at immortality, but more accurately it should be regarded as one of the greatest acts of human kindness imaginable.

The second, inevitably, is to extend financial support.

We've talked about the cure, but prevention is where we want to concentrate in the long run.

There's so much we don't know and we need money to find the answers.

We'd like you to fill in and send the coupon below so we can tell you more about the problems we face.

Then perhaps, you may care to help us realise our hopes for the future.

WITH SO MANY PEOPLE DESPERATE FOR ONE, IT'S A SHAME TO THROW THEM AWAY.

Royal Prince Alfred Hospital Dept. of Renal Medicine.

To: The Department of Renal Medicine, The Royal Prince Alfred Hospital, Missenden Road, Camperdown. NSW 2050.

I wish to help. Please send me:

☐ Kidney Donor Card(s).
(If more than one, write number.)
☐ Your regular information bulletins.

Your Name: _____

Address: _____

Post Code: _____

RADIO
FINALISTS

1985 Radio Finalists

Consumer Radio Single

244
WRITERS
Steve Hayden
Laurie Brandalise
CLIENT
Apple Computer
AGENCY PRODUCER
Jeff Palmer
AGENCY
Chiat/Day - Los Angeles

245
WRITER
Arthur Bijur
CLIENT
Wendy's
AGENCY PRODUCER
Peter Greco
AGENCY
Dancer Fitzgerald Sample

246
WRITER
Joy Golden
CLIENT
Fromageries Bel
AGENCY PRODUCER
Michael Pollock
AGENCY
TBWA

247
WRITER
Steve Smith
CLIENT
Club Med
AGENCY PRODUCER
Colleen O'Connor
AGENCY
Ammirati & Puris

248
WRITER
Mike Lescarbeau
CLIENT
Minnesota North Stars
AGENCY PRODUCER
Mike Lescarbeau
AGENCY
Fallon McElligott Rice/Mpls.

249
WRITER
Gary Rom
CLIENT
Southwestern Bell Telephone
AGENCY PRODUCERS
Michael Windler
David Henke
AGENCY
D'Arcy MacManus Masius/
St. Louis

250
WRITER
Richard Pels
CLIENT
Schweppes
AGENCY PRODUCER
Susan Shipman
AGENCY
Ammirati & Puris

244

(SFX: BABY SCREAM)

(MUSIC: UNDER ANNOUNCER THROUGHOUT SPOT)

ANNCR: From the moment little Albert entered this world, his parents somehow knew he was college material.

FATHER: What's the baby doing, honey?

MOTHER: The Times Crossword.

ANNCR: But Albert's parents soon realized their son's I.Q. was much bigger than their bank account.

ALBERT: Dad, can I go to M.I.T. and study theoretical physics?

FATHER: Have you ever thought about being a disc jockey?

ALBERT: What's a disc jockey?

ANNCR: As Albert's college days grew near, so did his family's financial nightmare.

FATHER: Forget about those exams, son, what do you say we go out . . .

MOTHER: Yeah . . .

FATHER: . . . shoot some pool, catch a rock concert?

MOTHER: Stay out all night.

ALBERT: What???

FATHER: Listen to your mother.

ANNCR: If only they'd known about Apple Computer's $50,000 Scholarship Sweepstakes. A chance to win $50,000 towards a higher education. And hundreds of other prizes. Like the Apple IIc personal computer. A more powerful version of the leading computer used in schools.

ALBERT: Folks, you know I'm getting older.

PARENTS: Nonsense.

ANNCR: If you're over twelve, see your participating Apple dealer by October 12th for details. No purchase necessary. Void where prohibited. Diploma not included.

FATHER: Come on, son, let's eat a bag of white sugar and watch a sitcom.

ALBERT: But I . . . uh . . .

(MUSIC: BUTTON)

MOTHER: Listen to your father.

245

ANNCR: It's after midnight. You're hungry. And your stomach is talking to you.

STOMACH: (GRUMBLING NOISES)
(CONTINUES UNDER)

ANNCR: Unfortunately, the refrigerator is empty.

STOMACH: Ohhhhhh
(GRUMBLING CONTINUES)

ANNCR: The supermarket is closed.

STOMACH: Ohhhhhhhh
(GRUMBLING CONTINUES)

ANNCR: And no one delivers at this hour.

STOMACH: Uh-oh
(GRUMBLING CONTINUES)

ANNCR: But you can drive to Wendy's where the pick-up window is now open late.

STOMACH: Oh?

ANNCR: So the next time your stomach talks to you after midnight, pick up a single or fries at Wendy's.

STOMACH: Ahhhhhhhhhhh. . . . .

ANNCR: Your stomach will thank you.

STOMACH: Oh, thank you.

ANNCR: Something later for Wendy's kind of people.

246

MOTHER: My son Arnold said he didn't want peanut butter and jelly for lunch anymore.
So I said, "I'll give you a little round laughing cow in a red net bag."
He said his teacher didn't allow animals.
I said, "Tell her it's cheese."
He said, "She'll know it's not cheese when it starts to moo."
I said, "It doesn't moo, it just sits on a cracker."
He said, "Even if it's quiet, she hates anything with 4 legs."
I said, "Hold up the bag and tell her that's what your mother gave you for lunch."
He said, "If my teacher sees that my mother gave me a laughing cow in a red net bag for lunch, she'll send me to a foster home."
I said, "Laughing Cow is cheese, Arnold. Five delicious bite-size cheeses freshly wrapped in wax with an easy-open zip. Mild Mini Bonbel and nippy Mini Babybel. Semi-soft delicious and natural. So they're good for you, Arnold."
He said, "You talked me into it, Ma."
So today Arnold went to school with the little round laughing cow in a red net bag. And tonight I have to pick him up at the foster home.

ANNCR: Mini Bonbel and Mini Babybel. Delectable cheeses by the Laughing Cow. They'll put a smile in your stomach. From Fromageries Bel. In your dairy case.

247

(SFX: HORNS BEEPING, PHONES RINGING, CLOCK RADIO BLARING)

ANNCR: Civilization has given us the telephone and unwanted phone calls. The newspaper and bad news. Money and money problems. Fortunately Club Med has given us an antidote.

(SFX: NOISE ENDS; CLUB MED THEME BEGINS.)

. . . the Club Med Vacation Village. Where all those prime disturbers of the peace like telephones, clocks and newspapers are gone. Where all the activities like waterskiing, windsurfing, sailing and tennis are each just a barefoot walk away from the other. And where everything is included for one, very reasonable price. So there are no money problems because there's no need for money. So call your Travel Agent or Club Med at 1-800-528-3100 and then hang up the phone and put the world on hold for a while.

(CLUB MED SONG:) *The Club Med Vacation The antidote for civilization.*

248

(SFX: WHALES UNDER THROUGHOUT)

ANNCR WITH FRENCH ACCENT: Fathoms deep, off the Atlantic Coast, roam the most intelligent creatures in the sea.
Huge, yet harmless, these pensive beasts live from day to day under the threat of another kind of animal. The whaler.
A fraction of the size, but infinitely more dangerous, the whaler is known for his cunning and ferocity, often claiming his prey as it lay sleeping.
The whalers must be stopped.
And the Minnesota North Stars are just the guys to do it.
Come out to the Met Center Saturday night as the North Stars take on the Hartford Whalers. We're going to give these people something to blubber about.

(SFX: WHALES UNDER)

249

ANNCR: Ever wonder what your parents do when you're away at school?

(MUSIC: SAD VIOLIN UP & UNDER)

DAD: What would you like to do this evening, Dear?

MOM: Oh, I thought I'd sit by the phone again. Perhaps our son, Larry, will call this month.

DAD: Would you like the light on?

MOM: No, I'll just sit in the dark.

ANNCR: You could've called, Larry. There's lots to talk about with your folks. Share with them why you changed your major to Recreation, explain what academic probation means or just ask 'em to send money.
And it's so easy . . . call between 11 P.M. Friday and 5 P.M. Sunday when rates are lowest. You can even call collect. And you can bet they'll be glad to hear your voice.

(SFX: RING! RING!)

MOM: Hello . . .

LARRY: Mom, it's me!

(MUSIC: DRAMATIC CRESCENDO)

MOM: Larry, is it really you?!

ANNCR: This message has been brought to you as a public service on behalf of parents everywhere by Southwestern Bell Telephone.

250

(SFX: BRITISH MARCHING MUSIC UNDER)

BRITISH ANNCR.: For many years it seemed, if there were a place in the world far too hot and altogether too sunny, then we British would inevitably make it part of our empire.
In fact, we practically cornered the market on deserts.
Making us, if not enormously wealthy, enormously thirsty. Thus creating a brisk demand for Schweppes Tonic Water, the Great British Bubbly.
From the parched Outback of Australia, where thirst-crazed Kiwi hunters virtually subsisted on Schweppes tonic water . . .
To the Saharan tungsten mines where we British would gratefully relish its cheeky little bubbles . . .
To the Manchurian Gobi Desert, where plucky yak traders would linger over its savory taste of lemons and Seville oranges.
Schweppes Tonic Water turned out to be just the thing.
So refreshing and Schweppervescent. So thirst-quenching, that even after we gave back all those blasted deserts, we British still thoroughly enjoy Schweppes Tonic Water. The Great British Bubbly.

251
WRITERS
Glenn Mabbott
Phil Collier
CLIENT
Byrne & Davidson Industries
AGENCY PRODUCER
Ted Robinson
AGENCY
John Clemenger Pty/
Australia

252
WRITER
Jim Parry
CLIENT
Reader's Digest
AGENCY PRODUCER
Bertelle Selig
AGENCY
Henderson Friedlich Graf &
Doyle

253
WRITERS
Jay Taub
Tod Seisser
John Cleese
CLIENT
Kronenbourg Beer
AGENCY PRODUCER
Bob Nelson
AGENCY
Levine, Huntley, Schmidt &
Beaver

254
WRITERS
Ric Cooper
Jay Pond-Jones
CLIENT
Kleenex Facial Tissues
AGENCY
D'Arcy MacManus Masius/
London

255
WRITERS
Hal Friedman
Brian Sitts
CLIENT
Burger King
AGENCY PRODUCER
David Schneiderman
AGENCY
J. Walter Thompson

256
WRITER
Stephen Bassett
CLIENT
Benihana of Tokyo
AGENCY PRODUCER
John Pace
AGENCY
McKinney Silver & Rockett/
N.C.

257
WRITER
Bill Johnson
CLIENT
Republic Telcom
AGENCY PRODUCER
Bill Johnson
AGENCY
Chuck Ruhr Advertising/
Mpls.

258
WRITER
Bill Miller
CLIENT
WFLD-TV
AGENCY PRODUCER
Bill Miller
AGENCY
Fallon, McElligott, Rice/
Mpls.

251

SANDRA (JEALOUS): Bert! The Finches have bought a new garage door.

BERT: I know, and it's not a B&D.

SANDRA: Last week it was a new car!

BERT: I know, my love, and in time we too will have all that, but we will not settle for cheap goods like their plastic lawn, plastic car and plastic inflatable children, because . . .

(SFX: MUSIC EXPLODES.)

BERT (OVERFLOWING WITH NATIONAL PRIDE): In this land of sweeping plains, koala bears and gum leaves in your drains . . .
A land of natural resources and echidnas
You probably got caught with a cheap garage door in the past din'n'yerz?
In this red and sometimes brown place,
Where a bloke's (or blokette's) dinkumness is written on their face . . .
In this continent of the occasional tree,
A garage door's gotta be what it's gotta be,
A B&D.

(SFX: MUSIC SWELLS.)

(MVO): B&D, Australia's top, number one, genuine, leading, original, favourite, best, most popular garage door.

252

(MUSIC UNDER)

ANNCR: It's the morning of March 3, 1984. In the Resch house in Columbus, Ohio, the stereo goes on, seemingly by itself. Tina Resch, age 14, unplugs it. The stereo still plays. As the day goes on, pictures tumble from their hooks, a set of stemware crashes, chairs seem to move on their own, couches upend themselves. What's happening? Tina's father remembers that today there *has* been one hour of calm—while Tina was out. The Resches call their minister . . . a newspaper . . . a team of psychic investigators. And objects keep moving in the Resch house. What *is* happening? Is it a poltergeist? Is it Tina? An original article in the December Reader's Digest examines the evidence. Every month, more people read—really read—The Digest than anything else and come away full of wonder. We make a difference in 53 million lives.

253

Hello. This commercial is for Kronenbourg, the largest selling bottle of beer in the whole of Europe, 'Better, not Bitter,' and thank you for all your calls saying how relieved you are to hear that we might be changing this awful slogan 'Better, not Bitter.' But at least you adore the beer. Mr. Jay Taub of Brooklyn writes, "This beer is real classy, but that slogan! The copywriter should be hung up by his . . ." Absolutely, Mr. Taub, we agree with you entirely, but it's the phraseology of 'Better, not Bitter' that's so ghastly; the thought itself is perfectly fine, it is a superior beer and it isn't bitter, so the advertising agency is playing around with variations on this theme like "Extremely nice and not at all pungent," and "A terrific beer that doesn't taste as though it's had a dead rat in it" and also "Have a Krony with your crony," which is . . . still in the running I am afraid. Mr. Bernie Lanigan of Boston suggests we use a jingle, yes, but the man who writes the jingles is the one who wrote the slogan, but if any of you out there have any ideas for slogans, they'd be very welcome, and meanwhile, well, carry on drinking superb Kronenbourg beer, imported by Kronenbourg USA, Greenwich, Connecticut, Europe's No. 1 bottle of beer, temporarily without a slogan.

254

MALCOLM: Hullo.
I'm Mad Malcolm, the Battersea Bruiser. Wrestling's a tough game, and when I get home nights, I like to relax with a romantic novel. Preferably an historical one.
And, of course, a big box of Kleenex For Men. So, when it looks like the Princess will never escape from the wicked Duke, I can sob into a nice soft Kleenex tissue.
(SNIFF)
Kleenex For Men.
They're just like me: amazingly strong and unbelievably soft.

FVO: Super-strong Kleenex Tissues.
The softest tissues money can buy.

255

(MUSIC: INTRO)

NARRATOR: Burger King presents—The Dawn of Burgers! In the beginning, when man was still living in caves, there were many dangers . . .

(SFX: ANIMAL GROWL, CAVEMEN: SCREAMS)

NARRATOR: . . . and not many pleasures.

(CAVEMEN: FORLORN SIGHS)

NARRATOR: So when you were lucky enough to get hold of something as special as a hamburger, you made the most of it—by cooking it over a new invention . . .

(SFX: MATCH LIGHTING)

CAVEMAN: Ouch!

NARRATOR: . . . Fire.
Even back then—before restaurants and cooking shows—people realized that flame-broiling made a burger taste special . . . seared just right, with flames licking up and those juices dripping down, for that rich, sizzling flavor. Today, some people have forsaken the flame, and turned to the practice of frying their burgers.

(SFX: PLOP—SSSSSSSSSSSS!)

NARRATOR: Society calls these people "Wendy's" and "McDonald's." But at Burger King, we say— when you have something that tastes as good as a flame-broiled burger, you stay with it for a long, long time.

SINGERS: *Aren't you hungry for Burger King now?*

(MUSIC: JAPANESE)

HE: So, this your first time at Behinana?

SHE: Well, no, actually . . .

HE: This is my first time too. 'Course being our first date, you might think I'd be intimidated.

SHE: No, no, no.

HE: You know, that clinkity-clink music . . .

SHE: Clinkity-clink?

HE: And those funny-looking bath robes . . .

SHE: Kimonos.

HE: Oh, and that thing the chef does with the big knife and fork . . .

SHE: Hibachi cooking.

HE: I think they call it hibachi cooking. But I'm worried. I've ordered in restaurants all over the world. Nome. Cancun. Fresno. I've got my own system.

SHE: No, no, you don't understand. Benihana's atmosphere is Japanese. But the menu is American. Like a steakhouse.

HE: Maybe I'd better order for both of us . . .

SHE: You really don't need to . . .

HE: You know, I'd hate to see you embarrass yourself.

SHE: Well, I think it's too late. I'll have the hibachi chicken.

HE: No problem.
(CLEARS THROAT, BEGINS SPEAKING SLOWLY AND LOUDLY.) I'll order. We Americans. No habla Japanese. Want food. Her, chicken.
(STARTS MAKING SOUNDS LIKE A CHICKEN.)

SHE: Don't do that!

HE: Me, steak.
(STARTS MAKING SOUNDS LIKE A COW.) Moooo! Moooo!

WAITRESS (IN PERFECT ENGLISH): Yes sir. One hibachi chicken and one hibachi steak.

HE: See, works every time.

SHE: Truly incredible.

HE: Yes, how about an appetizer?
I do a great scallop . . .

SHE: No, no, please . . .

HE: (STARTS MAKING "UNDERWATER" SOUNDS)

VO: Benihana. The American steakhouse with the Japanese flavor.

VO. ANNCR: If you were a rich man, maybe you could afford the rates AT&T charges for an 800 number.
But if you're a prudent businessperson, maybe you should check out a less expensive alternative.
The Respondability 800 Service of Republic Telcom.
With our Respondability 800 Service, your start-up costs are hundreds of dollars less. Your monthly fee is much less, too.
Yet the service is much, much more.
Republic Telcom's Respondability 800 Service. With the money you'll save, you could very well become a rich man.

LIVE ANNCR: For more information about Republic Telcom's Respondability 800 Service, or our low cost long-distance service, call toll-free 1-800-Respond.
That's 1-800-R-E-S-P-O-N-D.

(SFX: SOUTHERN POLITICIAN/PREACHER ADDRESSES THE CONVENTION; HELLFIRE AND BRIMSTONE SPEECH IS PUNCTUATED WITH CROWD CHEERS.)

ANNCR: My fellow Americans, a few weeks ago you had a choice to make. And you made it. You were asked to decide between watching the Democratic convention on network television or watching whatever you choose on WFLD-TV, Channel 32. And now, under the rules of equal time you are being called upon to make that decision again. Now, it's the Republicans' turn to try and dominate the airwaves. Is there a contest? Will it be Ronald and Nancy? Or will it be Alfred Hitchcock and The Birds? Will it be George Bush or Steve Martin and Richard Pryor? The delegates from Montana? Or the White Sox from Chicago? Watch the convention on network television and the choice is theirs. Or watch WFLD-TV, Channel 32, and the choice is yours. Oh yes.

Consumer Radio Single

259

(SFX: MOTORCYCLE CHANGING GEARS. MUSIC UNDER.)

ANNCR. VO.: Today there are any number of motorcycles that will rocket through the quarter mile in thirteen seconds or less. All the more reason to consider how fast these same machines are rocketing through the factories.
On any given day, Suzuki will spew out five thousand bikes, Yamaha nine thousand, and Honda an eyebrow-raising twelve thousand. Eyebrow raising at least to the BMW engineers who believe that mass production leads to mass compromise, and who limit the production of BMW's to less than one hundred machines a day. At BMW, we believe speed limits should be observed by the people who build motorcycles, not just the people who ride them.
BMW. The legendary motorcycles of Germany.

260

(MUSIC)

SALIERI: Are we going to appall you with something confidential and disgusting? Let's hope so. Because that is what you really like. Unconfessed crimes of buried wickedness. If that is what brings you to us . . . The prospect of hearing horrors . . . You shall not go unrewarded.

A: What a story!

B: What a scandal!

A: You hear it all over.

B: The cafes.

A: The opera.

B: The gutter.

A: I don't believe it.

B: Who can believe it?

A: What horror have you heard?

B: Tell us.

A: Tell us.

B: About Wolfgang . . .

A: Amadeus . . .

B: Mozart.

A: Mozart.

B: Mozart!

A: Mozart was dying.

B: He claimed he'd been poisoned.

A: Some say he accused a man.

B: Some say the man was Salieri.

A: Salieri.

B: I don't believe it.

A: Is it just possible?

B: Did Salieri murder Amadeus?

A: Amadeus. The man. The music. The murder. The madness. . . . And now, the motion picture.

B: The city hisses it from mouth to mouth.

A: Amadeus. Everything you've heard is true.

261

ANNCR: What you're about to hear is history in the making. The first time two car telephone systems have been put to the ultimate test. A road test. To see which one can carry a conversation further without static, fading or breaking up. In one car, Bell Atlantic's Alex; in an identical car, Cellular One.

(SFX: CARS STARTING THEIR ENGINES)

On April 12 they went north on I-95 from the Capital Beltway and this is the actual recording of what happened 14 miles up the road.

Hello . . . Hello . . . Hello, can you hear me? Hello, Bell?

(LOTS OF STATIC)

You are starting to break up. I can hardly hear you now. Bell. . . ?

Bell went off the air after just 14 miles, while Cellular One went more than 62 miles to Baltimore and beyond.

I just crossed from Baltimore into Harvard County and I hear you perfectly. You sound great.

So before you buy any car phone, take it for a drive. A long drive. And you'll discover that there's only one that goes the distance . . . Cellular One.

ANNCR: And now, the Amoco Radio Theater.

(MUSIC: ROCK SONG CONCLUDING AND FADING OUT)

D.J.: We're back with Chrissy, lead singer from the Bodily Functions. And that was a tune called . . .

CHRISSY: "Love."

D.J.: Off your latest LP "World War 19."

CHRISSY: That's right.

(INDIFFERENT ATTITUDE).

D.J.: Welcome aboard.

CHRISSY: Thanks.

D.J.: You just got back off a big tour.

CHRISSY: Hundred and fifty cities.

D.J.: Wow! That must've taken a while, huh.

CHRISSY: Week and a half.

D.J.: What is it about "The Road"?

CHRISSY: It's the driving.

D.J.: I see what your saying. Tramps like us . . . running against the wind . . .

CHRISSY: No, I mean driving.

D.J.: Right. What do you remember most about "The Road"?

CHRISSY (SIGHS): Amoco.

D.J.: Oh, I see what you're saying. The red, white, and blue—the strength—quality—the experience.

CHRISSY: No, Amoco gas stations.

D.J.: Right. Gasoline. Sure, sure.

CHRISSY: Yeah, we have an Amoco credit card.

D.J.: Ohhhh, plastic! That's sort of a thematic element in your work.

CHRISSY: No, well, we like it because it's an easy way to buy Amoco gasoline.

D.J.: I see what you're saying. There are places, places you've been . . .

CHRISSY: We drove to Amoco.

D.J.: Right. Well, let's uhh, go back to the L.P.

(MUSIC ROCK SONG UP AND UNDER)

ANNCR: Brought to you by Amoco—We go that extra mile.

JOEY: So I'm walking down the street yesterday, and I hear this guy yell, Hey, Joey!

(SONG:) *Seeing you now, again*

JOEY: My old roommate from college—hadn't seen him in years.

(SONG:) *Thinking of how*

JOEY: Almost didn't recognize him.

(SONG:) *I knew you when*

JOEY: He was wearing a tie.

(SONG:) *Though years have come between us*

JOEY: Kept his beard, though.

(SONG:) *We still see eye to eye with love that shines*

JOEY: Real good seeing him.

(SONG:) *As time goes by*

ANNCR: Remember the great times of your life on Kodacolor VR films. The sharpest, brightest, most dazzling line of color print films Kodak has ever made. There's no better, more beautiful way to color your memories.

JOEY: Then he showed me a picture of his kid.

(SONG:) *We're still a perfect fit*

JOEY: Is he cute!

(SONG:) *You haven't changed a bit*

JOEY: So I asked him what he named him.

(SONG:) *Looking fine . . .*

JOEY: Know what he said?

(SONG:) *As time . . .*

JOEY: Joey.

(SONG:) *Goes by*

ANNCR: Kodak. Because time goes by.

(SFX: TWO TEENAGE BOYS OBVIOUSLY HALF IN THE BAG AND ENJOYING THEMSELVES)

KID 1: Now where are those car keys?

KID 2: I don't know. Maybe they're back in the bar?

HAL D: When New Jersey raised its drinking age to 21, and New York's stayed at 19, a lot of Jersey teenagers found a new place to drink. New York.

(CAR STARTED) Because it's easy to drive across the border for a night of drinking.

KID 2: The light's red.

HAL: The hard part is the trip back.

KID 1: Hey watch out . . . we're gonna . . . !!!

HAL: Watch Jim Jensen's report: "Drinking and the Border War." Tonight on Channel 2 News at 6. The life you save may be your kid's.

265

265

BARRY: What time does the Walt Disney movie "Jungle Book" go on?

BOX OFFICE: "Jungle Book" is starting in five minutes.

BARRY: Oh great. I'll have one ticket, please.

BOX OFFICE: Adult or child?

BARRY: Uh—child.

BOX OFFICE: Where is the child?

BARRY: I'm the child.

BOX OFFICE: You're the child?

BARRY: Yeah, see my sucker? It's raspberry—

BOX OFFICE: Wait a minute. You're at least 16 years old.

BARRY: No I'm not. See, I even got a yo-yo—

BOX OFFICE: But you're not a child!

BARRY: Not so loud! Look, I'll pay for an adult, but give me a child's ticket, okay?

BOX OFFICE: Look, see this uniform? I can't do that!

BARRY: Shhhh!—Listen, if any of my buddies catch me going to see a Walt Disney movie like "Jungle Book," I'll be laughed right out of—

BOX OFFICE: So don't see "Jungle Book."

BARRY: Huh?

BOX OFFICE: Next door we got "The Incredible Zits."

BARRY: I don't wanna see "The Incredible Zits," I wanna see "Jungle Book."

BOX OFFICE: Yeah?

BARRY: When I was a kid, I remember Mowgli—

BOX OFFICE: Yeah.

BARRY: —and the bear—

BOX OFFICE: Sure.

BARRY: —and the snake—

BOX OFFICE: Okay.

BARRY: —and the tiger and the monkey—

(SFX: FOOTSTEPS ON)

ACE: Hey hey, Barry! You goin' to the movies too, huh?

BARRY: Oh, uh, hi, uh, Ace!
(AHEM) One ticket for "The Incredible Zits," please.

BOX OFFICE: There ya go. Next!

BARRY (GOING OFF): Uh, see you inside, Ace.

ACE: Oh yeah yeah right, uh—What time does "Jungle Book" start?

BOX OFFICE: In four minutes, and I can't sell you a child's ticket, either.

ACE: Why not?

BOX OFFICE: Look, you're at least 16 years old—

ACE: I am not—

BOX OFFICE: —you got wrinkles all over your face—

ACE: —do not—

BOX OFFICE (FADE): —look at the shoes you're wearing—!

ANNCR: Rated G. All ages admitted.

266

WOMAN: My daughter Tiffany said she wanted to do something totally awesome for her sweet 16.
I said I'll put a little round laughing cow in a red net bag on a silver platter and surround it with orchids.
She said that's cute, ma, but it isn't awesome. Better you should put it in mink and drive it up in a stretch limo.
I said, Tiffany, watch my lips. The laughing cow isn't an animal act, it's cheese.
She said will the girls be impressed with Laughing Cow cheese on a cracker?
I said, Tiffany, your girlfriends have so many birds on their antennae, they wouldn't be impressed with a dancing bear on a bagel. But they'll love the Laughing Cow. Mild Mini Bonbel and Nippy Mini Babybel. Five little round cheeses in their own red net bags. Delicious. Natural. Bite-size. Freshly wrapped in wax with an easy-open zip.
She said it sounds good to me, ma.
So we served the Laughing Cow at Tiffany's sweet 16 and all her friends were impressed except Heather Rubini who expected a real cow and brought a bale of alfalfa. So everybody had cheese with a roll in the hay. I want to tell you it was awesome.

ANNCR: Mini Bonbel. Mini Babybel. Just two in a selection of delectable cheeses by the Laughing Cow. Look for all of them in your dairy case. And put a smile in your stomach.

267

(SFX: BOB AND RAY WALKING DOWN A QUIET STREET, BIRDS CHIRPING, ETC.)

BOB: Are you sure this bullhorn idea is going to work?

RAY (THROUGH A BULLHORN): COME OUT, WE KNOW YOU'RE IN THERE. YOU! YEAH, YOU IN THE BROWN HOUSE. YOU REALLY NEED A HOME IMPROVEMENT LOAN.

MAN: Get outta here.

BOB: But what about The Arizona Bank?

RAY: Let them get their own bullhorn.

BOB: No, I mean everybody already knows The Arizona Bank has loans for everything. From blimps to boats . . .

RAY: Boats! That's a good one.
(BULLHORN) HEY YOU! IMAGINE HOW NICE A *BEAUTIFUL* BOAT WOULD LOOK IN FRONT OF THIS DUMP.

MAN (VOICE FAR AWAY): Get off my lawn!

RAY: Okay, okay.

BOB: And Ray, don't forget The Arizona Bank has terrific rates.

RAY: Well, once people realize that the Bank of Bob and Ray has (BULLHORN) DOUGH TO BLOW, they'll forget all about The Arizona Bank. Watch this.
(BULLHORN) HEY LADY, CAN WE LEND YOU SOME MONEY?

WOMAN (VERY UPSET): Leave me *alone!*

BOB: Nice work. Our first customer.

VO: For business or consumer loans, The Arizona Bank. It's pretty hard to beat. An equal housing lender. Member FDIC.

MILES: I have a solution to your sore ankle problems.

PAT: It's awright, it's awright, I got my own solution.

MILES: What's that?

PAT: Before I play tennis or if I go for a run, I stuff two cats into my sweat socks.

MILES: Live cats?

PAT: Biff 'n Rex.

MILES: And what supports your ankles?

PAT: Soon as ya start runnin', see, the cats they grab onto yer ankles. The quicker ya run the tighter they hold on, that's the more support that yer gettin' for yer ankles.

MILES: And you don't have any problems with Biff 'n Rex there?

PAT: Occasionally a little kitty litter, that's about it.

MILES: Well, look, I have a much better idea. It's called the All American S'port Wrap. It's the newest support system on the market. S'port Wrap's figure eight design makes it easy to put on, easy to adjust and you don't need pins or metal clips.

PAT: Found that I wear a size nine and a half siamese.

MILES: Well the S'port Wrap comes in sizes to fit any foot.

PAT: Okay where do I find it?

MILES: At your favorite drug store. Just look for the S'port Wrap display.

PAT: Another big advantage would be that you could wear S'port Wrap on both ankles and they'll never fight.

MILES: Fight?

PAT: Yeah, I was runnin' last week and for no reason Biff 'n Rex get into this fight. Well, before I knew it, I had cat spit all the way up to my knees.

MILES: Well, just get the All American S'port Wrap.

PAT: That cat spit, ya know, it defoliated my legs.

BILL COSBY: Today on the Bill Cosby Jell-O Pudding Show this is a test of the mom's-gonna-remember-to-make-Jell-O Pudding system. For the next few seconds you will hear the sound of a kid sighing because her mom forgot to make her smooth, creamy, easy-to-make Jello-O Pudding.

KID: Ahhh . . .

BILL COSBY: This was only a test. It was not a real mom-forgot-to-make-Jell-O Pudding situation 'cause you moms would never do that, would you? Nah.

ANNCR: Jell-O Pudding. It's probably on your shelf. Why not put it on your table?

BILL COSBY: This was only a test.

VO.: Did you know that your heart is a muscle? Most people think it's something much more exotic than that . . . but it's not . . . it's just a muscle. Now, grasp that large muscle on the underside of your leg. What do you feel? Is it hard and strong . . . or is it soft and flabby? That muscle in your leg has been around just as long as that muscle called your heart has been around. They were born on the same day. Everything you've done over the years to build and strengthen one, has built and strengthened the other one. And, sadly enough . . . if you've let one go, you've let the other one go. But the great thing about your body is, the day you start to do something about it, it responds. In fact, within 30 minutes of doing our exercise regime at Cosmopolitan, your body begins to reverse itself from all the years of too much food, too much stress and too little movement. Come on, give us a call. We've got the answer at Cosmopolitan Health and Fitness Centers.

("RAINDROPS" MUSIC ON INTERCOM OF CROWDED SCHOOL CAFETERIA)

MR. WILSON: Hi, Jamie.

JAMIE: Hi, Mr. Wilson.

MR. WILSON: Say, is that a Washington apple you have in your lunch?

JAMIE: Yep.

MR. WILSON: When I was a kid, we gave Red Delicious apples like that to our teacher.

JAMIE: Oh.

MR. WILSON: So how about it?

JAMIE: What?

MR. WILSON: Aren't you going to give me that apple?

JAMIE: No way.

MR. WILSON: Give it to me.

MRS. M.: What's going on here?

MR. WILSON: I was just trying to explain to Jamie that Washington apples are the apples picky apple pickers pick.

JAMIE: Yeah, And he was trying to pick mine.

MR. WILSON: I was not.

MRS. M.: Mr. Wilson, I think you should move to another table.

MR. WILSON: Fine.

(PAUSE)

MR. WILSON (FROM ACROSS ROOM): Hi, Billy, is that a Washington apple you have in your lunchbox?

ANNCR: A message from the Washington State Apple Commission.

272

INTERVIEWER: Today thousands of people will shop at Highland Appliance, but who and why? Let's find out. Sir, your name and what do you do?

DISCLAIMER: Phil Merlo. I'm a disclaimer-er.

INTVR: You mean you make disclaimers?

DISCLAIMER: Except in Arkansas and Nebraska.

INTVR: And you disclaim everything?

DISCLAIMER: While supplies last.

INTVR: I see. Now, Mr. Merlo, what do you know about Highland's Low Price Guarantee?

DISCLAIMER: It's at participating stores only. Void where prohibited.

INTVR: That's not true. It's available at every Highland store.

DISCLAIMER: Limit one to a customer.

INTVR: No. You see, if you buy something at *any* Highland . . .

DISCLAIMER: Allow four to six months for delivery.

INTVR: And then see it for less within 30 days . . .

DISCLAIMER: Minus shipping, handling and dealer prep.

INTVR: Ahem. Highland will refund you the difference plus 10% of the difference. And that's guaranteed in writing.

DISCLAIMER: Family and friends of employees are ineligible and may not apply for cash bonus or other prizes.

INTVR: Mr. Merlo, Highland's Low Price Guarantee always lives up to its promise.

DISCLAIMER (DISAPPOINTED): Oh . . .

INTVR: That's why it's such a good guarantee.

DISCLAIMER: And safe, when used as directed.

ANNCR: Highland. Everything you never expected from an appliance store.

DISCLAIMER: The characters in this commercial are fictitious. Any resemblance to real persons, living or dead, is purely coincidental.

273

Hello there. I want to tell you about a very fine imported beer called Kronenbourg—Kronenbourg Beer: 'Better, not Bitter'. . . that's the slogan, you see. Ah, but I hear you cry "Sorry partner, we've got 300 imported beers in the US of A already, shucks why should we try another?" Because Kronenbourg is the largest selling bottle of beer in the whole of Europe, a really superb imported beer. "Oh yea," you reply, "you're an Englisher, what do you know about beer, England has the worst beer in the world, nasty warm sticky stuff with various forms of pond life in it." Exactly! It is precisely because English beer is so awful that we are such experts on imported beers. So as an expert, I'm recommending Kronenbourg . . . Europe's No. 1 bottle of beer 'Better, not Bitter.' However there is one slight disadvantage to Kronenbourg . . . this advertising slogan 'Better, not Bitter.' Not the most exciting slogan I'm afraid, but never mind, you can't have everything and it doesn't affect the taste of this superb beer. So drink Kronenbourg beer, imported by Kronenbourg USA, Greenwich, Connecticut. 'Better, not Bitter' . . . and sorry about the slogan.

274

ANNCR: Time now for helpful tips for drive-up teller customers, brought to you by American Bank's Mint24.

(SFX: BING!)

FEMALE VOICE: One.

ANNCR: Check the sign above the lane. If it says "Closed," it could mean a long wait.

(SFX: BING!)

F.V.: Two.

ANNCR: Avoid lanes where the closer the drivers are to the teller, the more they need a shave.

(SFX: BING!)

F.V.: Three.

ANNCR: Avoid lanes in which all the cars' license plates are expired.

(SFX: BING!)

F.V.: Four.

ANNCR: Use Mint24 instead. With 52 locations in American Bank branches and 7-Eleven stores, Mint24 means banking when you want it, where you need it. Fast.

275

ANNCR: You're talking with your best friend. She says . . .

WOMAN: I'd love to go with you tonight, but I can't.

ANNCR: . . . but she says it with her hand to her mouth. Which is a signal that may mean . . .

WOMAN: I don't want to go with you tonight.

ANNCR: You tell her how disappointed you are. She says . . .

WOMAN: Oh, I know we'd have a great time.

ANNCR: . . . but she says it while she scratches her neck. Which is a signal that may mean . . .

WOMAN: I don't even know if we'd have a so-so time.

ANNCR: You tell her you'd love to go with her tomorrow, then. She says . . .

WOMAN: Yes, let's try for tomorrow.

ANNCR: . . . but she says it while she touches her nose. Which is a signal that may mean . . .

WOMANN: I'm not going to try very hard.

ANNCR: You tell her that, if she can't go, you won't go at all. She rubs her eye. Which is a signal that may mean . . .

WOMAN: Now *you're* lying.

ANNCR: All these signals are, of course, unconscious. But they may communicate more than words. And the December Reader's Digest shows how to interpret body language. Every month, more people read—really *read*—The Digest than anything else . . . and come away understanding the difference between what's said and what's meant. We make a difference in 53 million lives.

BILL COSBY: Today on the Bill Cosby Jell-O Pudding Show this is a test of the mom's-gonna-remember-to-make-Jell-O Pudding system. For the next few seconds you will hear the sound of a kid sighing because her mom forgot to make her smooth, creamy, easy-to-make Jell-O Pudding.

KID: Ahhh . . .

BILL COSBY: This was only a test. It was not a real mom-forgot-to-make-Jell-O Pudding situation 'cause you moms would never do that, would you? Nah.

ANNCR: Jell-O Pudding. It's probably on your shelf. Why not put it on your table?

BILL COSBY: This was only a test.

(SFX: PHONE, QUICK RING AND PICK UP:)

DANNY: Hello.

CATHI: Hi. You busy? You're busy.

DANNY: No, no. How are you?

CATHI: I dunno.

DANNY: I got a letter from your mother.

CATHI: You did? What'd she say?

DANNY: Oh nothin'. But, it was nice . . . y'know. She . . . she wanted to know if we were gonna get back together soon and stuff like that.

CATHI: Yeah.

DANNY: Hey . . . I got a new car.

CATHI: What did you get?

DANNY: A Camaro.

CATHI: What color?

(LAUGH)

BOTH: Black with tan interior.

CATHI: Well, sounds like you got what you wanted.

DANNY: Yeah . . . and I was wondering if . . . uh . . . you'd want to take a little drive, like Carmel for the weekend. And we'd be cruising along . . .

CATHI (OVER DANNY): In the Camaro.

DANNY: . . . Looking at the ocean and then, I was gonna ask if we could, uh . . .

CATHI: Get together?

DANNY (WITH CATHI): Get together. Yeah.

CATHI: Yes.

DANNY: Yes?

CATHI: Yes.

DANNY: Is that yes to getting together or yes to Carmel?

CATHI: Well, I figure we can go to Carmel to celebrate getting back together . . .

DANNY (OVER CATHI): Yeah. Great . . .

CATHI: . . . and your new Camaro.

DANNY: *Our* new Camaro.

CATHI: Oh. *Yes.* I like the sound of that.

(SFX: CAMARO SYNTHESIZER DRIVE AWAY)

DAVID: Life seems a little bit better in a Camaro by Chevrolet.

(MUSIC: UP AND UNDER)

ANNCR: And now, the Amoco Radio Theatre.

(MUSIC: FADES OUT)

MAN #1: Hey Tommy, great car!

TOMMY: Yeah, brand new—right off the lot.

MAN #1: Let's go for a spin.

TOMMY: All right.

(SFX: CAR DOOR OPENING)

CAR: Please fasten your seat belt.

TOMMY (LAUGHTER)

MAN #1: What?

CAR: Please fasten your seat belt.

MAN #1: What are you, a ventriloquist?

TOMMY: No, the car talks.

MAN #1: Terrific!

TOMMY: Check this out!

(SFX: CAR STARTING, RUNNING ENGINE UP & UNDER)

CAR: All working systems are in order.

TOMMY: Real high tech, huh?

MAN #1: Yeah.

CAR: A door is ajar.

TOMMY: No, a door is a door.

CAR: A door is ajar.

TOMMY: Close the door, close the door.

MAN #1: Oh yeah, sorry, got it.

CAR: Your gas gauge is low.

TOMMY: Oh thanks. I'll pull into this station right over here.

CAR: No —Amoco

TOMMY: What?

CAR: Amoco.

MAN #1: Why Amoco?

CAR: Amoco is rated the highest quality gasoline in America. Drivers across America overwhelmingly named Amoco as the brand they buy for quality.

TOMMY: I didn't know that.

CAR: Maybe that's why you've gone through 8 cars in the last 6 months.

TOMMY: Yeah, probably right, well, Amoco it is then. Amoco. Thank you.

MAN #1: Yeah, then maybe we'll get a bite to eat.

TOMMY: How about some Chinese, huh?

MAN #1: How about Italian?

CAR: There's a new sushi bar in town.

TOMMY: I don't know where it is.

CAR: No problem, I'll take you there.

(MUSIC: UP AND UNDER)

ANNCR: Brought to you by Amoco. We go that extra mile.

(MUSIC: UP AND OUT)

279

(SFX: MUSIC UNDER)

Japan's premier motorcycle journalist proclaimed them to be "motorcycles in which no flaws could be found." Japan's leading enthusiast magazine devoted an entire issue to their introduction. They were, in fact, the most honored motorcycles in Japanese history. But they weren't Japanese. BMW introduces the K-Series. The four-cylinder high performance bikes that offer the lightest weight, the lowest center of gravity, the broadest powerband, the best aerodynamics and the longest warranty of virtually any 1000cc machines in the world today.
The BMW K-Series. The most honored motorcycles in Japan are the legendary motorcycles of Germany.

280

ANNCR: Some people think that preseason games are boring. That might be true in some sports, but not hockey.
See, when a bunch of guys go out to play hockey, they start bumping into each other.
At first it's just a kind of an accident.
But then some player always mistakes one of those accidental bumps for an on-purpose bump, and he starts bumping into people on purpose real hard.
Then, pretty soon, all the guys are so busy bumping into each other real hard on purpose that they forget the game really doesn't count because it's an exhibition game.
And you can bet that's how things are going to work out when the North Stars play four tough teams at home this exhibition season.
Teams like Philadelphia, Edmonton, Washington and Chicago, they get mad real easy when you start bumping into them.
So, an exhibition game only means the other guys can't hurt you in the standings. It doesn't mean they can't hurt you on the ice.

281

CROWD/BACKGROUND: Let's toast the bride and groom, the happy couple.

WOMAN: Ah . . .

MAN: You're not toasting.

WOMAN: Ah . . . I'm . . . no . . . I'm not very fond of champagne, you know.

MAN: Really?

WOMAN: I hate to admit it, but I'm not. Ah . . . ah . . . anyway yours looks very different than mine, it's got a *big* head on it (LAUGHS) its . . .

MAN: Mine is very special champagne.

WOMAN: It's much more golden looking . . . (LAUGHS) what have you got there?

MAN: Imported from Canada!

WOMAN: I don't know any Canadian champagne.

MAN: They call it beer.

WOMAN (LAUGHS)

MAN: Beer . . . is what I wanted.

WOMAN: That's what I figured . . . (LAUGHS)

MAN: Wait a minute. Are you a friend of the bride or groom?

WOMAN: The groom, an . . . old friend.

MAN: So, you won't give me away . . .

WOMAN: No. (LAUGHS)

MAN: . . . if I offer you some Molson Golden.

WOMAN: Absolutely not!!!

HOMELESS: I've been sleeping on the street for about four months, but I can't really sleep because I'm afraid of getting killed. One time I had a .38 put up to my head. I could see the bullets on each side of the barrel. It's like living like a . . . like a hunted animal.

When I get hungry I steal food from the garbage and cut off the rotten parts. Sometimes I get lucky, hustle a buck or two for coffee. But most people pass me by like I'm not even alive. Like I don't even exist.

YUPPIE: Well I live on Gramercy Park. I live right on the park. I have a fabulous apartment. It's about nine and a half rooms. When I want to get away I just hop on a sea plane and go right to my house on Fire Island.

I work out each and every day. I run. I belong to several health clubs in New York. I think energy is a very important part of my life. My favorite restaurant is a little place off the Amalfi Coast in Italy. I'm a firm believer in living well.

ANNCR: There's a diversity of people and issues that continually shape New York City. And no one reflects that better than New York Magazine. After all, if we didn't read the city, the city wouldn't read us. New York Magazine.

YUPPIE: Life's been great to me.

HOMELESS: Somehow I will survive.

(SFX: SHOP BELL)

CUSTOMER: Hello . . .

ASSISTANT: . . . Dolly! Louis Armstrong 1964.

CUSTOMER: Er . . . yes . . . these tapes you sold me, the sound's starting to fade away.

ASSISTANT: "Fade Away," Buddy Holly '58. Flip side of "Peggy Sue."

CUSTOMER: Yes, that's all very well, but these tapes are no good.

ASSISTANT: "No good" . . . hard one that . . . Carol King 1968 er . . . February.

CUSTOMER (ANGRY): I demand some satisfaction!!

ASSISTANT: Bombombombombombombom . . . Stones '65, September, two weeks at No. 1.

CUSTOMER (VERY ANGRY): Look, these tapes have faded. They're useless! and I DEMAND YOU DO SOMETHING!

ASSISTANT (SINGING): *Something to me* . . . Connie Francis 1953.

VO: If your favourites are fading, it could be your tape.

Look for Sony's new range of see-through audio tapes and get true sound time after time. Remember Sony.

CUSTOMER: Right! Right! That's it! Okay! Come outside!

ASSISTANT (SINGING): *Come outside, there's a lovely moon out there.*
Mike Sarne, Wendy Richards.
Fabulous record. Gee, you got a good memory for songs.

VOCALS: *She's waiting there*
Like she has
A hundred times before

It's quitting time
And I can see her
Looking out the window
By the door.

Soon she'll be telling me,
How she spent her day,
With open arms
She'll just smile and say,

This Bud's for you
For all you do,
The king of beers
Is coming through

For all you do,
This Bud's for you
For all you do,
This Bud's for you.

ANNCR: Anheuser-Busch, St. Louis, Mo.

TELEVISION FINALISTS

1985 Television Finalists

Consumer Television Over :30 (:45/:60/:90) Single

285
ART DIRECTORS
Jeff Vetter
Richard Williams

WRITER
Mark Choate

CLIENT
Anheuser-Busch/Budweiser

PRODUCTION CO.
Kira Films

AGENCY
D'Arcy MacManus Masius/
St. Louis

286
ART DIRECTOR
Howard Benson

WRITER
Barry Biederman

CLIENT
ITT

DIRECTOR
Owen Roizman

PRODUCTION CO.
Roizman Short Visual
Productions

AGENCY PRODUCERS
Howard Benson
Jean Galton

AGENCY
Biederman & Company

287
ART DIRECTORS
Tim Mellors
Steve Grounds

WRITERS
Tim Mellors
Steve Grounds

CLIENT
British Airways

DIRECTOR
Tony Scott

PRODUCTION CO.
Ridley Scott Associates

AGENCY PRODUCER
Maureen Rickerd

AGENCY
Saatchi & Saatchi
Compton/London

288
ART DIRECTOR
Steve Ohman

WRITER
Harold Karp

CLIENT
W.R. Grace

PRODUCTION CO.
Steve Horn Productions

AGENCY PRODUCER
Mindy Gerber

AGENCY
The Marschalk Company

285

(MUSIC: BUDWEISER MELODY UNDER)

(SFX: CONTINUOUS MINING MACHINE)

COALMINER (VO): People in this part of the country's been minin' coal for a lot of years.
Me and the rest of these guys we learned from our Dads and our Grandads . . .

You know . . . kinda carryin' on the tradition.
It's like the guys on this shift.

We all grew up together.
They're good guys . . . and they know what they're doin' . . . and they're good at it.
I guarantee ya, aren't many men can do what we do, let alone do it as good.

(SFX: BAR PRESENCE)

ANNCR (VO): It's for guys like Dan Jagielski that we make sure every Budweiser is the best it can be. Made with the choicest ingredients, exclusive Beechwood aging, and brewed with the kind of pride Dan puts into his work.
So to Dan and all you guys out there like him . . .

SINGERS: *For all you do . . .*

ANNCR (VO): This Bud's for you.

286

ANNCR (VO): When a road is slippery, braking your car can cause skidding . . . or worse.

(SFX)

ANNCR (VO): You can see why on this test track. The surface is wet and slippery. When wheels lock here, your car can go out of control.

(SFX)

ANNCR (VO): Now Teves, an ITT company, has developed an anti-lock brake system that keeps wheels from locking when they shouldn't. The ITT Teves braking system has a built-in computer. It senses what's happening to your wheels. It automatically pumps the brakes faster than any driver could.

(SFX)

ANNCR (VO): This ITT brake system is beginning to reach cars this year. Not a winter too soon.

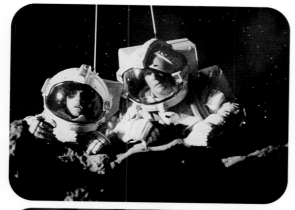

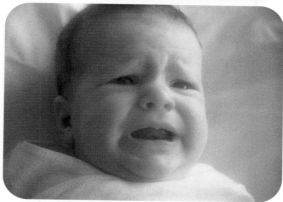

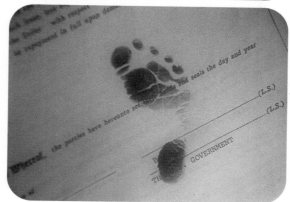

287

1ST ASTRONAUT: Go, go, go!!

2ND ASTRONAUT: Where is he going now?

ASTRONAUTS:: No!!!

(VO): When you're next away from home and in need of a little help, it's worth remembering British Airways has people in more places than any other airline.

TICKET AGENT: Smoking or non-smoking?

ASTRONAUTS: Non-smoking!!

(VO): British Airways.
The World's Favourite Airline

288

(SFX: FOOTSTEPS.)

MAN: Morning.
Shall we get down to business?

Now that you've joined us, you'll enjoy numerous rights and privileges. But you will share certain problems as well.

Specifically, you owe the United States government, in round numbers, $50,000.

BABY: Waaaaahhhhh.

ANNCR (VO): If federal deficits continue at their current rate, it's as if every baby born in 1985 will have a $50,000 debt strapped to its back.

MAN: Let us review these figures for you.

ANNCR (VO): At W.R. Grace & Co., we're not looking for someone to blame. We're too busy crying out for help.

Write to Congress.
If you don't think that'll do it, run for Congress.

289
ART DIRECTOR
Mary Means
WRITERS
Tom Mabley
Bob Sarlin
CLIENT
IBM
DIRECTOR
Stu Hagmann
PRODUCTION CO.
H.I.S.K.
AGENCY PRODUCER
Robert L. Dein
AGENCY
Lord, Geller, Federico,
Einstein

290
ART DIRECTOR
Alan Lerner
WRITER
Chris Matyszczyk
CLIENT
Grenvilles
DIRECTOR
Sid Roberson
PRODUCTION CO.
Sid Roberson
AGENCY PRODUCER
Ross McClellan
AGENCY
Ogilvy & Mather/London

291
ART DIRECTORS
Lou DiJoseph
Don Easdon
WRITER
Lee Kovel
CLIENT
Dr. Pepper
DIRECTOR
Bob Brooks
PRODUCTION CO.
BFCS
AGENCY PRODUCER
Laurie Kahn
AGENCY
Young & Rubicam

292
ART DIRECTOR
Ken Grimshaw
WRITER
John Donnelly
CLIENT
British Telecom
DIRECTOR
Paul Weiland
PRODUCTION CO.
Paul Weiland Productions
AGENCY PRODUCER
Nigel Foster
AGENCY
KMP Partnership/London

289

ANNCR (VO): In this rapidly changing world, even the
brightest and best manager in the company may
need more than a loyal staff to run a smooth
operation.
For, when headquarters calls and pressure
builds, it becomes harder to keep things rolling
without running into mixups, losing control of
the operation, and falling behind.
For rapid improvement, a manager could use a
tool for modern times, the IBM Personal
Computer . . . for smoother scheduling, better
planning, and greater productivity.
It can help a manager excel and . . . become a
big wheel in the company. The IBM Personal
Computer.
See it at a store near you.

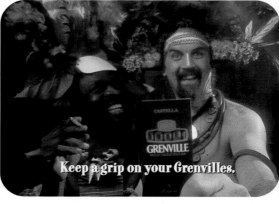

290

MAN (GARBLED): UGAMANAC?

WOMAN: KANTA GYA? CHIMAWOMO GYA?
HANSATOLEMO GYA. . . . . .
(Where's the dinner? Why haven't you put the
kids to bed? I'm out all day bringing home the
bacon. . . . .)

WOMAN: HAMA GRENVILLE GYA
(No Grenvilles tonight)

CONNOLLY: WHAAAT?

CONNOLLY (SINGS): ÍNSTALÁMAVANA
GRENVILLE. . . .
*(But if it wasnae for your Grenvilles
Where would you be?
In the grip of the jitters and baritone titters that
go with lunacy
Without this one indulgence there's no solidarity
So you've got to keep a grip on your Grenvilles.)*

(ALL MEN SING):
*(Coz if it wasnae for your Grenvilles
Where would you be?
Down and out
A layabout
Your tail between your knees
It's time to make a stand, d'ye ken?
And be what you want to be.
And just keep a grip on your Grenvilles)*

291

JAPANESE MAN: The monster! Godzilla! The monster.

AMERICAN REPORTER: We must stop Godzilla before he destroys the city.
I'm saying a prayer . . . a prayer for the whole world. What could he want? Unless we find something to appease him . . . We're doomed.

CHORUS: *Hold out, hold out for the out of the ordinary, hold out for Dr Pepper.*
Don't be sold out, hold out, it's a taste that's extraordinary, no doubt it's Dr Pepper, Dr Pepper.

GODZILLA (SFX) BURP!

292

CUSTER: Eat lead yew varmints.

(SFX: TELEPHONE BELLS.)

(VO): It's for you-ooo!

CUSTER: For me?

INDIANS: It's for you!

CUSTER: Hello?
It's reinforcements boys! . . .

INDIANS: Gasp!

CUSTER: And they'll be here in the mornin'!

INDIANS: In the mornin!

(VO): The phone.
It's for you to say you're on your way.

293
ART DIRECTOR
Dean Hanson
WRITER
Tom McElligott
CLIENT
Minnesota Federal Savings &
Loan
PRODUCTION CO.
James Productions
AGENCY PRODUCER
Judy Carter
AGENCY
Fallon McElligott Rice/Mpls.

294
ART DIRECTOR
Steve Gilbert
WRITER
Mike Gallagher
CLIENT
Anheuser-Busch/Budweiser
PRODUCTION CO.
Production Partners
AGENCY PRODUCER
·Craig MacGowan
AGENCY
D'Arcy MacManus Masius/
St. Louis

295
ART DIRECTOR
Bud Watts
WRITER
Greg Taubeneck
CLIENT
United Airlines
PRODUCTION CO.
Griner/Cuesta
AGENCY PRODUCER
Michael Rafayko
AGENCY
Leo Burnett USA/Chicago

293

(MUSIC)

(VO): All across Minnesota, banks are quietly
    notifying their customers that they're raising the
    price of checking . . . while their customers are
    not so quietly reacting.

(MUSIC CONTINUES)

(VO): If your bank is charging you more for
    checking, don't just get mad . . . get even.
    Call the Minnesota Federal checking hotline at
    333-1081, and you may be shocked to discover
    just how much you can save on checking.
    Minnesota Federal.
    We not only lower your cost of checking . . . we
    lower your blood pressure.

294

(MUSICAL FANFARE)

SINGER: *This Bud's for you.*

SINGER: *There's no one
    Else who does it
    Quite the way you do . . .
    So here's to you . . .*

SINGER: *You know it isn't
    Only what you say
    It's what you do*

(SFX: ENGINE REVS)

SINGER: *For all you do
    This Bud's for you.*

(SFX: ENGINE REVS)

SINGER: *For all you do*

(SFX: CRASHING DEBRIS)

SINGER: *For all you do*

SINGER: *This Bud's for you.*

(SFX: AIRPLANE ENGINES)

SINGER: *For all you do
    You know the king
    Of beers is coming
    Through . . .*

SINGER: *For all you do
    This Bud's for you.*

(SFX: AIRPLANE)

295

MUSIC: (UNITED HOOK)

FLIGHT ATTEND'T: Good luck.

GUY: Thanks

SINGERS: *You're not just another face*
Along the way
To another place

MAN #1: Sorry. Can't use 'em.

(MUSIC: ACCENT)

MAN #2: Maybe next year.

MAN #3: Don't need them. Great lunch.

SINGERS: *You're the pride of United's friendly skies.*

FLIGHT ATTEND'T: Dinner?

GUY: Oh, not just now.

FLIGHT ATTEND'T: Rough day?

GUY: Twice that!

FLIGHT ATTEND'T: Hey, tomorrow's another day.

GUY: (GRABS OLIVE)

MUSIC: (ACCENT)

MAN #4: Wish you'd been here yesterday.

MAN #5: No, they're not right for us.

MAN #6: Uh-uh.

SINGERS: *Got so many ways to fly ya*
We're United standin' by ya

FLIGHT ATTEND'T (TO GUY): Can you help out a dead
battery in eighteen B?

GUY: Sure. I got nothing to add up anyway.

OTHER GUY: Tough trip, huh? What business you in?

SINGERS: *You're not just flying*
You're flying the friendly skies

OTHER GUY: Now you're sure you can have three
hundred and fifty million of 'em to me on the
first?

SINGERS: *You're not just flying*

FLIGHT ATTEND'T: How was the trip?

SALES: Not bad.

SINGERS: *You're flying*
The friendly skies.

296
ART DIRECTOR
Bob Isherwood
WRITER
Jack Vaughan
CLIENT
Rentokil
DIRECTOR
Tony Williams
PRODUCTION CO.
Marmalade Films
AGENCY PRODUCER
Lois McKenzie
AGENCY
The Campaign Palace/
Australia

297
ART DIRECTOR
Gary Johnston
WRITERS
Steve Hayden
Laurie Brandalise
CLIENT
Apple Computer
DIRECTOR
Peter Smillie
PRODUCTION CO.
Robert Abel & Associates
AGENCY PRODUCER
Richard O'Neill
AGENCY
Chiat/Day - Los Angeles

298
ART DIRECTOR
Steve Gilbert
WRITER
Gerry Mandel
CLIENT
Anheuser-Busch/Budweiser
PRODUCTION CO.
Miller Mason & Associates
AGENCY PRODUCER
John Seaton
AGENCY
D'Arcy MacManus Masius/
St. Louis

299
ART DIRECTOR
Tony Dick
WRITERS
Alan Morris
Allan Johnston
CLIENT
Australian Tourist
Commission
DIRECTORS
Tony Dick
John Cornell
PRODUCTION CO.
Ross Wood Productions
AGENCY PRODUCERS
Tony Dick
John Cornell
AGENCY
MOJO Australia

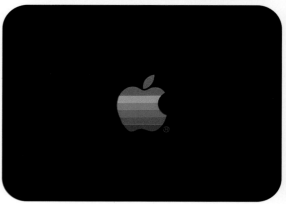

296

ANNC. (VO): Some household pests seem impossible
   to get rid of.
   So you learn to live with them.
   Even cockroaches, that, among other dirty
   habits. . . .
   . . . . carry disease organisms. . . .
   . . . . like salmonella.
   Cockroaches aren't alone of course.
(SFX: KNOCKING)
   Put up with them and you'll probably put up
   with their friends. Fleas that put the bite on
   you.
   And white ants that eat you out of house and
   home.
(SFX: CRUNCH)
   Nobody understands the nature of the beasts
   better than Rentokil.
   We can rid you of uninvited guests and keep
   them from coming back. Call Rentokil and we'll
   explain how.
   You *don't* have to live with them.

297

ANNCR VO: This is the Apple IIc Personal Computer.
   A more powerful version of the world's most
   popular personal computer.
   Even though it's rather small, it can handle an
   impressive amount of work.
   Now you'll probably use it to organize your
   personal finances . . . or your office files . . . or
   to help your kids get ahead in school.
   But with enough power to run an automated
   factory, there's no telling how far it can take
   you.
   The Apple IIc.
   It's a lot bigger than it looks.

298

(MUSIC: BUDWEISER FANFARE)

ANNCR (VO): To everyone in the spotlight before the show begins, this Bud's for you.

(MUSIC: JAMES INGRAM SOLO, VARIOUS SFX AND DIALOGUE THROUGHOUT)

SOLO VOCAL: *This Bud's for you, there's no one else who does it quite the way you do.*

CHORUS: *The way you do.*

SOLO: *So here's to you. For all you do, the king of beers is coming through.*

(MUSICAL ACCENT)

SOLO: *This Bud's for you.*

CHORUS: *For you.*

SOLO: *For all you do, the king of beers is coming through.*

ANNCR (VO): Hey, just for you, that distinctively clean, crisp taste that says Budweiser.

SOLO: *For all you do.*

INGRAM: Hey man, nice job.

ANNCR (VO): This Bud's for you.

299

PAUL HOGAN: America, you look like you need a holiday . . . a fair dinkum holiday.
In the Land of Wonder. The Land Down Under!
Now there's a few things I've gotta warn you about . . .
Firstly, you're gonna get wet.
Because the place is surrounded by water.
Ah, and you're gonna have to learn to say G'day.
'Cause every day's a good day in Australia.

GIRL: "G'day, Paul."

HOGAN: "G'day, love."
Course you'll have to get used to some of the local customs . . . like getting suntanned in the restaurant . . . playing football without a helmet . . . and calling everyone mate.
"Thanks, mate."

BARTENDER: "She's right, mate."

HOGAN: Apart from that, no worries. You'll have the time of your life in Australia . . .
'Cause we talk the same language. Although you lot do have a funny accent.
Ah, before you rush out to book your Aussie holiday, call this toll-free number for your copy of the Aussie Holiday Book.
Come on. Come and say G'day. I'll slip an extra shrimp on the barbie for you.

SINGERS: *Come and say G'day!*

300
ART DIRECTOR
Mike Fazende
WRITER
Bert Gardner
CLIENT
Control Data Institute
DIRECTOR
Greg Hoey
PRODUCTION CO.
Filmfair
AGENCY PRODUCER
Lisa Jarrard
AGENCY
Bozell & Jacobs/Mpls.

301
ART DIRECTOR
Nick Gisonde
WRITER
Charlie Breen
CLIENT
Miller Brewing/Lite
DIRECTOR
Bob Giraldi
PRODUCTION CO.
Giraldi Productions
AGENCY PRODUCER
Marc Mayhew
AGENCY
Backer & Spielvogel

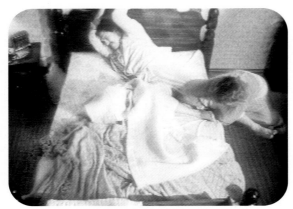

300

WIFE: Honey, you've got to go to work!

HUSBAND: No!

WIFE: Yes!

HUSBAND: No!

WIFE: Yes!

HUSBAND: No!

WIFE: Yes!

HUSBAND: No!

WIFE: Please?!

HUSBAND: No!!

ANNCR (VO): A lot of people don't look forward to
going to work in the morning.
Maybe they don't have a job they can look
forward *to*.
Maybe they don't have a job at all. Which can
make getting up even harder.
But if they like to work with their hands, they
could call Control Data Institute.
Control Data Institute has taught more than 30
thousand people the skills they need for *good*
jobs.
Jobs they can look forward to.
In a field experts say could grow 70% in the next
10 years. Computer technology.
In just 8½ months you can learn to repair
computers

You'll work with your hands, but you'll use your
head as well.
Which you can start using right now . . .
. . . by calling 1-800-TRAIN ME extension 100.
Ask about our (free) computer technology
seminar. Because going to the phone tonight can
make it easier to go to work tomorrow.

HUSBAND: Hello? Control Data Institute?

The First Lite Beer Camping Trip

MARV: This camping trip was a good idea.

GRITS: Yeah, it sure is relaxing.

BILLY: Peaceful.

CORKY: Groovy.

GUYS: Groovy.

MADDEN: Kind of dark though.

BUBBA: Man, I'm getting thirsty.

DICK: Yeah, let's have another Lite Beer from Miller.

RED: Yeah, Lite's less filling.

TASTE GREAT GROUP: Tastes great.

LESS FILLING GROUP: Less filling!

T.G.: Taste great!

L.F.: Less filling.

(SFX: HOWLING.)

TOMMY: What was that?

MICKEY SPILLANE: The creature.

DICK W: What creature?

MICKEY: Well, legend has it that a horrible thing stalks these woods.

LEE: Oooh, Mickey.

MICKEY: It comes out when the moon is full.

(SFX: HOWLING.)

RAY: What does this creature look like?

MICKEY (VO): It walks on two legs, but it isn't human.
It's got big eyes that bulge out and . . .

(SFX: FOOT STEPS.)

DICK B: It's the creature.

RODNEY: Hey guys, hey guys, where're you going?
Hey guys, where are the marshmallows?

(VO): Lite Beer from Miller. Everything you always wanted in a beer and less.

JOHN: Come on, it's after us.

BUBBA: Man, did you see that thing?

302

(VO): It's for you-ooo!

NEPTUNE: For me?

MEN ON BOAT: It's for you-ooo!

NEPTUNE: Oh . . . Hello?
Oh hello Son . . .
Happy birthday?
It's my birthday!

(VO): The phone.
It's for you to cheer someone up.

303

(VO): This is British Airways' Super Club Class seat.
The widest seat in the air. But being the widest
seat in the air, it isn't the easiest to fit through
the door.
Now on all our long-haul flights, the world's
widest airline seat.
From the airline that cares about everyone that
flies.
Super Club
From the world's favourite airline.

304

SOLO: *You can't get somewhere if you stop halfway*
You can't taste victory if you don't make the
play
And once you get rolling
Well, it's hard to stop
Pepsi taste goin' over the top!

CHORUS: *Taste that's bubblin' over, spillin' over*
Pourin' over, chillin' over ice
Over meltin', overwhelmin'
Over takin', over everybody.
Pepsi taste just not gonna stop
Pepsi taste goin' over the top!

SOLO: *Reachin' for the best*
You're leavin' the rest
Go halfway and you might as well stop
Come on up to Pepsi
Pepsi taste goin' over the top!

(CHORUS UNDER): *Bubblin' over, spillin' over,*
Pourin' over, chillin over . . .

SOLO: *Going over the top!*

(CHORUS UNDER): *Bubblin' over, spillin' over,*
Pourin' over, chillin' over . . .

SOLO: *Going over the top!*

(CHORUS UNDER): *Bubblin' over, spillin' over,*
Pourin' over, chillin' over . . .

SOLO: *Going over the top!*

305

(MUSIC UP)

SOLDIER: This is Army 2-1-2 seven miles northwest,
low fuel, heavy weather.

CONTROLLER: Army 2-1-2, radar contact turn right
heading 1-5-0.

ANNCR: With a fog bound helicopter hanging on your
every word it doesn't matter whether you're a
man or a woman, only that you're good.

CONTROLLER: Over landing threshold.

SINGERS: *Be all that you can be.*

SOLDIER: Thanks for your help.

CONTROLLER: Roger.

SINGERS: *You can do it in the Army.*

306
ART DIRECTOR
Pedro Gonzalez
WRITERS
Michael Lollis
Dan Hanover
CLIENT
United States Marine Corps
DIRECTOR
Phil Marco
PRODUCTION CO.
Phil Marco Productions
AGENCY PRODUCER
Jon Ambrose
AGENCY
J. Walter Thompson/
Washington, D.C.

307
ART DIRECTOR
Harvey Hoffenberg
WRITER
Ted Sann
CLIENT
Pepsi-Cola
DIRECTOR
Barry Meyers
PRODUCTION CO.
Sunlight Productions
AGENCY PRODUCER
Phyllis Landi
AGENCY
BBDO

308
ART DIRECTOR
George Euringer
WRITER
Tom Messner
CLIENT
MCI
DIRECTOR
Ross Cramer
PRODUCTION CO.
Elite Films
AGENCY PRODUCER
Mark Sitley
AGENCY
Ally & Gargano

309
ART DIRECTOR
Harvey Hoffenberg
WRITERS
Phil Dusenberry
Ted Sann
CLIENT
Pepsi-Cola
DIRECTOR
Bob Giraldi
PRODUCTION CO.
Giraldi Productions
AGENCY PRODUCER
David Frankel
AGENCY
BBDO

306

(SYNTHESIZED MUSIC AND SOUND EFFECTS
   THROUGHOUT)
ANNCR: You begin with raw steel . . .
   . . . shape it with fire . . .
   . . . muscle . . .
   . . . and sweat.
   Polish it to razor sharp perfection.
   What you end up with . . .
   is a Marine.
   We're looking for a few good men . . .
   . . . with the mettle . . .
   . . . to be Marines.

307

(SFX: BEACH SOUNDS, I.E., WIND, WATER.
   D. J. FROM RADIO.
   SOUNDS OF SPEAKERS BEING RAISED ATOP TRUCK.
   SOUNDS OF ICE CUBES BEING DROPPED INTO GLASS.
   SOUND IS HEARD ACROSS BEACH.
   SOUND OF POPPING TOP.
   SOUND OF POPPING TOP ECHOES OVER BEACH.
   SOUND OF POPPING CONTINUES.
   SOUND OF FIZZING SODA.
   SOUNDS OF FIZZING SODA ARE HEARD ACROSS
   BEACH.
   SOUNDS OF FIZZING SODA CONTINUE.)
BOY: Aah . . .
BOY: O.K. . . . who's first?
(CROWD NOISES)
(VO): Pepsi. The choice of a new Generation.

308

(MUSIC UNDER)

ANNCR (VO): This message is directed to the most important business and civic leaders in the city.

MAN: Uh, do you have . . . a phone I can use?

(MUSIC)

ANNCR (VO): Why don't you have MCI car phone service in your car?

MAN: Phone?

ANNCR (VO): With MCI car telephone service, you can call any other phone in the world from the comfort of the driver's seat.
The reception is crystal clear.
And because it's from MCI, it's not only on the leading edge of technology, it also costs a lot less than that conventional cellular phone service.
Up to 27% less on each and every call.
Call MCI.
The sooner you call, the sooner your car will have the one thing you wouldn't be without at home or in the office: a telephone.

309

(JACKSONS MUSIC)

JACKSONS: *You're a whole new generation*
Dancing through the day
Grabbin' for the magic on the run
A whole new generation
You're loving what you do. Put a Pepsi . . .
into motion
The choice is up to you
Hey-Hey-Hey, You're the Pepsi generation
Guzzle down and taste the thrill of today, and
feel the Pepsi way.
Taste the thrill of today, and feel the Pepsi way.
You're a whole new generation, You're a whole
new generation, You're a whole new generation.

310

ANNCR: In 1884 a woman immigrated into America.
Within her, people have seen all the good that is
within themselves.
She has given us hope and asked for nothing in
return.

WOMAN: I was eight years old when I first saw her. I
remember my father was squeezing my hand.
He just kept squeezing my hand. I just kept
looking at my father looking at her and I saw
him crying. I had never seen him cry before. The
sun was so bright. I have never seen the sun so
bright.

ANNCR: Can you ever picture her not being there?
Well neither can we.
We're Kodak . . . a founding sponsor of the
Statue of Liberty/Ellis Island Centennial
Restoration.
Now it's our turn to carry the torch.

SUPER: KEEP AMERICA'S IMAGE.

311

(SFX: SMALL ORGAN, LAST CHORD OF SONG)

(VO): It can be intimidating to step up to a new
technology. At Wang, we make computers not to
intimidate, but to *enhance* one's performance. So
when *we* put technology at your fingertips it's
not just the power.
It's the glory.

(SFX: MAGNIFICENT ORGAN MUSIC)

(VO): Wang. We put people in front of computers.

312

ANNCR (VO): Vietnam. When it was over, 58,022 never made it back. And America is still asking why. Time-Life Books and Boston Publishing bring you the Vietnam Experience. The first book series that puts the war in historical perspective and begins to give you the answers. These are the books that let you feel what it was like to be there. From the Tet offensive to the siege at Khe San. From the rice paddies of the Mekong Delta to the jungles of the Ho Chi Minh Trail. Join the men who fought as bravely as any Americans in any war. Fighting an enemy who was nowhere and everywhere. Men who won every major battle they were in. Yet came home to no parades. Beginning with *America Takes Over*, each book lets you re-examine those years. This is the one book series no American can afford to miss. The Vietnam Experience. Only now can we begin to understand a war that took 58,022 lives. A war that is still touching us all.

313

HUNCHBACK: Oh why was I born so ugly?

(SFX: RING RING.)

HUNCHBACK: The bells!?

VO: It's for you-ooo!

HUNCHBACK: For me??

CROWD: It's for you-ooo!

HUNCHBACK: Hello. It's Esmeralda!

(TO GARGOYLE) She loves me! Smack!

VO: The phone.
It's for you to make someone feel wanted.

Consumer Television
:30 Single

314
ART DIRECTOR
Mike Moser
WRITER
Brian O'Neill
CLIENT
Businessland
DIRECTOR
Mike Cuesta
PRODUCTION CO.
Griner/Cuesta
AGENCY PRODUCER
Richard O'Neill
AGENCY
Chiat/Day - San Francisco

315
ART DIRECTOR
Jerry Whitley
WRITER
Mark Silveira
CLIENT
BMW of North America
DIRECTOR
Tibor Hirsch
PRODUCTION CO.
THT Productions
AGENCY PRODUCER
Stephen Labovsky
AGENCY
Ammirati & Puris

316
ART DIRECTOR
Sam Scali
WRITER
Ed McCabe
CLIENT
Perdue
DIRECTOR
Henry Holtzman
PRODUCTION CO.
N. Lee Lacy
AGENCY PRODUCER
Carol Singer
AGENCY
Scali McCabe Sloves

317
ART DIRECTOR
Ray Groff
WRITER
Jim Lawson
CLIENT
Dorsey Laboratories
DIRECTOR
Dick Clark
PRODUCTION CO.
Stone-Clark Productions
AGENCY PRODUCER
Wende Sasse
AGENCY
Needham Harper Worldwide

314

MAN: This micro has macro modelling and comes with multiple mini modems.

MAN: It'll format, forecast, ferret, file, figure and form formulations.

ANNCR (VO): Some computer salespeople seem to know more about buzzwords than about computers

MAN: It's compatible and expandable, it's . . .

ANNCR (VO): But at Businessland, our people have an average of four years experience in the computer industry, and years of business experience. Which is why our salespeople don't sound like . . .

MAN: . . . infallible.

ANNCR (VO): Salespeople.

(VO): Businessland. Where business people are going to buy computers.

315

ANNCR. (VO): Not long ago, Japan's premier motorsports magazine for the first time devoted an entire issue . . . to a motorcycle.
But even more astonishing is that this, the most honored motorcycle in Japanese history . . . isn't Japanese.
BMW . . . The legendary motorcycles of Germany.

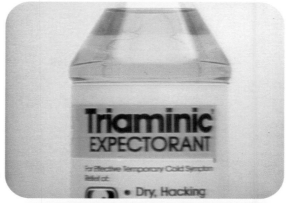

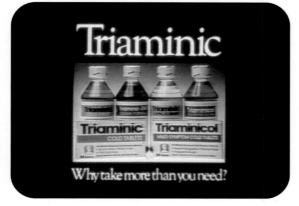

316

(SILENT)

FRANK PERDUE: This is not a frozen chicken according to U.S. Department of Agriculture standards.

(SFX: DRILL)

(SILENT)

Because it hasn't reached zero degrees at its deepest point. If this meets *your* standards for a non-frozen chicken, go ahead and buy one.

(SFX: CLICK)

My chickens are considerably warmer than that.

(SILENT)

317

ANNCR (VO): Almost no one has *every* symptom of a cold.
    You may have a
(ANNOUNCER SNEEZES) . . .
    . . . but not a
(ANNOUNCER COUGHS DRYLY).
    Or a
(ANNOUNCER BLOWS HIS NOSE) . . .
    . . . but not a
(ANNOUNCER HOLDS HIS TEMPLE IN PAIN).
    Or even a
(ANNOUNCER SNIFFS) . . .
    . . . but no sign of
(ANNOUNCER SHIVERS).
    That's why Triaminic products come in *four* formulas, recommended by doctors and pharmacists *for just* the symptoms you have. So you don't take more medicine than you need. Triaminic, in liquids and tablets.
    Why treat
(ANNOUNCER REPEATS EVERY SYMPTOM) when all you want is a simple
(SIGN OF RELIEF)?

318
ART DIRECTOR
David Jenkins
WRITER
Jon Jackson
CLIENT
Hershey Foods
PRODUCTION CO.
Production Partners
AGENCY PRODUCER
Susan Birbeck
AGENCY
Ogilvy & Mather

319
ART DIRECTOR
Dean Hanson
WRITER
Tom McElligott
CLIENT
Minnesota Federal Savings &
Loan
DIRECTOR
Lee Lacy
PRODUCTION CO.
N. Lee Lacy
AGENCY PRODUCER
Judy Carter
AGENCY
Fallon McElligott Rice/Mpls.

320
ART DIRECTOR
Tony DeGregorio
WRITER
Lee Garfinkel
CLIENT
Subaru
DIRECTOR
Rick Levine
PRODUCTION CO.
Rick Levine Productions
AGENCY PRODUCER
Bob Nelson
AGENCY
Levine Huntley Schmidt &
Beaver

321
ART DIRECTOR
Phil Silvestri
WRITER
Joe Della Femina
CLIENT
Continental Tire
DIRECTOR
Jim Johnston
PRODUCTION CO.
Johnston Films
AGENCY PRODUCER
Peter Yahr
AGENCY
Della Femina Travisano &
Partners

318

BOY: My sister is the pretty one—my brother is the
smart one—and me, I'm the klutz.
When my mother says, "Nobody's perfect," I
know just who she means.
After yesterday I expected bread and water for
lunch—but look: today Mom gave me a Kiss—a
little Hershey's Kiss.
When my mother says "Nobody's perfect"—she
could mean my sister.
ANNCR: Hershey's Kisses.
They're only little 'til you taste them.

319

VO: Does it seem, like the only time your bank isn't
happy to see you . . . is when you want to
borrow money?

(MUSIC BEGINS AND CONTINUES: HIT THE ROAD, JACK)

(MUSIC BUILDS)

VO: Next time, come to Minnesota Federal . . .
With millions of dollars to lend . . .
. . . we're not about to tell you to take a walk.
Minnesota Federal.

320

(MUSIC: TARANTELLA)

(SFX: HORRIBLE THUNDER CLAP)

OLD WOMAN (RISING WITH HER POCKET BOOK): Let's go home.

(SFX: THUNDER CONTINUES.)

DAUGHTER (CRYING TO FATHER): Daddy!

FATHER (IN DESPERATE HOPE TAKES MICROPHONE FROM BAND LEADER): Please, stop! Nothing is going to ruin this wedding. So if it takes all night - I'll personally drive each of you home in my car . . . my Subaru.

(PAUSE-ABOUT 4 BEATS)

(MUSIC: TARANTELLA STARTS UP UPROARIOUSLY.)

ANNCR: Drive a Subaru with on-demand four-wheel-drive. And don't let the weather spoil a good time.
SUBARU. INEXPENSIVE. AND BUILT TO STAY THAT WAY.

321

MAN: At Continental we spare no expense designing great tires for Germany. But we won't spend one extra cent on commercials.
Our tire in action.
Designed for 170 days of rain a year in northern Germany.
Limitless speeds on the autobahn.
And tons of snow in the Alps.
So, imagine what they can do on American roads.
At Continental, we don't make great tire commercials, we make great tires.

322
ART DIRECTOR
Rich Silverstein
WRITERS
Andy Berlin
Jeff Goodby
CLIENT
Oakland Invaders
DIRECTOR
Jon Francis
PRODUCTION CO.
Bass/Francis
AGENCY PRODUCER
Debbie King
AGENCY
Goodby Berlin & Silverstein/
San Francisco

323
ART DIRECTOR
Sal DeVito
WRITER
Steve Penchina
CLIENT
WNBC Radio
DIRECTOR
George Gomes
PRODUCTION CO.
Gomes-Loew
AGENCY PRODUCER
Jane Liepschutz
AGENCY
Penchina, Selkowitz

324
ART DIRECTOR AND WRITER
Steve Kasloff
CLIENT
Body Double
DIRECTORS
Steve Kasloff
Richard Greenberg
PRODUCTION COS.
Richard Greenberg
Columbia Pictures
AGENCY
Columbia Pictures
Advertising

325
ART DIRECTOR
Frank Nicholas
WRITER
Steve Turner
CLIENT
Star-Kist Meaty Bone
PRODUCTION CO.
Eggers Films
AGENCY PRODUCER
Wil Fieldhouse
AGENCY
Leo Burnett USA/Chicago

322

PLAYER 1: We're Oakland Invaders . . .

(SFX)

PLAYER 2: Not the kind from outer space . . .

(SFX)

PLAYER 3: We play professional football . . .

(SFX)

PLAYER 4: All over the place . . .

(SFX)

PLAYER 5: We run the ball . . .

(SFX)

PLAYER 6: We pass the ball . . .

(SFX)

PLAYER 7: We're gone without a trace . . .

(SFX)

PLAYER 8: We want you to see us . . .

(SFX)

PLAYER 9: We'll save you a place . . .

(SFX)

PLAYER 10: So call us up for tickets . . .

(SFX)

PLAYER 11: Or I'll break your face.

ANNCR (VO): The second season opens at home,
March 4th. For season tickets, call 638-7800
now. Operators are standing by.

323

RANDY BONGARTEN: Because of certain indiscreet
remarks by Don Imus and Howard Stern,
WNBC Radio apologizes to the following:
The National Organization for Women
New York Chapter of Hadassah
Governor Cuomo
The New York Jets
The United States Congress - both Houses
Nassau Community College
The Gay Men's Choir
Sons of Italy
Rabbi Arthur Selkowitz
My Wife

IMUS (VO): 66 WNBC. If we weren't so bad, we
wouldn't be so good.

RANDY: Queen Elizabeth
Mayor Koch

(SFX: SOUND FADES)

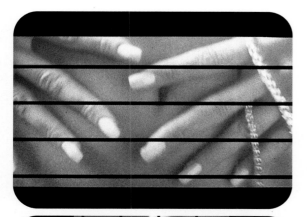

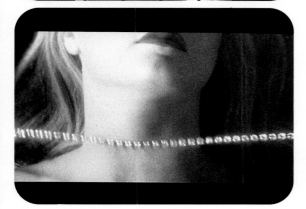

324

ANNCR: He thought he was watching her.
But she was watching him.
He thought it was private.
But he was invited.
He knew he had gone too far.
He couldn't stop.

(SFX: A WOMAN'S SCREAM)

Brian de Palma, the modern Master of
Suspense, invites you to witness a seduction,
a mystery, a murder.
Body Double.
You can't believe everything you see.

325

MAILMAN: Hey, Max. What's going on?

MAX: I'm stocking up on Meaty Bone Dog Biscuits.

MAILMAN: Meaty Bone? Any good?

MAX: You kiddin'?! Meaty Bones are great.

MAILMAN: Aw C'mon.

MAX: Look, Meaty Bone's crunchy
(CRACK) like ordinary biscuits.
But, Meaty Bone bakes on . . . a rich, meaty
sauce . . . my customers love.

MAILMAN: Hey, these even taste better than Milk
Bones! You know your meat, Max.

MAX: 'Course. What? Do I look like a carpenter?

ANNCR (VO): Meaty Bone Dog Biscuits. The meaty
taste, tastes better.

MAILMAN: Hey Max, how'd you like a partner?

MAX: Sure. And watch you eat all the profits?

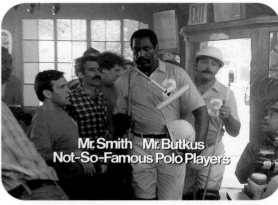

326

ANNCR (VO): When things are out of control . . . *a simple solution* is the personal computer software in IBM's Assistant Series.
Start by entering facts and figures into Filing Assistant.
Then move the facts around to work up a plan . . . or draw a graph.
There's Writing Assistant to help you handle words . . . and Reporting Assistant to pull everything together.
The Assistant Series from IBM.
Getting all your ducks in a row has never been easier.

327

DICK: I'll tell ya, playing is a lot tougher than it looks.

BUBBA: Sure is.

DICK: And even though the horses do the running, you can still work up a thirst.

BUBBA: So after a chucker or two, we equestrians drink Lite Beer from Miller.

DICK: Yeah, Lite tastes great and it's got a third less calories than their regular beer.

BUBBA: And, it's less filling.

DICK: And that's important. Because tomorrow, we're gonna try our hand at water polo.

BUBBA: Yeah. I sure hope these horses can swim.

DICK: Me too.

ANNCR: Lite Beer from Miller. Everything you always wanted in a beer . . .

(SFX: HORSE WHINNY, WATER SPLASHING) . . . And less.

328

(MUSIC AND SFX)

(MUSIC)

(MUSIC UNDER)

ANNCR. (VO): With a cargo bay of 71 cubic feet and a life expectancy of 16.5 years, this is the space vehicle that could transport you into the 21st century.

(SFX: SLAM OF HATCH)

(SILENT)

Volvo

329

(SFX MUSIC THROUGHOUT UNDERNEATH)

WALT: Hello, Fred.

FRED: Mornin', Walt.

VO: There ought to be something useful we can do . . .

FRED: Better hurry, Henry.

VO: . . . with all this garbage.

HENRY: I got it, I got it!

VO: Well, beginning next year, in Tampa, Florida, Waste Management will be taking the city's trash and turning it into . . .
. . . electricity.

HENRY: Take it easy, fellas.

VO: Now ask yourself . . .

FRED: See you tomorrow, Henry.

VO: . . . isn't that better than just throwing it all away? Waste Management. Helping the world dispose of its problems.

330

ORSON WELLES VO: To the Danes, it must appear that
    those clever-clogs, the Swedes, have everything.
    Probably one of the sturdiest cars in the world.
    Probably the most successful pop group.

(SFX: ABBA SINGING "MONEY MONEY MONEY")
    And probably the greatest tennis player.

(SFX: "BJOINK")

Still, the Danes don't seem too upset.
    Carlsberg.
    Probably the best *lager* in the world.

331

(SFX MUSIC: 'WE'RE IN THE MONEY')

VO: Stella Artois
    Reassuringly expensive.

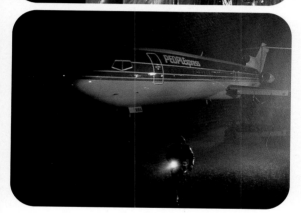

332

(VO): There's a certain kind of guy who'll never say, "It's Not My Job". Because everything is his job. You know what you call someone like that . . . an owner.
There's a company where each and every employee is an owner, with an average of $40,000 of stock. People Express Airlines. At People Express each of us feels like we own the airline.
Because we do.

333

ANNCR VO: This is a highly sophisticated business computer. And to use it . . . all you have to do is learn this . . .
This is Macintosh from Apple. Also a highly sophisticated business computer.
And to use it, all you have to do is learn this . . .
Now . . . you decide which one's more sophisticated.
Macintosh.
The computer for the rest of us.

Consumer Television :30 Single

334
ART DIRECTORS
Charles Cilo
Conrad Malotak
WRITER
Gene Schinto
CLIENT
Nissan Motor Corporation
DIRECTOR
Peter Miranda
PRODUCTION CO.
May Day Productions
AGENCY PRODUCER
Bob Ammon
AGENCY
William Esty

335
ART DIRECTOR
Steve Scholem
WRITER
Sharon Vanderslice
CLIENT
WNBC-TV
DIRECTOR
Jim Paisley
PRODUCTION CO.
Normandy Film Group
AGENCY PRODUCER
Susan Rosenberg
AGENCY
Lord, Geller, Federico,
Einstein

336
ART DIRECTOR
Sam Scali
WRITER
Ed McCabe
CLIENT
Perdue
DIRECTOR
Henry Holtzman
PRODUCTION CO.
N. Lee Lacy
AGENCY PRODUCER
Carol Singer
AGENCY
Scali McCabe Sloves

337
ART DIRECTOR
Stan Schoffield
WRITER
Martin Puris
CLIENT
Schweppes
DIRECTOR
Bob Brooks
PRODUCTION CO.
Brooks Fulford Cramer
Seresin
AGENCY PRODUCER
Ozzie Spenningsby
AGENCY
Ammirati & Puris

334

(SFX: FANFARE)

COP: Nissan 300 ZX . . . Turbo.
   Looks fast.

(SFX: SPEEDING CAR SOUNDS)

(SFX: VROOM)

(SILENT)

(SFX & MUSIC)
ANNCR (VO): The Nissan 300 ZX *is* Major Motion . . .
   even standing still.

GUY: What's that for?

COP: Speeding!

GUY: Oh!

SINGERS (VO): *Come alive, come and drive*
(SFX: WHOOSH) *Major motion from Nissan.*

ANNCR (VO): At your Datsun dealer.

335

(EERIE MUSIC UNDER.)

VO: Go ahead. Get into this cab.
   It's waiting.
   But what if the driver doesn't know the way?
   Or thinks you don't and takes you for a ride?
   What if you don't have the right change?
   Or the right look?
   Will he refuse to take you anywhere at all?
   Mike Taibbi reports: "How to Take a Taxi
   Without Getting Taken." This week at 6 on
   News 4 New York.

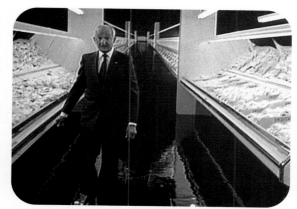

336

(SFX: FRANK PERDUE PICKS UP ONE PACKAGE OF
    CHICKEN, REPLACES IT.)

FRANK PERDUE: Have you noticed how many chicken
    companies have packages that look like Perdue?
    Do you suppose they could be? . . .
    Nooo. They wouldn't.
    But I'd suggest you be careful not to pick up the
    wrong yellow and red package.
    Otherwise I'll have to take drastic measures to
    keep you from becoming confused.
    Don't make me do it!

337

DUKE: Being a Duke is not what it used to be.
    Opened the house to tourists . . .
    Sold the family silver ., . .
    Auctioned the 17th Duke.
    Fact is, nearly everything's gone . . .
    Except the old family favorite . . .
    Schweppes Tonic.
    Essence of fresh fruit . . . cheeky little
    bubbles . . .
    Schweppes.

VISITOR: Thank you very much, your lordship.

DUKE: My pleasure.

VO: Schweppes. The Great British Bubbly.

338
ART DIRECTOR
Mike Moser
WRITER
Brian O'Neill
CLIENT
Businessland
DIRECTOR
Mike Cuesta
PRODUCTION CO.
Griner/Cuesta
AGENCY PRODUCER
Richard O'Neill
AGENCY
Chiat/Day - San Francisco

339
ART DIRECTOR
Mike Cheney
WRITER
George Kase
CLIENT
Turtle Wax
DIRECTOR
Toni Ficalora
PRODUCTION CO.
Toni Ficalora Productions
AGENCY PRODUCER
Marea Tesseris
AGENCY
Lou Beres & Associates/
Chicago

340
ART DIRECTOR
Don Keller
WRITER
Phil Raskin
CLIENT
Kellogg's
PRODUCTION CO.
Eggers Films
AGENCY PRODUCER
John Scott
AGENCY
Leo Burnett USA/Chicago

341
ART DIRECTOR
Martin Connelly
WRITER
Patricia Malkin
CLIENT
Bonkers
PRODUCTION CO.
Charlex
AGENCY PRODUCER
Christine Cacace
AGENCY
Dancer Fitzgerald Sample

338

ANNCR (VO): Some computer salespeople seem to have a superficial knowledge of computers.

MAN #1 (IN PARROT VOICE): User-friendly . . . wrawk . . . user-friendly . . .

WOMAN: . . . Pooooortable . . . . . . Powwwwwrful . . .

MAN #2 (SQUAWKY.): Programmable . . . . . . Expandable . . . . . . Incredible . . .

ANNCR (VO): But at Businessland, our people have an average of four years experience in the computer industry, and years of business experience. And *that* kind of knowledge . . .

MAN #2 (WRAWK.)

ANNCR (VO): is impossible to imitate.

(VO): Businessland. Where business people are going to buy computers.

339

ANNCR VO: New Turtle Wax Clear Guard vinyl protectant . . . clearly outshines them all!

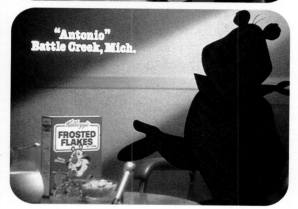

340

WOMAN: I'm thirty-two years old . . . and I love Kellogg's Frosted Flakes.

ANNCR: Brave adults are coming forward to challenge the notion that Frosted Flakes is just a kids' cereal.

MAN: I know there's a tiger on the box. I like the taste. Okay?

ANNCR: Because you loved them as a kid doesn't mean you can't love them as an adult.

COUPLE: One day our neighbor saw the package on the table. And we don't even have children!

ANNCR: With that extra crunch in milk. That frosting just right. That taste as great as ever.

TONY: Well, they've always been my favorite.

(SFX: CLICK)

TONY: So dig in! Frosted Flakes have the taste adults have grown to love. They're gr-r-eat!

341

RUTH: Some folks don't believe the super-fruitiness of Bonkers fruit candy.
They learn soon enough.

(SFX: BONK!, LAUGHTER)
Some folks think Bonkers is gum.

(SFX: BONK!, LAUGHTER)
They know it's candy now. With this extra fruity inside, Bonkers is so super-fruity . . . OOPS!

(SFX: BONK!, LAUGHTER)

ANNCR (VO): Bonkers bonks you out!

RUTH: Some candy!

342
ART DIRECTOR
Ervin Jue
WRITER
Dean Hacohen
CLIENT
Volkswagen
DIRECTOR
Terry Bedford
PRODUCTION CO.
Jennie & Company
AGENCY PRODUCER
Lee Weiss
AGENCY
Doyle Dane Bernbach

343
ART DIRECTOR
Joe Matamales
WRITER
Mike Abadi
CLIENT
USA Network
DIRECTOR
Greg Ramsey
PRODUCTION CO.
Landeck/Pelco Editorial
AGENCY
Marsteller

344
ART DIRECTOR
Gary Larsen
WRITER
Rick Colby
CLIENT
Center Theatre Group
DIRECTOR
Marc Feldman
PRODUCTION CO.
Tempest
AGENCY PRODUCER
Nancy Kissick
AGENCY
Larsen Colby Koralek/
Los Angeles

345
ART DIRECTOR
Pam Cunningham
WRITER
Carol Ogden
CLIENT
American Honda
DIRECTOR
Henry Sandbank
PRODUCTION CO.
Sandbank Films
AGENCY PRODUCER
Joel Ziskin
AGENCY
Needham Harper Worldwide

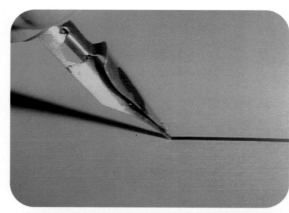

342

(SFX: WIND)

(SFX: CAR NOISE)

(SFX: WIND)

SFX: CAR NOISE)

(SFX: WIND, CLICKETY CLACK)

SFX: CAR NOISE)

(SFX: WIND, CRASH)

(SFX: CAR NOISE THROUGHOUT)

ANNCR (VO): The 1985 Volkswagen Scirocco. German
engineering.

(SFX: MUSIC STARTS TO BLEND INTO CAR NOISE)
Precision handling. Outstanding performance.
And you're about to see the most exciting thing
of all. Scirocco. It's not a car. It's a Volkswagen.

343

(SFX: PEN SCRATCHING PAPER)

ANNOUNCER (VO): Where can you get a kind
word . . .

MAN: You're such a pretty nurse, Rita.
(WOMAN SCREAMS)

(SFX: PEN SCRATCHING)

ANNOUNCER (VO): Some fun in the sun . . .

DROWNING BOY (CRYING OUT): Mom! Mom!

(SFX: PEN SCRATCHING)

ANNOUNCER (VO): A helping hand . . .

(SFX: POWER DRILL BUZZING)

(SFX: PEN SCRATCHING)

ANNOUNCER (VO): Even a breathtaking view.
(WOMAN SCREAMS)

(SFX: HITCHCOCK THEME MUSIC)

ANNOUNCER (VO): The Alfred Hitchcock Hour. On
USA. Six nights a week.

(SFX: USA THEME MUSIC)

SINGERS: *It's a great place to stay. USA!*

USA ANNOUNCER (VO): The USA Cable Network.

344

(SFX: RESTAURANT NOISES)

WOMAN #1: I just saw "The Hands of Its Enemy" at the Huntington Hartford.

WOMAN #2: Oh . . . was that fabulous or what!!?

WOMAN #1: Oh . . . no wonder Gary Franklin gave it a ten!

WOMAN #2: Wasn't Phyllis Frelich terrific? The whole cast was terrific! Especially . . . uh . . .

WOMAN #1: What's his name . . .

WOMAN #2: . . . Oh . . . he made me laugh . . .

WOMAN #1: . . . He made me cry . . .

WOMAN #2: . . . What'shisname . . .

WOMAN #1: He won an Oscar . . .

WOMAN #2: . . . Right . . . right . . . big movie star . . .

WOMAN #1: . . . Robert! . . .

WOMAN #2: . . . No . . . Richard . . . something . . .

WOMAN #1: . . . yeah . . . Richard What'sname . . .

RICHARD (SNEEZES): Dreyfussss!!!

VO: Don't miss "The Hands of Its Enemy" with Phyllis Frelich . . . and . . . uh . . . uh . . . Richard Dreyfuss.

345

VO: A Honda Civic Wagon has such nice features.
It's very clever.
It's smart about money.
It's always there when you need it . . . and can keep your secrets.
It's very neat, even cleans up after itself.
And it looks . . . well, it has a great personality.

SINGERS: *Honda!*

346
ART DIRECTOR
Mike Fazende
WRITER
Bert Gardner
CLIENT
Control Data Institute
DIRECTOR
Greg Hoey
PRODUCTION CO.
Filmfair
AGENCY PRODUCER
Lisa Jarrard
AGENCY
Bozell & Jacobs/Mpls.

347
ART DIRECTOR
Jean Robaire
WRITERS
John Stein
Brent Bouchez
CLIENT
Pizza Hut
DIRECTOR
George Gomes
PRODUCTION CO.
Gomes-Loew
AGENCY PRODUCER
Elaine Hinton
AGENCY
Chiat/Day - Los Angeles

348
ART DIRECTOR
Joe Minnella
WRITERS
Dale Silverberg
John DeCerchio
CLIENT
Art Van
PRODUCTION CO.
Ron Castorri
AGENCY PRODUCER
Sheldon Cohn
AGENCY
W.B. Doner & Company/
Michigan

349
ART DIRECTOR
F. Paul Pracilio
WRITER
Jeffrey Atlas
CLIENT
American Express
DIRECTOR
Steve Horn
PRODUCTION CO.
Steve Horn Productions
AGENCY PRODUCER
Ann Marcato
AGENCY
Ogilvy & Mather

346

ANNCR (VO): This is a message for people who don't
like their jobs.
People who went to college to have a good
future. But got locked into jobs with no future at
all. These people *could* call Control Data
Institute and train for careers in computer
programming. Control Data Institute can train
them in just 6½ months.
Call this number today.
Don't be chained to a dead end job.

347

(VIENNA BOYS CHOIR SINGING THE "TWELVE DAYS OF
CHRISTMAS")

CHORUS: *On the first day after Christmas my true
love gave to me . . .
. . . left over tu-r-key.
On the second day after Christmas my true love
gave to me . . .
. . . turkey casserole that she made from leftover
turkey.
On the third day after Christmas . . .*
(CHORUS FADES, INSTRUMENTS AND FA, LA, LA'S
CONTINUE.)

ANNCR VO: If the holidays are lingering longer than
you expected . . .
We have a suggestion.
A Pan Pizza from Pizza Hut.
With pepperoni . . . mushrooms . . . almost any
topping . . . except one.

(CHORUS COMES UP AGAIN LOUDLY.)

CHORUS: *. . . flaming turkey wings.*
(FADING) *Fa, la, la, la, la
Fa, la, la, la, la.*

348

CROWD (CHANTING): Open the doors! Open the
  doors . . .

MANAGER: Well, Frank, who's gonna open the
  doors?

FRANK: Not me. I opened the doors last year.

VO: Announcing one of the biggest furniture sales of
  the year.

MANAGER: Tom?

TOM: I opened the doors two years ago.

(CHANTING CONTINUES AND FADES)

VO: Art Van's Pre-Holiday Sale. The best brand
  names in furniture at 15% to 60% off.

MANAGER: Someone's gotta open them.

JOHNNY: Hi, guys.

MANAGER: Johnny

(OTHERS ECHO IN . . . JOHNNY)

JOHNNY (UNDER): Oh . . . nnnnooooo . . .
  aaahhhhh . . .

VO: Art Van's Pre-Holiday Sale . . . Friday and
  Saturday only. It's the sale everyone's been
  waiting for. Well almost everyone.

349

STEPHEN KING: Do you know me?
  It's frightening how many novels of suspense
  I've written.
  But still, when I'm not recognized, it just kills
  me.
  So instead of saying I wrote *Carrie*, I carry the
  American Express Card.
  Without it, isn't life a little scary?

ANNCR: To apply for the Card, look for this display.
  And take one.

STEPHEN KING: The American Express Card.
  Don't leave home without it.

350
ART DIRECTOR
Mary Means
WRITERS
Tom Mabley
Bob Sarlin
CLIENT
IBM
DIRECTOR
Stu Hagmann
PRODUCTION CO.
H.I.S.K.
AGENCY PRODUCER
Robert L. Dein
AGENCY
Lord, Geller, Federico,
Einstein

351
ART DIRECTOR
Tony Angotti
WRITER
Tom Thomas
CLIENT
BMW of North America
DIRECTOR
Henry Sandbank
PRODUCTION CO.
Sandbank Films
AGENCY PRODUCER
Ozzie Spenningsby
AGENCY
Ammirati & Puris

352
ART DIRECTOR
Jim Handloser
WRITER
Helayne Spivak
CLIENT
Ciba-Geigy
DIRECTOR
Ross Cramer
PRODUCTION CO.
The Power & Light Company
AGENCY PRODUCER
Mark Sitley
AGENCY
Ally & Gargano

353
ART DIRECTOR
David Christensen
WRITER
Alfredo Marcantonio
CLIENT
Whitbread-Heineken
DIRECTOR
Roger Woodburn
PRODUCTION CO.
Park Village Productions
AGENCY PRODUCER
Mike Griffin
AGENCY
Lowe Howard-Spink
Campbell-Ewald/London

350

vo: In these modern times, even the best manager needs help to succeed. For when pressure builds, it becomes harder to keep things rolling without losing control and falling behind.
A manager could use the IBM Personal Computer for smoother scheduling and greater productivity. It can help a manager become a big wheel in the company.
The IBM Personal Computer, at a store near you.

351

ANNCR (VO): Every day, BMW presents a comprehensive report . . . on the state of automotive technology.
Not through some dry dissertation . . . or the theoretical vacuum of a laboratory . . . but rather through a more appropriate vehicle.
The BMW 733i. The luxury sedan that translates the intricacies of technology . . . into that very elusive commodity . . . called fun.
BMW 733i.

352

ANNCR (VO): It's nighttime. That 12-hour appetite
    suppressant you took this morning just wore off.
    You're all alone with your refrigerator.

(EERIE MUSIC & SFX UNDER)

(MUSIC & SFX)
Next time try Acutrim.
    Acutrim lasts longer than any other appetite
    suppressant . . .
    . . . a full 16 hours.
    Because you never know when temptation's
    going to strike.
    Acutrim. It's at its strongest when you're at
    your weakest.

353

(SFX: MUSIC "THE GREAT PRETENDER")

VO: Heineken refreshes the parts other beers cannot
    reach.

354
ART DIRECTOR
Norman Tanen
WRITER
Mark Ezratty
CLIENT
MCI
DIRECTOR
Dick Loew
PRODUCTION CO.
Gomes-Loew
AGENCY PRODUCER
Charlotte Rosenblatt
AGENCY
Benton & Bowles

355
ART DIRECTOR
Gary Johns
WRITER
Jeff Gorman
CLIENT
Nike
DIRECTOR
Joe Sedelmaier
PRODUCTION CO.
Sedelmaier Films
AGENCY PRODUCER
Morty Baran
AGENCY
Chiat/Day - Los Angeles

356
ART DIRECTOR
Marv Lefkowitz
WRITERS
Tony Isidore
Bob Elgort
CLIENT
Sharp Electronics
DIRECTOR
Joe Sedelmaier
PRODUCTION CO.
Sedelmaier Films
AGENCY PRODUCER
Peter Yahr
AGENCY
Isidore & Paulson

357
ART DIRECTOR
Gary Yoshida
WRITER
Bob Coburn
CLIENT
American Honda
DIRECTOR
Henry Sandbank
PRODUCTION CO.
Sandbank Films
AGENCY PRODUCER
Joel Ziskin
AGENCY
Needham Harper Worldwide/
Los Angeles

354

(SFX: BELL HUMMING)

ANNCR: If Alexander Graham Bell were alive today,
he'd have a big problem with his creation.

BELL: Watson, come here! My phone bill.

ANNCR: Call MCI. The only national interstate long
distance service offering volume discounts
without monthly fees or minimums while saving
businesses hundreds of millions of dollars versus
AT&T.

355

(MUSIC THROUGHOUT)

ANNCR: Nike Hijacks.
They're not for everyone.

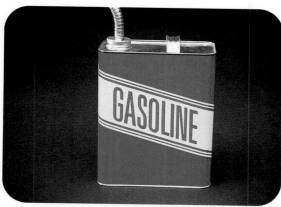

356

ANNCR (VO): Sharp introduces a video tape recorder so personal everybody thinks it's theirs. That's why they call it "My Video."
It has video search . . . uses 8 hour tapes . . .
Yet it's small enough . . . to move from room to room, house to house, even out of doors.
Sharp's "My Video."
We replaced a half million transistors and diodes with one tiny chip.
Sharp.

357

(MUSIC)

BURGESS: The EPA figures say you can get 49 miles out of a gallon of gas.
If you aren't getting this kind of mileage from your gasoline, maybe you should change your brand of car.
We recommend you try the number one mileage car, the Honda Civic CRX HF.
The right car for your gasoline.

358
ART DIRECTOR
Tod Seisser
WRITER
Jay Taub
CLIENT
Citizen Watches
DIRECTOR
Henry Sandbank
PRODUCTION CO.
Sandbank Films
AGENCY PRODUCER
Rachel Novak
AGENCY
Levine Huntley Schmidt &
Beaver

359
ART DIRECTOR
David Bigman
WRITER
Marc Deschenes
CLIENT
3M
DIRECTOR
Alan Blake
PRODUCTION CO.
Jennie & Company
AGENCY PRODUCER
Richard O'Neill
AGENCY
Chiat/Day - San Francisco

360
ART DIRECTORS
Rick Steinman
Bert Hoddinott
WRITERS
Rick Steinman
Bert Hoddinott
CLIENT
Sunkist
AGENCY PRODUCER
Chuck Bauer
AGENCY
Foote Cone & Belding/
Chicago

361
ART DIRECTOR
Roger Cazemage
WRITER
Chris Browne
CLIENT
Times Newspapers
DIRECTOR
Graham Baker
PRODUCTION CO.
Baker Bierman More
O'Ferrall
AGENCY PRODUCER
Wendy Hills
AGENCY
Grandfield Rork Collins/
London

358

ANNCR: This is Big Ben. And this is the man who
    sets it. It's his job to keep this clock so accurate,
    you could set your watch by it. As millions of
    Londoners do.
    The big question is, how does he check the
    accuracy of Big Ben? With a Citizen. The watch
    so accurate, you could set a clock by it.
    Citizen Watches. The smartest engineering ever
    strapped to a wrist.

359

ANNCR: Are you worried about being audited next
    Thursday?

WOMAN: Not at all.

ANNCR: Are you worried that a woman has never
    made it to Senior V.P.?

WOMAN: No.

ANNCR: Worried about your daughter going out with
    the punk rocker?

WOMAN (LAUGHS): Not really.

ANNCR: Are you worried about a floppy disk losing
    all your payroll records?

WOMAN: Noo . . .

ANNCR: If you had 3M diskettes, you wouldn't have
    to worry. 3M floppies are certified 100% error-
    free. No floppy is more reliable. So don't worry.
    Get 3M.

(VO): 3M diskettes. One less thing to worry about.

360

SINGERS: *Gotta keep those Sunkist vibrations a happenin' with you.*
Good, good, good, good vibrations
Sunkist Orange Soda taste sensations
Good, good, good (I'm drinkin' up good vibrations) good vibrations.
(Sunny Sunkist excitations)
Good vibrations
Ahhhhh!
Good, good, good, (Bubbly orange jubilation)
Good vibrations!

361

MEL SMITH: See, we're all playing the stock market this morning?
Thought I'd have a go. Well I thought this week's £20,000 might come in handy.
All going well is it?

MVO: Play the stock market without the risk. Play Portfolio in The Times.

Consumer Television :30 Single

362
ART DIRECTORS
Lee Clow
Brent Thomas
WRITERS
Steve Hayden
Penny Kapousouz
CLIENT
Apple Computer
DIRECTOR
Mark Coppos
PRODUCTION CO.
Directors Consortium
AGENCY PRODUCER
Morty Baran
AGENCY
Chiat/Day - Los Angeles

363
ART DIRECTOR
Mark Hughes
WRITER
Neal Gomberg
CLIENT
Volkswagen
DIRECTOR
Ross Cramer
PRODUCTION CO.
The Power & Light Company
AGENCY PRODUCER
Lee Weiss
AGENCY
Doyle Dane Bernbach

364
ART DIRECTOR
Michael Tesch
WRITER
Patrick Kelly
CLIENT
Federal Express
DIRECTOR
Patrick Kelly
PRODUCTION CO.
Kelly Pictures
AGENCY PRODUCER
Maureen Kearns
AGENCY
Ally & Gargano

365
ART DIRECTOR
Tony LaMonte
WRITER
Michael Shevack
CLIENT
Black & Decker
DIRECTOR
Patrick Morgan
PRODUCTION CO.
Fairbanks Films
AGENCY PRODUCER
Nancy Perez
AGENCY
BBDO

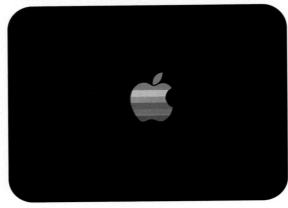

362

ANNCR (VO): Introducing Macintosh. It does all the things you'd expect a business computer to do. It does a lot of things you wouldn't expect a business computer to do. And it does some things no other business computer has ever done before . . .
Of course, to do all this, you *will* have to learn to do this . . .
Macintosh
The computer for the rest of us.

363

(MUSIC THROUGHOUT)

ANNCR (VO): What's the biggest difference between the Volkswagen Vanagon and those new mini-vans? Well, in the Vanagon, seven people can take a vacation. And, of course, in a mini-van, seven people can take a vacation. They just can't take very much else. Vanagon. It's not a car. It's a Volkswagen.

364

ANNCR: Ten years ago, Federal Express changed the way America did business.

GUY: I need it tomorrow, or it's all over!!! How did they do this?

ANNCR: Now we're going to do it again.

GUY: Listen Bill, I'm in serious trouble, tomorrow's not soon enough. Bill, I need it today. Seriously, Bill.

ANNCR: Introducing ZapMail. A copy of practically anything sent coast to coast in just two hours.

GUY: Seriously. How did they do this?

ANNCR: Federal Express introduces ZapMail.

(SFX: CRASH)

(LIGHTNING BOLT)

It's absolutely, positively incredible.

365

This is Car Vac . . . from Black & Decker's Car Care series.
Plug it in, rev it up, feel its power.
Black and Decker's Car Vac starts fast.
It's great on the curves, great in the straightaways.
Its 16 foot cord really goes the distance.
Watch it corner, maneuver through tight spots.
Car Vac handles like a dream and even stops on a dime.
Car Vac. It's got great pick-up because it's the only car vacuum that's built like a Black & Decker.

Consumer Television
:30 Single

366
ART DIRECTOR
Harvey Hoffenberg
WRITER
Ted Sann
CLIENT
Pepsi-Cola
DIRECTOR
Ridley Scott
PRODUCTION CO.
Fairbanks Films
AGENCY PRODUCER
Phyllis Landi
AGENCY
BBDO

367
ART DIRECTOR
George Euringer
WRITER
Helayne Spivak
CLIENT
MCI
DIRECTOR
Dick Stone
PRODUCTION CO.
Stone-Clark Productions
AGENCY PRODUCER
Linda Kligman
AGENCY
Ally & Gargano

368
ART DIRECTOR
Bill Puckett
WRITER
John Schmidt
CLIENT
Thermos
DIRECTOR
Geoffrey Mayo
PRODUCTION CO.
Geoffrey Mayo Films
AGENCY PRODUCER
Frank DiSalvo
AGENCY
Calet, Hirsch & Spector

369
ART DIRECTOR
Michael Tesch
WRITER
Patrick Kelly
CLIENT
Federal Express
DIRECTOR
Patrick Kelly
PRODUCTION CO.
Kelly Pictures
AGENCY PRODUCER
Jerry Haynes
AGENCY
Ally & Gargano

366

MOTHER: Laura . . . who drank all the Pepsi?
. . . And don't tell me it was some . . . strange
creature from another planet either . . . o.k.?

LAURA: Yes, Mom.

(LIGHT MYSTERIOUS MUSIC)

VO: Can anyone resist . . . the sparkling taste of
Pepsi? . . . Anyone?

(SFX: SYMPHONIC MUSIC.)

LAURA: Hey, take it easy on the Pepsi . . . o.k.?

ALIEN: I'm sorry.

VO: Pepsi. The Choice of a New Generation.

367

JOAN: Have you heard AT&T's latest promise? Now
they're not just reaching out. Uh, uh.
They're reaching out in new directions. Oh,
please.
They're reaching out in the same direction they
always have. For your wallet. Am I right?
Look, take my advice. Do what I did. Switch to
MCI.
They'll save you money on every long distance
call you make to any other state from coast to
coast. And they'll keep their hands to
themselves.

ANNCR (VO): Call MCI. Now there's no monthly fee,
so you can save over AT&T on all your out-of-
state calls, anytime, 24 hours a day.

368

(MUSIC: UNDER)

WIFE: Honey, you forgot the cooler.

ANNCR VO: Thermos would like to remind you: when it's 95 on the beach, it's 107 on the sand . . . 114 on the pavement . . . and over 125 degrees in the car. But inside a Thermos cooler . . . it's always ice cold.
Thermos. The hottest name in coolers.
For a limited time, save up to $5 on selected Thermos coolers.

369

MAN 1: Dick, send this by Emery to Pittsburgh, and if it's not there by 10:30 tomorrow, I'm holding you personally responsible.

MAN 2: Send this by Airborne to San Diego, and if it's not there by 10:30 a.m. Dick, you're in big trouble.

MAN 3: Send this by Purolator to Seattle, and it better get there by 10:30, Dick.

ANNCR: If you were in Dick's shoes, you'd probably do what Dick's going to do.

DICK: Helloooooooooo Federal.

ANNCR: Federal Express. Why fool around with anyone else?

Consumer Television :30 Single

370
ART DIRECTOR
Neil Leinwohl
WRITER
Kevin McKeon
CLIENT
Eagle Telephonics
DIRECTOR
Ken Matson
PRODUCTION CO.
Bean/Kahn Productions
AGENCY PRODUCER
Milda Misevicius
AGENCY
Korey Kay & Partners

371
ART DIRECTOR
George Euringer
WRITER
Helayne Spivak
CLIENT
MCI
DIRECTOR
Dick Stone
PRODUCTION CO.
Stone-Clark Productions
AGENCY PRODUCER
Linda Kligman
AGENCY
Ally & Gargano

372
ART DIRECTOR
Bob Needleman
WRITER
Jim Murphy
CLIENT
AT&T
DIRECTOR
Steve Steigman
PRODUCTION CO.
Steve Steigman Productions
AGENCY
NW Ayer

373
ART DIRECTORS
Martha Holmes
Don Schneider
WRITER
Martha Holmes
CLIENT
Pepsi-Cola
DIRECTOR
Howard Guard
PRODUCTION CO.
Iris Films
AGENCY PRODUCER
Jeff Fischgrund
AGENCY
BBDO

370

GUY: Notice anything unusual about my office? Sure you do! There's no phone on my desk! It's being replaced by a much better phone system. An Eagle. It does things like hold on to my messages if I'm out. Then displays them when I return. With this new system, not even an executive can mess up a call. Soon, Eagles will be landing in everyone's office. Hopefully, on their desks.

ANNCR (VO): The Eagle One. Now all other phone systems are endangered species.

371

JOAN: Have you noticed how friendly AT&T is lately?
Oh sure, now that you have a choice of long distance phone companies it's "Hello. Thank you for calling. Have a nice day."
And why? Grow up. It's not because they love you.
It's because they're afraid you'll do what I did, which is switch to MCI.
Because MCI saves me up to 30, 40, even 50% on long distance calls to any phone in any other state from coast to coast.
Now that's what I call a friend. Who needs Hello . . . Hello . . .

ANNCR (VO): Call MCI. Joan Rivers and nearly two million others are saving up to 30, 40, even 50% on their out-of-state calls.

EVERYONE'S SAYING THEY'RE CHEAPER THAN AT&T.

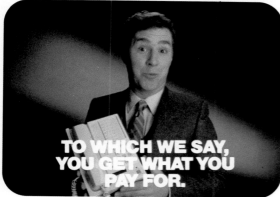

TO WHICH WE SAY, YOU GET WHAT YOU PAY FOR.

diet

372

1st man: Do you want to buy a phone? It's cheaper than AT&T?

2nd man: You won't get anything this cheap from AT&T.

1st woman: Cheap, we're the cheapest.

2nd woman: What you really need is cheap long distance.

3rd man: And, of course, our business systems are much cheaper than AT&T.

4th man: We're cheaper than AT&T. What more can I say.

vo: Everyone's saying they're cheaper than AT&T. But no one is saying they're better. All they can say is they're cheaper . . . to which we say,. "You get what you pay for"

anncr. (vo): Whether it's telephones, long distance, information systems or computers . . . AT&T.

373

woman I: So I finally get to meet him.

woman II: He'll be here any minute.

woman I: You've been keeping him a secret.

woman II: Oh, come on . . . here, hold this.

woman I: Diet Pepsi does taste better than it used to. Hard to believe that's one calorie.

woman II: They improved it.

woman I: With NutraSweet.

woman II: Don't drink it all!

woman I: Are those my shoes?

woman II: No!

(sfx ding dong)

woman II: Here he is!

woman I: I'm ready.

woman I: I'll probably steal him from you during dinner.

woman II: Not a chance.

woman II: Hi, daddy!

woman I: Hi!

374

BUSINESSMAN: DA DA DA DA DA DA DA DA DA DA DA DA DA DA DA DA DA

BUSINESSMAN & SECRETARY: DA, DA, DA, DA, DA, DA, DA, DA, DA, DA, DA, DA, DA, DA, DA, DA!!

ANNCR (VO): Federal Express introduces the biggest thing we've done in years. It's a new service that lets you send a copy of any letter or document coast to coast in just two hours.
All you do is pick up the phone, we do the rest.

BUSINESSMAN: DA DA DA DA DA!!!

ANNCR: Federal Express introduces ZapMail.

(SFX: CRASH)

(LIGHTNING BOLT)

It's absolutely, positively incredible.

375

AVO: Somewhere in this room is a beautiful antique, hidden under layer upon layer of paint.
Now Black & Decker will find it with Heat'n Strip, the remarkable paint stripper that works with hot air, not caustic chemicals.
Heat'n Strip bubbles away years of paint with less work and a lot less mess.
It makes all other ways of stripping paint antique.
Heat'n Strip . . . It's built like a Black & Decker.

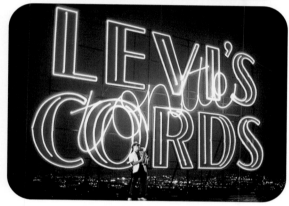

376

MERV: When I first heard of MCI, I didn't sign up right away.

Oh, I believed they'd cut my long distance bills; and I knew that millions of people already liked MCI and that all I had to do was call MCI and start saving.

But the fact was I continued to use AT&T. Then I remembered a piece of advice my grandmother gave me years ago:

"Mervin," she said, "don't be a jerk."

ANNCR (VO): Call MCI. Join Merv and millions of others saving up to 30, 40, even 50 percent.

377

(MUSIC UP)

MALE SINGER: *The night is young and*
   The fever is high
   I got room to move
   Nothing but time
   My Levi's Cords
   Spark, sparkle and shinin'

MALE SINGER W/GRP. SINGERS: *On a night turn*
   Right turn

MALE SINGER: *Levi's Corduroy night*

GROUP SINGERS: *Burnin', burnin'*

MALE SINGER: *Night turn*
   Oh, right turn
   Levi's Corduroy night

GROUP SINGERS: *Burnin', burnin*

(MUSIC FADES)

Consumer Television
:30 Campaign

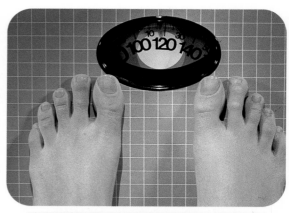

378

MR. HURD: Hi. Uh, I'm supposed to tell you about
the trucks at Rosen Novak. Now usually trucks
scare the pants off of me, but these are nice
trucks. There are new trucks, and used trucks,
and you can take them for a ride . . . you don't
have to! So get on over to Rosen Novak . . . if
you wanna . . . you don't have to if you don't
wanna. I'm sorry. I hope I wasn't too pushy.

379

ANNCR (VO): Anorexia Nervosa begins innocently
enough with a desire to lose weight.
But something goes wrong.
(SFX: HEAVY BEAT) And no matter how thin this
young woman is, she wants to be thinner still.
Obsessed with losing weight.
(SFX: AS ABOVE) Moody. Hyperactive. And trying to
hide what is a very serious problem.
But the Charter Treatment Program can help.
(SFX: AS ABOVE)
Their highly-acclaimed program treats not only
Anorexia, but a wide range of other eating
disorders as well.
So call the Charter Answerline.
Because there's a thin line between a starvation
diet—and starvation.

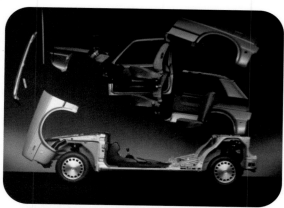

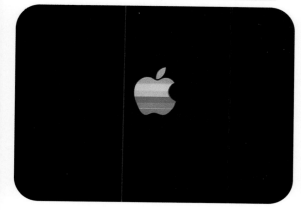

380

ANNCR (VO): This is a highly sophisticated business
computer. And to use it . . . all you have to do is
learn this . . .
This is Macintosh from Apple. Also a highly
sophisticated business computer.
And to use it, all you have to do is learn this . . .
Now . . . you decide which one's more
sophisticated.
Macintosh.
The computer for the rest of us.

381

(MUSIC THROUGHOUT)

VO: The new 1985 Volkswagen Golf has arrived.
Drop in for a test drive.
Golf. It's not a car, it's a Volkswagen.

**Consumer Television
:30 Campaign**

382
ART DIRECTOR
Lloyd Allen
WRITER
Daryle Rico
CLIENT
Portland General Electric
DIRECTOR
Mike Van Ackeren
PRODUCTION CO.
Mike Van Ackeren
AGENCY PRODUCER
Lloyd Allen
AGENCY
Gerber Advertising/Oregon

383
ART DIRECTOR
Gary Gibson
WRITER
Rich Flora
CLIENT
Texas Rangers
DIRECTOR
Rich Flora
PRODUCTION CO.
Group Seven
AGENCY PRODUCER
Greg Gibson
AGENCY
The Richards Group/Dallas

384
ART DIRECTOR
Dana Dolabany
WRITER
Dan Brown
CLIENT
NYNEX
DIRECTOR
Joe Sedelmaier
PRODUCTION CO.
Sedelmaier Films
AGENCY PRODUCER
Lou Stamoulis
AGENCY
Cabot Advertising/Boston

385
ART DIRECTORS
Chris Blum
Leslie Caldwell
WRITER
Mike Koelker
CLIENT
Levi Strauss
DIRECTOR
Leslie Dektor
PRODUCTION CO.
Petermann/Dektor
AGENCY PRODUCER
Steve Neely
AGENCY
Foote Cone & Belding/
San Francisco

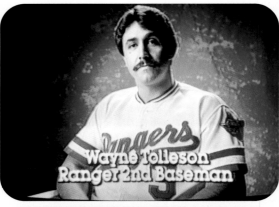

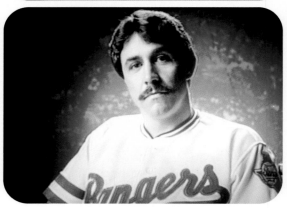

382
MAN: How many slices of toast can you get for a
    penny?
    If you're a PGE customer, the answer is about 7.
    Seven slices of toast for only a penny. Now
    that's an awful lot of bread for very little dough.
ANNCR: When you consider all it does for you,
    electricity is a mighty good buy.

383
TOLLESON: It all started when I was just a kid. I
    wondered what stealing was like.
    So I tried it. And I got good. But then it got to
    be a way of life—people expected me to steal.
    Oh sure, I've been caught.
    But it doesn't matter. I'll steal again.
ANNCR (VO): How 'bout those Rangers. Watch 'em
    take on the Tigers.

384

(MUSIC: VIOLINS)

ANNCR (VO): Imagine, if you couldn't advertise in the NYNEX Yellow Pages . . . you could end up talking to a lot of people who are . . .

MAN: Just Looking.

MAITRE D': Just Looking.

WOMAN: Just Looking.

MAITRE D': Just Looking.

WAITER (SNAPS FINGERS): Just Looking.

BUSBOY: Just Looking.

ANNCR. (VO): Fortunately, the NYNEX Yellow Pages gets you serious customers. Because four out of five people who pick it up are ready to buy. They're not . . .

MAN: Just Looking.

ANNCR (VO): NYNEX Yellow Pages for New York Telephone. Where would you be without it?

385

BLUES SINGER: *Ain't no body*
Like my body
That's about the size of it, Ummhhh.
So I personalize my size, with
Levi's 501 Blues . . .
They shrink to fit.
They're the Blues that make
me feel good.
Levi's 501 Blues . . .
Love them Blues, Oh Yeah!

386

ANNCR (VO): Before you give up on computers . . .
try the computer you already know how to use.
Take Macintosh out for a free . . .
. . . overnight test drive.

387

(MUSIC UNDER)

ANNCR (VO): Every day, millions of people place
their important photos in the hands of the
experts.

LAB GUY #1: What's that?

LAB GUY #2: Eggplant special.

LAB GUY #3: Is that this guy's nose or is he eatin' a
banana?

OLD LAB MAN: Comin' thru. This is that one-hour
stuff . . .

ANNCR (VO): With results often less than hoped
for . . .

LAB GUY #4: I think they're running a little blue.

LAB GUY #5: They're running a little blue.

ANNCR (VO): Maybe that's why there are millions of
others who keep the outcome of their important
pictures in their own hands . . . with Polaroid
Instant Cameras.

388

ANNCR: Ten years ago, Federal Express changed
the way America did business.

GUY: I need it tomorrow, or it's all over!!!
How did they do this?

ANNCR: Now we're going to do it again.

GUY: Listen, Bill, I'm in serious trouble, tomorrow's
not soon enough. Bill, I need it today. Seriously,
Bill.

ANNCR: Introducing ZapMail.
A copy of practically anything sent coast to coast
in just two hours.

GUY: Seriously. How did they do this?

ANNCR: Federal Express introduces ZapMail.

(SFX: CRASH)

(LIGHTNING BOLT)

It's absolutely, positively incredible.

389

WOMAN I: So I finally get to meet him.

WOMAN II: He'll be here any minute.

WOMAN I: You've been keeping him a secret.

WOMAN II: Oh, come on . . . here, hold this.

WOMAN I: Diet Pepsi does taste better than it used
to. Hard to believe that's one calorie.

WOMAN II: They improved it.

WOMAN I: With NutraSweet.

WOMAN II: Don't drink it all!

WOMAN I: Are those my shoes?

WOMAN II: No.!

(SFX: DOOR BELL)

WOMAN II: Here he is!

WOMAN I: I'm ready.

WOMAN I: I'll probably steal him from you during
dinner.

WOMAN II: Not a chance.

WOMAN II: Hi, daddy!

WOMAN I: Hi!

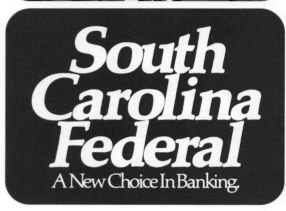

390

JOAN: Have you heard AT&T's latest promise? Now they're not just reaching out. Uh, uh.
They're reaching out in new directions. Oh, please.
They're reaching out in the same direction they always have. For your wallet. Am I right?
Look, take my advice. Do what I did. Switch to MCI.
They'll save you money on every long distance call you make to any other state from coast to coast. And they'll keep their hands to themselves.

ANNCR (VO): Call MCI. Now there's no monthly fee, so you can save over AT&T on all your out-of-state calls, anytime, 24 hours a day.

391

(SFX: ROCK GRINDING AGAINST ROCK)

ANNCR. (VO): If your banker seems a little . . . set in his ways . . . come see one who isn't. At South Carolina Federal. A new choice in banking.

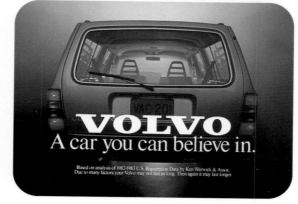

392

VO: Some people will put up with anything . . .
when they have to pay for TV repairs . . .
Rent from Granada and all repairs are free.

393

(MUSIC UNDER)

ANNCR (VO): With a life expectancy of 16.5 years,
this is the space vehicle that could transport you
into the 21st century.

(SFX: SLAM OF HATCH)

394
ART DIRECTOR
Bill Murphy

WRITER
Vashti Brotherhood

CLIENT
MSL

DIRECTOR
Barry Bransfield

PRODUCTION CO.
Viz Wiz

AGENCY PRODUCER
Maggie Hines

AGENCY
Hill Holliday Connors
Cosmopulos/Boston

395
ART DIRECTOR
Jim Brock

WRITER
Bill Martin

CLIENT
WXEX TV8

DIRECTOR
Jon Parks

PRODUCTION CO.
Mirage Productions

AGENCY PRODUCER
Bill Martin

AGENCY
Finnegan & Agee/Virginia

396
ART DIRECTOR
John Henderson

WRITER
Joe Di Stefano

CLIENT
Hertz Rent A Car

DIRECTORS
Alan Cole
John Henderson

PRODUCTION CO.
Iloura Productions

AGENCY PRODUCER
John Henderson

AGENCY
Scali McCabe Sloves/
Australia

394

JOHN HOUSEMAN: A select few of you shall go on to
fame and fortune. The rest of you had better
play Megabucks. It's worth over 4 million
dollars.

395

(SFX: SOUND OF RAIN)

ANCR: Any TV weather forecaster can predict rain.
John Bernier's forecasts are somewhat more
precise.

JOHN: Now . . .

(SFX: LARGE CLAP OF THUNDER)

396

(MUSIC THROUGHOUT: "THANKS FOR THE MEMORY")

ANNCR: The hardest thing about renting the new
   BMW 318i from Hertz, is saying goodbye.

HERTZ GIRL: There, there Mr. Davis, there's always
   next time.

397

ANNCR. (VO): Next time you look for ham, look for the Boar's Head Brand.
It's your assurance that the ham you buy isn't a turkey.

398

ANNCR (VO): Why learn all of this . . .
(SFX: THUD) . . . when you can use Macintosh by simply learning this.
Macintosh.

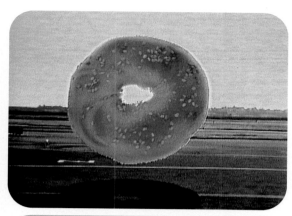

399

ANNCR: When their planes are full, they roll out one
of these. When ours are full, we roll out one of
these.
The Eastern Air Shuttle to Boston and
Washington, guaranteed seats.

INDEX

Index

Art Directors

Writers

Clients